Lawyers on Trial

Other books by Philip M. Stern

THE GREAT TREASURY RAID

THE SHAME OF A NATION
 (With photographs by George de Vincent)

THE OPPENHEIMER CASE: Security on Trial

THE RAPE OF THE TAXPAYER

PHILIP M. STERN

Lawyers on Trial

Times
BOOKS

Published by TIMES BOOKS, a division of
Quadrangle/The New York Times Book Co., Inc.
Three Park Avenue, New York, N.Y. 10016

Published simultaneously in Canada by
Fitzhenry & Whiteside, Ltd., Toronto

Library of Congress Cataloging in Publication Data

Stern, Philip M
  Lawyers on trial.

  Bibliography: p. 221
  Includes index.
  1. Lawyers—United States. I. Title.
KF297.S73   340'.023'73   79-91667
ISBN 0-8129-0904-6

Manufactured in the United States of America

This book is dedicated first and foremost

to Helen

the most special, touching friend
and partner any man ever had . . .

. . . and also to those courageous and public-spirited lawyers whose first object is to serve the public good, and who lend nobility to their profession.

Preface

This book grew out of my enrolling as a law school freshman at the age of 49.

I was not sure where it would all lead when I walked into that first class with students half my age. I certainly had no thought of a book; quite the contrary, I had high hopes of entering a profession I had always respected. Not only are some of my best friends lawyers, but many of my heroes, too: men and women I had seen using their lawyering skills to right wrongs.

But one day, midway into that grueling freshman year (at Georgetown University, in Washington, D.C.), a conversation with a friend and contemporary put law school in a new light. A highly successful Washington attorney, he had attended Harvard Law School nearly twenty-five years earlier. When I mentioned that I was studying landlord-tenant law in my course on Real Property, my friend expressed surprise. That had not, he said, been taught in his freshman property course at Harvard.

"Really?" I said. "What *did* you study?"

"Well," he said, "we spent the first two months studying the medieval antecedents of modern property law"— legal concepts such as Fee Tail and The Rule in Shelley's Case that have little relevance to modern-day clients.

Since landlord-tenant law is one of the cardinal areas of property law that affects a broad slice of the population (the tens of millions of renters), I wondered: if so recently at Harvard they bypassed that subject, whose property law *did* they teach?

The question prompted me to reexamine my own courses and to ask, "Whose law are *we* learning? What

vii

kinds of clients are we being prepared to serve?" True, unlike the Harvard students of the early fifties, we spent some time on tenant law, but our property law course also devoted about as much time to the Rule Against Perpetuities—a legal wrinkle that essentially defines the circumstances under which the handful of people wealthy enough to bypass their children and grandchildren can legally leave their property to their great-grandchildren, as a means of avoiding inheritance taxes.

As I viewed law school against that "whose law" question, the preponderance of legal problems to which we freshmen were exposed seemed to be those of business and the well-to-do. Moreover, our first-year indoctrination to the courtroom—the only such experience that would be required in our three years of law school—was in a mock court *of appeals,* the kind of court used mostly by the few wealthy enough to afford the enormous expense of a legal appeal. If, before graduation, we were to get the kind of trial court experience that most clients would need, it would be happenstance.

But was I drawing a premature conclusion, based only on the first of three law school years? Apparently not, for when it came time for us to map out our second- and third-year curricula, the emphasis on preparing to serve the tip of the economic pyramid was, if anything, more clearly underlined. Not only were the course offerings predominantly business oriented; we were also told that if we were like classes before us, 90 percent of us would sign up for a package of courses on business and commercial law. Few of us would elect to learn consumer or poverty law.

All of that raised questions: to what extent does the legal profession mirror the emphasis on business and commercial interests so apparent in the law school setting? To what extent do lawyers serve only the peak of the pyramid, leaving the rest of the population underrepresented? And if legal services *are* unfairly distributed, to what degree is that caused—and perpetuated—by the policies of the Organized Bar?

Those questions seemed so compelling that after completing my freshman year I decided to explore and write a book about them.

This book is about the dark side of the legal profession. It does not hold itself out to be a "balanced" presentation (in the sense of giving the profession's virtues equal space with its shortcomings) any more than the pronouncements of the American Bar Association emphasize the bar's defects as much as its strengths. There are, of course, many public-spirited lawyers (I would never have entered law school but for them) and many fine things to be said about the profession which are not, admittedly, fully catalogued here. If you are looking to learn more about the profession's strong points, you should not seek them in this book, any more than you should turn to the press releases of the ABA if your object is to discover the bar's deficiencies.

While emphasizing the profession's shortcomings, I have sought to avoid the aberrational and to illuminate, through the facts and examples I have chosen, what I believe to be more the rule than the exception.

It has not always been easy to be sure that is the case. The profession is large and varied, and divided into a multitude of separate systems (the fifty state bar associations plus hundreds of county and city bar groups), each with its own rules and practices. Moreover, there is a dearth of comprehensive information about those many systems. It would not surprise me, therefore, if some lawyers were to find their local practices at variance with those described in this book. Nevertheless, I believe that the picture I have drawn here is an essentially correct one, and I would be surprised (and apologetic) if it could be demonstrated that the points I have made were based more on the exception than the rule.

In fairness to the Organized Bar, a special note is in order regarding an extensive revision of the profession's Code of Professional Responsibility that has been suggested by an American Bar Association Commission on Evaluation of Professional Standards. On January 30, 1980, that Commission released a 134-page Discussion Draft of Model Rules of Professional Conduct. Some of the suggestions contained in that document address particular problems discussed in this book (for example, the proposed rule on lawyer advertising would permit all but deceptive advertising by attorneys, rather than the more restrictive rule described on page 57).

This book does not, however, attempt to take into account the Commission's proposed rule changes, but deals with the existing Code, for two principal reasons. First, the ABA Commission emphasized that its proposals have "not been adopted by the (ABA) House of Delegates and do not represent the policy of the American Bar Association." On the contrary, they were expected to be the subject of extensive public hearings, to be submitted in "final version" to the House of Delegates in February 1981.

More importantly, the proposed changes, even if adopted in their entirety, would not affect the fundamental points made in this book. They do little, if anything, to reduce the basic powers of the Lawyers' Monopoly or to make the profession more accountable to the general public via, say, subjecting it to control by a majority of non-lawyers. (Indeed, these rules changes themselves were drafted by a panel made up predominantly of lawyers.) They do not purport to address the problems inherent in legal education, the bar exam or the character and fitness screening process.

In short, many of the proposed changes are, in my view, constructive and deserve commendation. But they are subject to change before their final adoption; and even if all of them were to be approved, they would not alter in any fundamental way the problems to which this book is addressed.

You will see numerous references in this book to "the Organized Bar" (or, at times, to "the Lawyers' Monopoly"), by which I mean the official bar—the various bar associations, national, state, and local, as distinct from the rank-and-file members of the bar. Just as I find reason to be critical of the former, I find reason to be sympathetic with the latter.

It is important to distinguish between the two,* not merely because less than half of all lawyers belong to the American Bar Association and not just because many who do belong do not subscribe to the ABA's stands. There is an even more important reason to distinguish—and sympathize with—the vast majority of individual lawyers. Most of them are not richly rewarded for their work (see page 7) and their interests have, in my view, often been badly served by the bar elite and by the rules its leaders have imposed on the bar as a whole. To take but one example, the ban on lawyer advertising that prevailed prior to its invalidation by the Supreme Court in 1977 may have been all very well for established law firms that had little difficulty making themselves known in business circles. Yet it prevented a large number of solo practitioners and small-firm lawyers from making themselves known to a vast unserved market of middle-income clients.

A word about the gender of the pronouns used in this book. I am, like many, offended by the automatic use of the masculine pronoun "he." I wish that a genderless pronoun had been invented to circumvent the awkward "he/she" "his/hers," etc., or alternatively, that we had come to the point where a lawyer or judge could be called "she" interchangeably with "he" without distracting or interfering with communication. Since, regrettably, neither has come to pass, I have tried to avoid the he/she dilemma where I could and have used "he or she" wherever I could do so gracefully. But there are instances where I have, in the interest of simplicity, resigned myself

---

*It is to emphasize that distinction that the terms *Organized Bar* and *Lawyers' Monopoly* bear capital letters.

to the masculine pronoun. This paragraph is simply intended to convey my discomfort in doing so.

In my view, the concern about the unequal distribution of lawyers' services and talents expressed in this book is not merely a "do-gooder" worry; nor is it confined to the plight of the "disadvantaged." The well-heeled—and the well-represented—have as much to be concerned about injustice as the unmoneyed and unrepresented.

Martin Luther King put the point well when, writing from a Birmingham jail, he stated, "Injustice anywhere is a threat to justice everywhere."* His argument applies to the injustices, large and small, that are the inevitable result of rationing legal help (which is to say, access to justice) and confining it to those able to pay for it.

I have written this book in the hope it will, to some degree, however small, contribute to a lessening of injustice.

Philip M. Stern
New York, N. Y.
January 1980

*Atlantic Monthly, August 1973

Contents

xiii

Introduction

Two sentences sum up this book.

One is from a *New Yorker* cartoon, in which a lawyer says to an anxious client: "You have a pretty good case, Mr. Pitkin. How much justice can you afford?"

The other is the statement by President Carter that "ninety percent of our lawyers serve ten percent of our people."*

Justice for sale to the highest bidder, with the highest bidders—the richest among us, giant corporations and some wealthy individuals—getting most of it.

Hardly the ideal proclaimed, daily, by our school children, of "One nation . . . indivisible, with . . . justice for all."

If it is true that lawyers predominantly serve the rich, they are not unique among professionals. What sets them apart is that they exclusively control access to an entire branch of government: the judicial branch. For, as a practical matter, when you have a legal problem, you can't get through the courtroom door without a lawyer.†

So when the American Bar Association makes the remarkable admission that it "has long been aware that the middle seventy percent of the population is not being reached or served adequately by the [legal] profession,"

*The source for this and other facts throughout this book may be found in the Notes and Sources section, pp. 221–56.
†Technically, you can, as a layman, represent yourself. But in most contests against an experienced lawyer, only the foolhardy would try.

it is acknowledging that nearly three-quarters of the American people lack full access to the system of justice.

The profession's failure to serve "the middle seventy percent" is not for lack of lawyers. On the contrary, this country alone has two-thirds of all the lawyers on earth. Three times as many, per capita, as England. Twenty-one times as many as Japan. And law schools continue to pour out new attorneys at an unprecedented rate.

Yet, by the profession's own admission, nearly three-fourths of Americans are not being adequately served.

Astounding.

In the criminal arena of law, we *are* coming closer to realizing the ideal of "justice for all," for the courts have established the right to counsel, even where a criminal defendant cannot pay. But in the arena of civil law, with which this book is exclusively concerned, it's "how much justice can you afford?"

What is more significant than that 90 percent of lawyers serve 10 percent of the people is the fact that *the legal profession has done its best to keep it that way.* The Organized Bar has deliberately kept the price of legal help up and has kept competition down. For decades, the bar deemed it *unethical* for a lawyer to charge less than the bar prescribed. Finally, the Supreme Court said that was illegal. Yet even today there is price fixing among lawyers —in the buying and selling of homes, for example.

The Bar has fought ways of doing away with lawyers as expensive and needless middlemen—has fought, for example, the self-help probating of wills. In America, people pay lawyers nearly one billion dollars a year for probate —three times what they pay in funeral expenses. In England, people generally handle the matter themselves, without lawyers, up to one hundred times more cheaply and seventeen times more quickly than in America.

The bar has resisted virtually every new idea for making legal help available to people at prices they can afford. For instance, it greeted the launching of the first legal clinic—that promised to help with divorces, bankruptcies, and other common legal problems for a fraction of the going rate—not by congratulating the inventors of that new idea, but by charging them with "dishonesty" and "moral turpitude" and by trying to suspend their licenses to practice law.

How do lawyers get away with it? The answer is simple: they have a monopoly—a state-approved monopoly, like a public utility. Utilities, however, are subject to public control, by a public utilities commission. Not the legal profession, which in essence is answerable to no one.* It writes its own rules and enforces (or fails to enforce) them as it sees fit. If you have a complaint against your lawyer, you have only one place to turn: your local bar association, where it will be passed upon by your attorney's brethren in the profession. Hardly the most objective of judges.

In a variety of ways, the legal profession points its members toward the service of the wealthiest ten percent.
    You see it everywhere.
    You see it in the way lawyers are trained, in what they are—and are *not*—taught in law school. Corporation law, commercial law, securities law—yes, in abundance. Consumer law? Tenant law? The rights of debtors? Rarely.
    You see it in the selective way in which the profession's rules, the so-called Canons of Ethics, are written. To take one example: the rules regarding lawyer advertising, while limiting the means for reaching the general public, explicitly approve advertisements aimed at corporations, banks, insurance companies, and other businesses. So if you get behind in paying your bills, a local merchant can instantly locate an expert and efficient debt-collection

*In the last analysis, the Bar is answerable to the courts and the judges —who are, without exception, themselves members of the legal profession.

lawyer to sue you. But if you try to find an attorney to defend you—or perhaps bring an action against a store that has gypped you—the bar rules leave you little choice but to flounder in the sea of lawyers' names in the Yellow Pages of your telephone directory.

Think of what that means: while the merchant may well be able to sue you over an uncollected bill as small as, say, $50, you may have an open-and-shut grievance of $100 or $500 and not be able to find a lawyer who will take on your case for a fee that makes sense. *What would we think of a medical system in which no doctor would treat a cut or a burn because it was too small to handle?*

You also see the Bar's bias in the manner in which the Canons of Ethics are enforced or not enforced; in the kinds of lawyers and the kinds of offenses that stir the Bar's ire. Let Lennox Hinds, president of the National Conference of Black Lawyers comment on a criminal trial he thinks unfair and the Organized Bar initiates a formal complaint against him. But let Hoyt Augustus Moore, of the Wall Street firm of Cravath, Swaine & Moore, publicly admit having paid a $250,000 bribe to a federal judge and not one disciplinary finger is raised against him. For fourteen years after acknowledging his clear-cut felony, Moore was allowed to pursue his highly lucrative practice, as if he had never been involved in a blatant obstruction of justice.

In one sense, the lengths to which the bar goes to favor the well-to-do are quite unnecessary, because the legal system itself operates in such a way as to stack the deck in favor of the "haves." It is not enough that they enjoy marked superiority in sheer dollar power and the capacity to outlast the "have-nots" in legal battle; or that they have first claim to the Best and the Brightest in the profession. There's more to the advantages they possess: as Chapter 13 recounts, woven into the legal system are imbalances so substantial—and so subtle—that even if the have-nots were, suddenly, to enjoy parity of legal representation, they would still enter most legal battles with several strikes against them.

Given this inherent deck-stacking against the have-nots, does the legal profession behave in a way that lessens the imbalances? Or does it make them worse?

All too often it's the latter. The best lawyers, far from playing a neutral or passive role, are the inventive, active instruments for perpetuating the power of the haves and preserving their leverage over the have-nots. As recounted in Chapter 14, lawyers devise legal fictions (such as a $120 million bank "branch" operating out of a broom-closet office in the Bahamas) to secure special tax advantages for their prosperous clients; or they resort to legal delaying tactics they know to be unwarranted, to wear down a less well-heeled opponent or, perhaps, merely to postpone the day of judgment against a profitable arrangement of their client's; or they defend client actions (such as selling dangerous drugs without the proper warnings, with fatal consequences to the innocent purchasers) that they would never dream of sanctioning as private, conscience-bound individuals.

In defense of such actions, lawyers often argue that they are merely doing their duty, which is to represent their clients "zealously." And that indeed, is what the Bar, via its Canons of Ethics, instructs lawyers is their sole duty. If innocent people are injured as a consequence of what they and their clients do, that is someone else's responsibility, not theirs. But are lawyers saying that it reduces them to mere puppets, slaves to their clients' interests? If so, is that the way we want lawyers to think and behave?

And what of the American Bar Association's assertion that "ours is a profession and not a mere money-getting trade"? Or Chief Justice Warren Burger's statement that "our boast has been that as a profession we place the public interest ahead of private gain"?

Ironically, for the vast majority of attorneys, the amount of "private gain" is by no means exorbitant, for in general the law is not a lucrative profession. In 1977, the median income for lawyers belonging to the ABA was $32,000, far below the median income for doctors ($55,000). Fewer than one lawyer in six made over $75,000. (A 1974 survey of Chicago lawyers revealed that nearly half of those responding made less than $30,000.) The vast majority of lawyers work prodigiously hard but do not end up wealthy; yet their fees are generally out of reach for most. It is a no-win situation for everyone.

There is a stark, two-word question that forms the basis for the most piercing appraisal of any public institution.

The question is: *for whom?*

For whom is the legal profession run? For whom are its rules of conduct written, its standards of admission fashioned, its school curricula designed?

For the members of the profession?

For the courts and judges?

For a select category of clients?

Or for the general public?

For whom? It is the question that, I think, lies behind the anger felt by so many who have had to deal with lawyers in times of trouble. It is the question that prompted me to write this book.

Lawyers on Trial

A Note on Standards for Judging the Legal Profession

Some may feel that this book holds the legal profession to unfair and unrealistic standards—to norms to which no large group of humans can reasonably be expected to adhere.

They are not, however, norms solely of my making. On the contrary, *they are standards the profession has set for itself,* as proclaimed by the Organized Bar, by the courts, and by eminent members of the profession. The following are but a few of many examples:

> The purposes of the [American Bar] Association are to . . . promote . . . the administration of justice [and] to apply the knowledge and experience of the [legal] profession to the promotion of the public good.
> —Constitution of the American Bar Association, Section 1.2

> . . . the [legal] profession is a branch of the administration of justice and not a mere money-getting trade.
> —American Bar Association Canons of Ethics, Canon XII

> Lawyers, like others, must support and educate families, but our boast has been that as a profession, we place the public interest ahead of private gain.
> —Chief Justice Warren Burger, speech to the American Law Institute, May 21, 1974

The Bar . . . is guided by the desire to serve the country, not itself.
> —Leon Jaworski, President,
> American Bar Association,
> 1972, citing statement
> by an earlier ABA president
> "exactly thirty years ago."

Members of the [legal] profession, although profit-motivated, have a broad social responsibility.
> —The American Bar Association,
> Brief to the U.S. Supreme Court
> in *Bates* v. *Arizona Bar,* 1977

The goals of the bar . . . are "to inculcate in its members the principles of duty and service to the public, to improve the administration of justice, and to advance the science of jurisprudence."
> —Speech by Florida Chief Justice
> Arthur England to the Florida bar,
> June 16, 1979

If the Bar is to become a method of making money in the most convenient way possible, but making it at all hazards, then the Bar is degraded.
> —Samuel J. Tilden, addressing the first
> meeting of the Association of the Bar
> of the City of New York, February 1870

A basic tenet of the professional responsibility of lawyers is that every person in our society should have ready access to the . . . services of a lawyer of integrity and competence.
> —American Bar Association, Code of
> Professional Responsibility, Ethical
> Consideration 1–1

You are invited to judge for yourself as you read the following pages whether or not the legal profession has lived up to those standards.

1

A Legal Parable

George Rowan was plenty steamed up. His attorney, Henry Thompson, had told Rowan he had a legally airtight case against the AAA Transfer Company, which had ruined some of Rowan's furniture (and, what's more, refused to release the rest of Rowan's household goods until Rowan paid the moving bill). The damages were about $500, but Thompson said it would cost *at least* that much, and maybe as much as $1,000, to take the case to court—the only way, he said, that Rowan would get any satisfaction from AAA. What's more, Thompson added, he wouldn't touch the case without the $500 in cash, up front.

Laying out $500 to $1,000 to get back $500 was clearly a losing proposition. So Rowan figured he had no choice but to drop his claim against AAA, pay the damn moving bill, and swallow his loss (and his anger) even though he was dead right and AAA dead wrong.

When he told his wife what Thompson had said, she recalled that only a year ago, when they had gotten behind on a $50 hospital bill, the hospital had actually filed a lawsuit against them—official court summons and all.

How was it, she wanted to know, that the hospital could hire a lawyer and bring a court action on a paltry $50 claim when her husband couldn't pursue *his* $500 claim —ten times as much—without losing money paying lawyer's fees?

A good question.

It's a large part of what this book is all about.

5

2

Who Lawyers Do — and Don't — Serve

As of the late 1970's, there were about 500,000 lawyers in America—as noted, three times as many, per capita, as in England, and *twenty-one* times as many as Japan. (There are, in fact, more lawyers in Washington, D.C., than in all of Japan.)

Whom does this plethora of lawyers serve? Who commands the legal talent in the United States?

For the first time in our history, it is possible for people to get government help in solving their noncriminal legal problems. But to get that help, a family has to be very poor. If a family of four takes in more than $8,375 a year, or about $165 a week, they're not eligible for a free Legal Services lawyer, for they are above the "poverty line." So when it comes to getting legal help, the large bulk of Americans are on their own.

Furthermore, to serve the thirty million or so people who live below the "poverty line," the government provides a total of five thousand lawyers*—the same number as work for the twenty-five largest law firms in America.

As of 1975 (the last time the comparison was made), *three* Wall Street law firms, whose main clients are big corporations, employed more attorneys than all the public-inter-

*The Legal Services Corporation concerns itself only with civil (that is, noncriminal) legal problems, so this figure does not include lawyers in Legal Aid, public defenders' offices and the like, who provide criminal defense for the poor.

est law firms in the entire country, whose main clients are
consumers, citizen groups, environmental organizations,
and the like.

Ralph Nader's Public Citizen Litigation Group has
packed a powerful legal wallop. To cite but one of its
achievements, it brought the landmark suit that persuaded the U.S. Supreme Court to strike down a decades-
old rule forbidding lawyers to compete with one another
and charge lower fees to get new clients.

The entire 1978 budget of the Litigation Group was
about $214,000, about half the amount earned by a sin-
gle partner in one of the many Washington law firms
that mainly serve the corporate world. (Joseph Califano
earned $505,490 in his last year in private practice be-
fore becoming Secretary of Health, Education and Welfare.)

In 1979, the starting salary for a fledgling, just-out-of-
law-school attorney at a large Wall Street firm was $28,-
000 a year. The starting salary for a lawyer in the government's Legal Services program for the poor was
about $13,000.

After five years, the Wall Street lawyer could expect to
be making about $40,000. After five years, most Legal
Service lawyers could expect to make $18,000 to $20,000.

The Federal Communications Commission (FCC) in
Washington is in charge of regulating the policies and
activities of radio and TV stations across the country.

In 1978 there were, in Washington, only seven lawyers
representing the interests of viewers and citizen groups
before the FCC. In that same year there were, in Washington, more than *seven hundred* lawyers representing
the interests of broadcasters before the FCC.

The lawyering power of major American corporations
dwarfs that of even the United States government itself.
For example, in 1977 corporations spent $24 *billion* on

legal services. By contrast, the budget of the U.S. Department of Justice, which is in charge of enforcing the antitrust laws and other laws affecting business, totals one-tenth as much.

According to a mid-1979 report in *The New York Times,* lack of enforcement manpower was a vital factor in confining the Carter administration's promised crackdown on corporate and white-collar crime to "a handful of cases" in two years. The *Times* said the cost of such crime has been officially estimated at $44 billion a year— eleven times the cost of robberies, burglaries, and other crimes against property.

"One of our biggest problems is lack of investigative resources," the U.S. Attorney for New York told the *Times.* The *Times* noted there are just sixty government lawyers assigned to review some twenty-four hundred cases of alleged criminal tax evasions each year, quoting one government official as saying, "We're missing good cases against big corporations because we lack the manpower."

The legal resources of a single corporation can outweigh those of the United States government. Take, for example, IBM, against whom the government brought antitrust charges in 1969. In 1979, IBM had on its own staff some 243 full-time lawyers*—about half the total number of attorneys in the Antitrust Division of the U.S. Department of Justice.

Even with that large complement of staff lawyers, IBM delegated its defense against the government's charges to the Wall Street law firm of Cravath, Swaine & Moore, which opened two special branch offices just for the IBM case alone: one near the U.S. courthouse where the trial has been proceeding since 1975 (manning that office on

---

*At a Senate hearing, IBM General Counsel (and former Attorney General) Nicholas Katzenbach observed, "It does seem strange to me . . . to think that a private corporation might have more resources than the government of the United States."

a three-shift, around-the-clock basis when court is in session) and another near IBM's headquarters in Armonk, New York.

A *New York Times* account of the trial reports that "Cravath brings only seasoned lawyers to the court. Several times, [the Department of] Justice has stuck a fresh-faced lawyer right out of law school in court and had him question witnesses." The inexperience of government lawyers has often vexed the trial judge, according to *New Times* magazine.

As of 1979, the highest-paid trial attorney in the United States Justice Department made $47,500 a year. Thomas Barr, who heads up IBM's defense for Cravath, made more than three times that much. And IBM's own general counsel, former Attorney General Nicholas Katzenbach, made $362,815—not counting $168,538 in retirement and other benefits.

Such salary discrepancies can be a crippling handicap to the government in maintaining continuity of personnel in the years-long investigation and prosecution of a major, complex antitrust case,* as the following history of another such case illustrates:

July, 1973: U.S. Federal Trade Commission (FTC) brings major antimonopoly case against the eight largest oil companies.

July, 1976: Peter A. White, age thirty, chief FTC attorney in the slow-moving case (only now, after three years, moving into the preliminary investigative stage) leaves government to join Houston law firm headed by Watergate and Koreagate prosecutor Leon Jaworski. (The firm lists "oil and gas" and "antitrust" among its fields of legal specialty.)

White is succeeded by Roger B. Pool, also thirty, who, according to *The New York Times,* "has had only slight involvement in the case."

---

*As of mid-1979, ten years after the indictment was brought, the trial of the IBM case was entering its fifth year.

June, 1978: The New York Times reports that "Roger B. Pool [plans] to leave [government] in August to join a San Francisco law firm. Two other key [FTC] lawyers [in the oil case] quit last winter."

The public's stake in vigorous antitrust enforcement is immense. According to government estimates, when the cost of illegal price fixing is figured in, the total cost of corporate crime comes to *$200 billion* every year.

In a 1978 legal battle over the question of whether the major oil companies should be allowed to keep alleged overcharges amounting to $1.3 billion or should be required to refund the overcharges to consumers, the court documents listed *thirty* separate attorneys for the various oil companies (and one participant says at one time they numbered more than one hundred) and just *three* lawyers (one for Consumers Union and two representing the U.S. government) arguing for the consumer refund.*

One oil company attorney startled his adversary by stating his firm was charging its client $350 an hour (nearly twice its normal charge) in this case. Asked how such an extraordinary fee could be justified, the attorney smiled and said, "Do you know what the *interest* on $1.3 billion is every *day?*"

The answer (assuming, conservatively, that the oil company can earn ten percent on its money): more than $350,000—or about $2.5 million every week.

THE LEGAL PROFESSION AND "THE MIDDLE SEVENTY PERCENT OF THE POPULATION"

Many may believe that it is only the very poor in America who lack the legal help they need. Unhappily, that is not the case. The underrepresentation extends, by the bar's own admission, to a broad majority of the population.

The Organized Bar went to considerable effort and expense to document that very fact. The American Bar As-

---

*This case is described more fully on pages 19 and 20.

sociation, through its research arm, the American Bar Foundation (ABF), launched a nationwide survey to determine "The Legal Needs of the Public." Six years and $750,000 later, the study emerged. Among its striking findings was that among Americans with legal problems serious enough to consider consulting an attorney, *nearly three out of four had either never consulted a lawyer, or had done so only once in their lives.*

Among other things, the ABF surveyors asked those who had encountered common legal problems how often they had actually *used* a lawyer to help them. Here are the findings:

Type of problem experienced	*Rough proportion of those experiencing problem who had actually used a lawyer*
Dispute with home improvement or home repair contractor	1 in 6
Attempted eviction by landlord	1 in 4
Other serious dispute with landlord	1 in 8
Difficulty in obtaining services from the city (for example getting garbage collected, getting street paved, etc.)	1 in 33
Serious dispute with someone you owe money to	1 in 8
Your property seriously damaged or stolen by someone else	1 in 12
Your child seriously injured by someone else	1 in 4
Yourself seriously injured by someone else	1 in 3

The failure of the legal profession to engage itself in the

day-to-day problems of the general public is summed up
in two statements emanating from the Organized Bar
itself.

In 1974, Orville H. Schell, Jr., then president of the
Association of the Bar of the City of New York, told a
Senate committee: "[A] high percentage of people in this
country are not receiving adequate legal services. The
estimated percentages run from 60–90% of the population. *Whatever estimate you take, the numbers are stag-
gering.*" [Emphasis added]

Two years earlier, the American Bar Association had
acknowledged not only the gap but its own long-standing
awareness of the legal profession's deficiencies. As noted,
it said:

> The [ABA] has long been aware that *the middle 70
> percent of our population is not being reached or
> served adequately by the legal profession.* [Emphasis
> added]

Many people I have talked to consider the concentration
of legal help for corporations and the well-to-do a natural
state of affairs. After all, they say, rich people and corporations have more legal problems than poor and middle-
class people. Most families lead comparatively simple
lives—why do they need lawyers all that much?

Consider the following, which are composites based on
real-life cases, and decide for yourself whether less affluent people "don't need lawyers all that much" or whether
it's the case, for *everyone,* that "for want of a lawyer," a
great deal can be lost.

For-Want-of-a-Lawyer Case No. 1: To Grace Thompson, age seventy-nine, the unavailability of a lawyer was
literally a life-and-death matter.

Ms. Thompson was a Medicaid patient in a nursing
home whose staff, responding to orders from the State
Welfare Department to cut down on Medicaid outlays,
decided to transfer her to another, less costly, facility. The

nursing home staff had heard of a medical phenomenon known as "transfer trauma" that had been shown, in one study, to increase by 500 to 900 percent the chances of a patient's death within four months of transfer. But the pressures to economize were considerable, and they did not take that danger into account in deciding to transfer Grace Thompson. Moreover, Ms. Thompson, being lawyerless, was unaware of her right, under Medicaid law, to a hearing on her transfer; thus, she failed to demand it and was not granted it. She also had no way of knowing that the few patients who *had* requested and obtained a hearing had had near-total success in blocking the transfer where their lawyers could show that the transfer-trauma danger had not been properly considered.

So Grace Thompson was shifted to a facility that saved the Medicaid program ten dollars a day for her care and subjected her to the hazards of transfer trauma. Five months later, she was dead.

For-Want-of-a-Lawyer Case No. 2: Charles Christian an unemployed Philadelphia factory worker, age forty-two and in good health, sought one of the openings as a city guard but was not permitted to take the requisite examination because, by virtue of a city directive, those positions were closed to people over age forty-one. The directive violated federal employment-discrimination laws, but Charles Christian, lacking both a lawyer and (he thought) the means to hire one, knew nothing of that. He was also unaware of laws providing for payment of his legal fees in employment-discrimination cases such as this one.

Ignorant of his rights, he concluded he had no choice but to return to pounding pavements, even though in eighteen months of trying that method had not produced a single job.

For-Want-of-a-Lawyer Case No. 3: Henry Swanson, an insurance agent in Maryland, missed two payments on his car. The dealer repossessed the car and refused to return it until Swanson had paid the *entire* purchase price. Not represented by a lawyer, Swanson was not aware that the dealer's demand was illegal under state law (a mere catch-up of missed payments, which Swanson was in a position to pay, was enough, under the law, to get the car back). *Result:* Swanson needlessly lost the car—*and* the $1,000 he had already paid on it.

For-Want-of-a-Lawyer Case No. 4: Frank Lacuzzi, a Philadelphia policeman, fell badly behind on his bills. As his creditors began harassing him with growing ferocity, he fell into an acute depression.

With no lawyer to guide him (he was convinced there was no attorney he could afford), Frank Lacuzzi was unaware that a legal escape route—filing for bankruptcy—was available to him. Like eight out of every ten Philadelphians surveyed, he had always believed that only *businesses* could file for bankruptcy, that individuals like himself were trapped.

Seeing no way out, Frank Lacuzzi tried to take his life, failed, and was hospitalized. Even in his hospital bed he was not free of his creditors: the harassment continued. Then he read a newspaper ad for attorney Mitchell Miller's Bankruptcy Clinic, offering help at half the ordinary going rate, and within a few days, with Miller's help, he embarked on a course that had been available to him all along: bankruptcy—a chance for a fresh start.

For-Want-of-a-Lawyer Case No. 5: Sarah Ellsworth, a Hartford, Connecticut, high school student with an unblemished record, was suddenly expelled for what was called a "disciplinary offense." No hearing, no chance for her to explain her side of an argument with a teacher reputed to be unusually vindictive.

In other cities, student expulsions without a hearing had been held illegal. But Sarah's parents had never heard of such rulings and, accustomed to accepting "official actions" as final and unchallengeable and not having a lawyer readily at hand to consult, it never occurred to them that they could bring a legal action.

Sarah was sent off to an "alternative learning facility," made up wholly of children with "disciplinary problems."

For-Want-of-a-Lawyer Case No. 6: If you accept stereotypes, few groups fit the "plain-folks-have-scant-need-for-lawyers" argument more neatly than middling to poor blacks in the rural South.

But that stereotype is belied by the dramatic fact* that in just two decades (1954–74) the number of black landowners in the South shrank from 175,000 to 40,000. Why, in a time of booming land prices, should blacks be selling at bargain-basement prices to corporations and well-to-do white speculators? Because, historically, rural blacks, to whom attorneys seemed unapproachable strangers, didn't write wills. Thus, when they died their land became the property of the assorted relatives spelled out in state law. Over the years those relatives scattered to places unknown, and when the survivors living on the land found themselves unable to pay the taxes and the other heirs couldn't be located to exercise their option to pay the taxes and keep the land, it went on the auction block.

As of 1978, there were just four million acres still owned by blacks (less than one-third of the fifteen million acres they had once owned). It was being sold off at the rate of 500,000 acres a year.

For want of a will . . .

For want of a lawyer . . .

THE LEGAL PROFESSION
AND "PUBLIC INTEREST" LAW

The legal interests of unmoneyed people can also be defended by so-called public-interest lawyers—a new breed of attorneys who usually represent, not individual clients, but groups and organizations: civic, consumer, religious,

*Unearthed by CBS-TV's enterprising reporter Marlene Sanders, aided by the Emergency Land Fund in Atlanta.

minority, environmental groups, and the like. By and large, the lawsuits they bring are designed to benefit some broad sector of the population or the community at large.* As a rule, those whose interests they represent would, but for public-interest lawyers, be without a legal voice.

Here are some causes that public interest law firms have recently taken on:

In 1979, attorney Robert Gnaizda of Public Advocates, a six-lawyer public-interest firm in San Francisco, filed a petition on behalf of the Gray Panthers (a senior citizens' organization) protesting what it called discriminatory federal regulations that put a ceiling of 5 to 5½ percent on small savings accounts but permitted interest rates of 10 percent and more for those who had enough to deposit $10,000 or more in such accounts. Warning that "Savings Accounts May Be Dangerous to Your Wealth," the Gray Panthers contended that with the cost of living rising 8 percent a year, the 5 percent interest ceiling was actually resulting in a $10 billion annual *loss* to small savers. Within months of the Gray Panther petition, federal credit regulators, acknowledging that small savers had been underpaid by some $42 billion in the past decade, announced that they were phasing out the decades-old interest ceiling and instituting an immediate rate boost for small savers of one-quarter of one percent which, while inadequate in Gray Panther eyes, did mean $1.2 billion of added interest for small savers. Newsmen attributed the increase to the Gray Panther lawsuit.

NOTE: The total annual budget of the Public Advocates law firm is about $450,000—the equivalent of the yearly earnings of two successful Wall Street law partners.

---

*In the middle and late seventies, the public-interest label was also adopted by legal entities, such as the Pacific Legal Foundation, that derived most of their support from business firms and groups, and concentrated their legal efforts on combatting what they viewed as excessive governmental interference in business and private affairs.

In 1964, attorneys acting for public-interest church and citizens' groups challenged the license renewal of TV station WLBT in Jackson, Mississippi. Although Jackson's population is about 45 percent black, the station had but one black employee ("Slim," the janitor). It permitted its lobby space to be used by the arch-segregationist White Citizens Council for the sale of its literature. Station newscasters habitually referred to blacks as "niggers" (the news director contended this was not a question of discrimination but solely of the newscasters' inability to pronounce the word *Negro*). WLBT systematically declined to carry network documentaries dealing with racial integration. On one occasion, the appearance on NBC's "Today" television show by Justice Thurgood Marshall (then an attorney for the National Association for the Advancement of Colored People) was interrupted by a mysterious case of WLBT "cable trouble."

After a five-year court battle, then appeals-court judge Warren Burger, in an unheard of move, ordered the WLBT license transferred to a nonprofit group that has since substantially increased news and public affairs programming (including a racially integrated program for preschool children), has a racially balanced staff—and the first black station manager in the country.

But the victory was far broader. At the time of the challenges, the Federal Communications Commission not only treated behavior such as WLBT's as irrelevant to license renewals, it took the position that viewer and citizens' groups were not entitled to be *heard* at renewal proceedings, no matter how offensive they found the station's programs and practices. The WLBT challenge changed that. Viewer groups won the right to be heard; and a station's programming and employment practices are now integral to its entitlement to continued use of the public airwaves. As a result of these victories, broadcasters are now readier to meet with and respond to the programming complaints of citizen groups; and the FCC has adopted one of the most effective equal-opportunity-employment standards of any federal regulatory agency.

(The proportion of minority employees in the broadcast industry almost doubled between 1971 and 1977.)

NOTE: The combined budgets of the Media Access Project and the Citizens Communication Center—two public-interest law groups in Washington that help citizen groups monitor broadcasters' activities and bring license challenges—comes to about $500,000 annually. One single law firm in Washington that specializes in representing broadcasters before the FCC receives fees nearly four times that amount from broadcaster clients alone.

From 1970 to 1977, there were seven explosions in American coal mines that caused more than two hundred miners' deaths—often resulting not directly from the explosions themselves but from the ensuing lack of oxygen in the mine. Some experts believe many lives would have been saved if American miners had carried an oxygen-generating breathing apparatus that has been used in Europe for years, replacing the less expensive and usually ineffective "self-rescue" device traditionally carried by miners here. The introduction of the oxygen kit was opposed as too costly not merely by the big coal companies, *but also by the miners' union.* Thus, the matter would have been dropped but for lawyers for the Center for Law and Social Policy, a public-interest firm in Washington, who fought a two-year battle—and ultimately won. (The Labor Department ordered the gradual introduction of the effective European-type apparatus for all American miners.)

NOTE: The cost of litigating that case amounted to an estimated $40,000—the equivalent of one and a half *beginning*-lawyers' salaries in a large law firm.

In the post-Watergate era came revelations of multimillion-dollar corporate "slush funds"—funds accumulated in secret (often overseas) and dispensed by a tight inner circle of corporate executives, largely to pay illegal bribes and payoffs to secure government contracts (mostly overseas). Occasionally, though, bits and pieces of these slush funds would find their way into domestic political campaigns (for example, $20,000 that the Northrop Corporation gave illegally to Richard Nixon's lawyer, Herbert Kalmbach, when Kalmbach was raising "reassurance" money for Howard Hunt and other Watergate conspirators).

In protest against such practices, the Center for Law and the Public Interest in Los Angeles filed lawsuits against Northrop and Phillips Petroleum. Not only did the lawyers establish the right of shareholders to make corporate executives accountable for such actions; as a result of the lawsuit, the companies also agreed to put outside directors on their boards, theretofore dominated by "inside" directors (company executives and employees answerable to the president and chairman). Thus, not only were independent watchdog-directors placed on key corporate committees to spot illegal uses of corporate funds, but those corporations also adopted policies against continuations of the illegal bribes and payoffs.

NOTE: The Center for Law and the Public Interest operates on a total annual budget of about $600,000. The nation's *five* largest law firms alone receive nearly three hundred times that amount in annual fees.

According to the most recent nationwide survey of public-interest legal work, undertaken by the Council on Public Interest Law, the total of funds available to the entire public-interest law movement in 1975 was equivalent to the fees paid that year to just two large American law firms.

That same report found that as of 1975, out of 400,000 attorneys practicing in the U.S., only about 600—or less than two-tenths of one percent—were working in public-interest law firms and centers surveyed by the Council.

From the public's viewpoint that is too bad, for just one public-interest lawyer at the right place at the right time *can* make a colossal difference. In one case, it could have made a *$1.3 billion difference.*

It happened this way: late in 1976, Martin Lobel, a Washington public-interest lawyer expert in the intricacies of federal oil price regulation, spotted amid the daily torrent of new federal regulations one that didn't look quite right. Lobel knew that regulators had accused the major oil companies of misapplying an earlier edict so as to give themselves unwarranted price increases (amounting, it later developed, to $1.3 billion.)* Yet this new regulation that Lobel spotted appeared to allow the companies to keep the profits, rather than requiring them to be refunded to consumers.

Lobel, acting on behalf of Consumers Union, promptly lodged a legal protest and succeeded in getting federal regulators to retreat in haste.† While the oil companies ultimately won on procedural grounds having nothing to do with the propriety of the $1.3 billion, the lawsuit produced important dividends: the Department of Energy changed its procedures to give public-interest lawyers added opportunity in the future to spot and to protest oil price increases. Beyond that, the case has two indisputable lessons: first, that well over one billion dollars can hinge on a single, densely worded federal regulation buried among hundreds of others; and second, that such regulations can slide by, wholly unchallenged—as this one would have but for the eye of a lone, expert public-interest lawyer in Washington.

The story of another public-interest legal expert shows how crucial one man and a comparative handful of dollars can be in public-interest law.

In 1969, Albert Kramer (the product of a lower-class Los Angeles family and a man endowed with an extraordinary public conscience) resigned from the influential

*The companies claimed that the earlier regulation was ambiguously worded. Strikingly, small independent oil companies had no trouble understanding the government's meaning and did not interpret the regulation in the generous way the "majors," with their battery of sophisticated lawyers, did.

†Under the regulators' revised decree, in order to keep the unintended price increases, the oil companies would have to prove "hardship" on a case-by-case basis.

Washington law firm of Covington & Burling and, with a $25,000 grant from the Midas International Foundation, founded the Citizens Communication Center. At the time, citizen challenges to the renewal of broadcasters' licenses were unheard of and, with the FCC accustomed to giving virtual rubber-stamp approval to renewal requests (approving 98.8 percent of AM, 99.4 percent of FM and 97.7 percent of TV stations in the years 1972–77), broadcasters felt free to use the public airwaves as they saw fit (as the WLBT example illustrates). Kramer taught local citizens' groups how to monitor broadcasts for abuses; what questions to ask station managers; how to comb station files in search of information that might form the basis for a "petition to deny" a station's license—an action that, if nothing else, shifted the burden of proof to the station and required it to provide information to show why it deserved a license renewal. The citizen challenges raised the prospect of protracted and expensive FCC hearings, and gave Kramer and his clients strong negotiating leverage with broadcasters to improve their programming in exchange for withdrawal of the petition. In one instance, Kramer exacted an agreement from Capital Cities Broadcasting, a major multistation owner, to spend $1 million for minority programming employment for blacks and Hispanics on broadcast stations in Philadelphia, New Haven, and Fresno.

For four years, operating solely with funds from charitable foundations, Kramer, an eighteen-hour-a-day worker, built the Citizens Center. But the most he felt justified taking, by way of salary, was not enough to meet soaring housing costs and to give his two children the education he felt they needed. And so in 1975 Kramer returned to the service of large corporate clients as an associate of the large and influential Washington firm of Arnold & Porter.

The salary difference—the difference between Albert Kramer, singular public-interest lawyer and Albert Kramer, just-another-among-tens-of-thousands-of-corporate lawyers: about $15,000—about half the starting salary of a just-out-of-law-school Wall Street junior.

Why is money for public-interest lawyers so scarce?

First, the groups they represent are usually too poor or too diffuse to come up with more than token payments to lawyers. Second, the legal remedy sought in a public-interest lawsuit is often a *non*money kind (that is, where the goal is to block a license renewal or the building of an oil pipeline or nuclear plant), and in such cases, the usual device for financing lawsuits by the unprosperous—attorneys undertaking a case in return for a share of whatever money damages are awarded—is unworkable.

As a result, public-interest lawyers have had to lean largely on charitable foundations for their support. But the foundations have proved a fragile reed. Public-interest law firms are an unfamiliar breed of applicant and, as the Council on Public Interest Law found in its 1976 study, most foundations "prefer to give to projects . . . run by people they know . . ." Only a select few foundations have ventured into this area, and the beneficiaries have largely been firms working on national issues.

What's more, most public-interest lawyers are in the business of boat rocking, often distasteful to foundation boards. One firm told the Council it was convinced it had lost a grant after filing a discrimination suit against a college whose president sat on the foundation's board.

Even venturesome foundations often have an avowed policy of providing start-up funds for new projects for just a limited period of time, so as to leave themselves free to respond to "new initiatives, new ideas and new people" as they come along. That policy rules out the sort of long-term support that might attract lawyers such as Albert Kramer to a career in public-interest law.

"The foundations," the Council concluded in 1976, "clearly cannot form the principal funding source for public interest law."

There was a flicker of hope in the 1960's, that federal courts would tap a new source of support for public-interest lawyers: court-awarded fees for attorneys who succeed either in enforcing some broad public policy (environmental protection, for instance) or in winning other broadly shared benefits. The prospect of such court-bestowed fees prompted public-interest attorneys to challenge the building of the proposed Alaska oil pipeline because of the feared environmental dangers—and to devote 4,455 man-hours in pursuing that challenge to victory. A lower court agreed they should be recompensed for their work, but the United States Supreme Court closed the door on that new avenue by ruling that judges are not empowered to make such awards unless specifically authorized to do so by an act of Congress.

Congress *has* specifically authorized fee awards in civil rights cases, and such cases (especially employment-discrimination suits) have helped underwrite some public-interest firms. Nonetheless, funds remain scarce, and important legal battles have had to be abandoned solely for lack of money. For example, after a seven-year fight to force the Nuclear Regulatory Commission to adopt stricter rules for the disposition of highly radioactive wastes, a Michigan environmental group finally had to give up for want of funds.

In August 1976, a year after the Supreme Court decision curbed court-ordered fees for public-interest lawyers, the House of Delegates of the American Bar Association considered a resolution urging Congress, in effect, to undo the damage of that ruling by authorizing attorney fee awards in cases that "vindicate a significant public interest."

The ABA House of Delegates voted the resolution down.

The Alaska pipeline ruling was a devastating blow to public-spirited lawyers such as one in Seattle who had donated $75,000 worth of time fighting construction of a freeway that would put 400 poor people out of their homes—families who were only able to collect $4,300 to pay him. He won his case; the judge invited him to request reasonable compensation; but before he could rule, the Alaska decision barred any fee award.

Not surprisingly, that lawyer's firm, estimating its loss at about $56,000, decided to cut back sharply on its public-interest work. "I just spent two years of my life fighting a freeway," the lawyer said. "As a result . . . the homes of thousands of people were saved. The taxpayers were saved millions of dollars. And I was paid less than three dollars an hour. I can't afford to do it again."

THE LEGAL PROFESSION AND THE POOR

On the eve of this country's two hundredth birthday, *The New York Times* observed in an editorial: "No society can properly claim it is governed by a system of law when millions of its citizens are denied access to the legal system because they are poor."

Every year, an estimated seven million poor people have a legal problem (apart from their need to defend themselves against *criminal* charges). The only way they can get a lawyer's help in handling those noncriminal problems is (a) if the government pays for it; or (b) if some charitable organization does so.

As for government help, during the first 190 years of this country's existence (that is, prior to 1965), the government did not provide one cent for legal aid for the poor (once again, exclusive of aid to criminal defense lawyers). That is astonishing, considering that those who cannot afford attorneys are, for all intents and purposes, denied access to one of the three branches of government (the judicial branch).

As for charitable funds, in 1919 a key founder of Legal Aid, attorney Reginald Heber Smith, convinced that his profession had a special duty to the unrepresented, argued that Legal Aid should find its "chief financial source" in the private bar. To that end, he proposed a levy of just five dollars a year on every lawyer in the country.

His proposal went nowhere.

As for his hope that the Bar would be the "chief financial source" of Legal Aid, the total donations to that cause from private attorneys—counting both cash *and* donated services—came to $3,338,000 in 1975 (the last year the sum was publicized). That amounted to three one-hundredths of one percent of the total earnings of the private bar.

In 1965, as part of President Lyndon Johnson's War on Poverty program, the Office of Economic Opportunity began providing civil legal help for the poor. While the program began with a few million dollars, by 1979 it had grown to $270 million.

That sounds like a lot of money (and it is); yet even with $270 million, as of October 1978 there were still nearly eight million poor people who lacked even minimum access to government legal aid, and government-paid lawyers could only handle about one-fifth of the legal problems of the poor, with 80 percent of their legal needs still unattended to.

The government's goal is to expand the Legal Services program to the point where there will be, on the average, two government-paid lawyers for every ten thousand poor people. That surely seems a modest goal: it would provide the poor with just one-seventh as many lawyers as the rest of the population already enjoys.*

Viewed from one other perspective: in 1977, a single company—American Telephone and Telegraph—spent more than twice as much for legal help (over $26 million) as the United States government spent to care for the legal needs of two million poor people in New York State ($11 million).

The dearth of lawyers for the poor can mean long, long delays. In Brooklyn, for example, there are so few Legal Services attorneys that any of Brooklyn's half-million poor

*There are now fourteen lawyers for every ten thousand Americans above the poverty line.

people desiring a divorce must wait twelve to eighteen months *just to get an interview* with one of the government-paid lawyers.

By contrast, if IBM has a legal problem, it doesn't have to wait eighteen *minutes* to get help (what with 243 lawyers on its staff, plus the services of Cravath, Swaine & Moore and others when needed).

For a single corporation: more than 240 full-time lawyers, plus Cravath—and instantaneous legal help. For a half-million poor in Brooklyn: about ninety lawyers—and long waits.

The bar statistics only begin to measure the disparities. There is also the matter of lawyer seasoning and experience. Among Legal Services attorneys, the turnover rate is very high: more than thirty-five percent every year. The result: a preponderance of inexperienced lawyers. The average staff attorney's experience in the Legal Services Corporation is just two and a half years in practice. The average on the IBM staff is about eleven years.

A prime cause of the high turnover among Legal Services lawyers is a phenomenon known as "burn-out," the result of heavy caseloads and pressure, pressure, pressure: from clients, from harassed judges, from opposing attorneys, to hurry, settle, move on to the next case and the next. It is not conducive to pride or ease of mind to hurry when the fate of others is at stake.

At IBM there is pressure, too, of course. But if the load gets too heavy, other shoulders are put to the wheel—from Cravath or one of a number of other large firms.

Another critical disparity: legal help for Brooklyn's poor almost always comes after the fact. It's usually an I've-got-the-court-summons-so-what-do-I-do-now crisis. Who among Brooklyn's poor would dream of consulting a lawyer *before* signing an apartment lease or *before* contracting to buy that bedroom suite, not knowing the merchant, under the fine print, can whisk the goods away if they're late on a single payment? With IBM, of course, it's entirely different: with 240 full-time lawyers on its staff, it can look ahead, send out early warning signals to company executives approaching a legal minefield, keep abreast of trends and prospective changes in the law. Specialists do that: specialists in tax law, in patent law, in foreign-trade law —in a myriad of specialties.

A few lawyers in the Legal Services program fulfill that function. They work in specialty law centers (one for the handicapped, another for housing law, another for migrant law, for example) where they are cushioned against the crushing day-to-day caseloads and are able to analyze root causes, detect trends, and initiate test cases in an effort to set new legal precedents.

Altogether in 1978, nationwide, a total of 114 lawyers worked in such centers—fewer than half the number of salaried attorneys at IBM.

Could the United States *afford* to provide more legal help for its unmoneyed citizens?

Sweden, with per capita income about 15 percent greater than ours, spends *four* times as much as we do on government-supported legal help.

The per capita income in England is just half that of the United States. Yet the British government spends three times as much as America's on civil legal aid for its citizens.

3

Some Recent Changes — Apparent or Real?

On the surface at least, the 1970's gave promise of considerable change in the legal profession. The Supreme Court struck down decades-old American Bar Association rules that had forbidden lawyers to engage in price-cutting competition and to advertise their prices to the general public. Some lawyers did indeed begin to advertise, especially the enterprising attorneys who launched legal "clinics"—multibranch offices, much like H & R Block tax services, conveniently located in neighborhood shopping areas and able, by sheer volume, to perform certain routine legal tasks at lower-than-normal prices. A few groups, mainly labor unions and credit unions, banded together to buy their legal help at a volume discount. And the first government-supported legal program to help with the noncriminal problems of the poor was launched.

It must have seemed to some like a revolution. But how much had *really* changed? That is, for the ordinary person with a legal problem and no contacts in the profession, was it any easier to find the right lawyer for the problem at hand? And had prices come down significantly?

To find out, I decided, early in 1979 to test the waters, ostensibly as an uninformed newcomer to the legal arena, seeking help with some commonly experienced problems: a divorce, buying a home, probating a will, forming a corporation to start a small business. My search took place among lawyers chosen at random in and around New York City, where I live.

I decided to start with one of the big Wall Street firms,

not wanting to rule out arbitrarily the possibility of enlisting the Best and Brightest in my behalf. So I called the prestigious, 183-lawyer firm of Cravath, Swaine & Moore and said I wanted help getting a divorce. I didn't get past the switchboard. "Oh, honey. You've got the wrong place. We only have big corporate clients. What you need is the bar association. They'll refer you to the right lawyer."

Next stop (acting randomly at her suggestion), the Nassau County Bar Association, which covers part of Long Island. Here was a chance to find out what effect lawyer advertising had had on prices, for in that county, where the going rate for an uncontested divorce had been $500 or more, some lawyers were offering the service for $195 and some do-it-yourself divorce centers, manned mainly by nonlawyers, would sell the forms in a kit and help you fill them out for just $95. But the one lawyer to whom the bar association sent me (I'd been told they'd give me a choice of several) charged the same old rate: $500.

Was he typical? To find out, I called several area attorneys, chosen at random from the Yellow Pages. I did turn up one who would handle my case for $250—and who said that the competitive ads had forced his rate down—but the beneficent effects of lawyer advertising were far from widespread. Of the four other lawyers I telephoned, two quoted $500, one $750, and the other $750 to $1,000, "depending on the details of your situation."

How about buying a home? I was aware of the custom among lawyers of charging, not on the basis of the time or work involved in a home purchase, but on a percentage of the price of the house. That meant that the fee on a $100,000 purchase was automatically twice that for a $50,000 house, even if the work involved was identical in the two transactions—hardly the kind of arrangement you would expect in a competitive, free-enterprise market that might have developed with the advent of lawyer advertising. By the time of my survey in early 1979, such advertising had been permitted for nearly two years. It seemed likely to me that some fledgling lawyers, eager to meet the overhead, would by now be clamoring to do the

job on other than a percentage-of-purchase-price basis.
Indeed, there *were* lawyer ads in the New York area offering a flat rate of $250. Yet when I began calling around
at random, I found only one attorney willing to help me
for $250. All the rest quoted the old one-percent-of-pur-
chase-price.

Forming a corporation for a new business venture is not,
of course, as commonly sought after as a divorce or a
home purchase, but I had a particular reason for wanting
to know how much lawyers would charge, in 1979, for
that service. An attorney friend had told me it was common practice for lawyers to farm out the work to a specialty company, manned almost entirely by nonlawyers.
The company would draw up and file all the necessary
documents (even including writing minutes of the new
corporation's board of directors); the lawyer would pay
the company $160—and then turn around and charge the
client several hundred dollars, *without doing a lick of
work himself.* Could that really be true in 1979?
   It was. All but one of the lawyers I talked to quoted
between $300 and $450 for a job they could get done for
$160.* That piqued my curiosity. If specialists could make
a profit selling to lawyers for $160, why wouldn't they be
delighted to sell directly to me and other members of the
public for, say, $200? They'd make more money and I'd
save money—classical free enterprise. I called the U.S.
Corporation Company, a leader in the field. Would they
form a corporation for me? No, they dealt only through
lawyers. Why? They didn't want the local bar association
initiating charges against them of unauthorized practice
of law (in many states a crime punishable with a prison
sentence).

---

*My lawyer friend assured me that the rationale offered by other
attorneys for this practice—that they earned the huge markup by
"reviewing" the papers to make sure they were "in order"—was sheer
nonsense, that lawyers routinely handed on the packet of papers from
the corporation-forming company without so much as a glance at
them.

Quite an arrangement: not only do lawyers have a monopoly on the rendering of legal services; the unauthorized-practice lever also gives them, in effect, *the power to define the boundaries of their own private turf.* That power, it seemed, was intact at the end of the 1970's—the decade that had given the appearance of bringing such changes to the legal profession.

While broad-scale advertising was too expensive for the individual practitioners of the sort I'd been calling, I knew from watching TV that multibranch legal clinics were reaching out to the public, and from their fee schedules, I knew they were undercutting traditional rates for certain kinds of standard legal tasks that could be handled on a high-volume, mass-production basis. But what if a person had a problem that was likely to be resolved only in court—a dispute with a landlord or a merchant, for instance. Small-claims court springs to mind as a lawyerless solution—but it's not that simple: most such courts sit at times and places onerous for working people; procedures are complex and court staff scarce; and even if a person wins, collecting the money is yet another obstacle course that usually ends up in frustration. So where small-claims court is not the answer and a regular court trial is the only alternative, can the mass-production savings of a legal clinic help there, too? I learned of a lady in Brooklyn whose brand-new Buick, despite at least ten visits to the dealer's repair shop, persisted in swerving dangerously into the opposite lane whenever she applied the brakes. The dealer was adamant against an exchange of cars. A breach-of-warranty lawsuit seemed the only answer, but no lawyer could help my friend at a price she could afford. I took the problem to the largest of the legal clinics, founded by the pioneers of the movement, Jacoby & Meyers. They were sympathetic, but acknowledged that, when it came to litigation, they couldn't quote flat fees as with their other services, but would have to charge by the hour. And since in this case the dealer had said he would involve General Motors and its battery of attorneys, there was no telling how many hours the case would require. The Jacoby lawyer also had little doubt that if the Buick dealer and GM decided to stand their ground (in order to discourage other complaining customers from bringing lawsuits), they could easily outlast and outlitigate the Brooklyn lady. So, like it or not, she had no choice but to live with her dangerous car. That, too, was a fact of legal life that hadn't changed, even with the advent of lawyer advertising and legal clinics and the other "reforms" of the 1970's.

4

 Where There's a Will,
There's a Probate Lawyer

Few areas of the law affect as many Americans as the probating of wills and the legal costs of buying and selling homes, the subjects of this and the following chapter.

Those very fields were singled out for special attention in 1974 by the Chief Justice of the United States, Warren Burger, as examples of what once were "relatively simple tasks" that have become "encrusted with procedural complications" that "often add unreasonably to costs."

Speaking to the American Law Institute—the cream of the legal profession—the Chief Justice saw "an imperative need" in those two fields to "re-examine and improve."

To what extent has the legal profession heeded his admonition?

Fiorello LaGuardia, the colorful one-time mayor of New York City, once termed the probate court "the most expensive undertaking establishment in the world." He was on target. The last time the Internal Revenue Service provided solid figures, Americans paid two and a half to three times as much to lawyers for probating wills as they paid to the funeral industry for burying the dead.

The lawyers' bills came to over three-quarters of a *billion* dollars—and, projecting that 1972 figure forward in time, the figure must by now be over the billion-dollar mark.

What is more striking is that probate expenses in the United States are as much as one hundred times what they are in England, according to University of Missouri law professor and probate expert William F. Fratcher. What's more, Fratcher says, probate typically takes seventeen times as long here as in England. The explanation: British probate procedures are vastly simpler, and do-it-yourself probate, without a lawyer, is the rule rather than the exception, as it is here.

Here and there in the United States, one catches hints of the savings that can be realized when probate can be wrested from the grip of the lawyer. Author Murray Teigh Bloom has described how, with the aid of a simplified state probate law enacted over the stormy opposition of the Organized Bar, Wisconsin resident Adele Conway was able to probate the $100,000 will of her husband *on her own,* for a total outlay of just $45 (not counting the 30 hours she personally devoted to the task.* The usual legal fee would have been $5,000.

In Maryland, even without a specially simplified probate law, Mrs. Barbara Thompson of Bethesda probated her husband's $140,000 estate with a couple of hours' coaching from lawyer-legislator (and ardent probate reformer) David L. Scull. Ordinarily the legal fee for such an estate would have been about $7,000. Mrs. Thompson paid Scull $150.

Imagine paying fees of $5,000 to $7,000 for settling estates that nonlawyers handled competently. It seems incredible until you realize that lawyers' probate fees are based not on time spent but on the size of the estate, no matter how simple the legal work involved. Thus, as with home purchases, the fee for handling a million-dollar estate would be close to double the fee on a $500,000 estate, even if the larger one was in apple-pie order and required a minimum of legal work. That can result in generous fees. One Wisconsin lawyer told CBS's *60 Minutes* of earning probate fees that came to as much as $481 an

---

*Bloom also reported that not one among four hundred do-it-yourself probate cases resulted in any subsequent legal difficulties, further testimony to the feasibility of self-help probate.

hour—six to eight times his normal hourly rate. And in 1979, Tom Goldstein, legal affairs reporter for *The New York Times* reported that probate fees on the estates of the very rich in Florida sometimes amount to more than $1,000 an hour.

Nowhere is the Lawyers' Monopoly's power more manifest than in the persistence of the percentage method of calculating probate fees. Traditionally, that method had its basis in the minimum-fee schedules promulgated by local bar associations. Yet even after those were outlawed by the U.S. Supreme Court in mid-1975, the uniform-percentage charges here persisted. A 1977 Commerce Clearing House Estate Planning Guide noted that the "toll" the "probate process . . . exacts" is "generally based on the [size of the] gross estate." The uniform percentage quotations I found in my telephone survey of New York lawyers in 1979 showed that, notwithstanding the Supreme Court ruling, the practice lives on.

The percentage method typically finds sanction in state probate statutes—and many probate attorneys have found a way of using those laws to exact the last full measure of fees from their clients. In most state laws the percentage is supposed to be a *ceiling,* but many probate attorneys would have their clients believe it is *the* fee prescribed by law. Some certainly treat it that way. In the District of Columbia, where the "statutory fee" is 10 percent, lawyer Charles Iverson charged precisely $6,077 for probating a $60,774.24 estate—a precision topped by the firm of Houston & Gardner, whose fee for handling a $47,516.95 estate was calculated, to the penny, at $4,-751.69.

Not all Washington attorneys, of course, push the law to its limits, but a survey of fee claims undertaken by Maryland legislator David Scull disclosed that nearly half of them charged between 90 and 100 percent of the statutory ceiling.

A similar survey by Scull in two Maryland counties near Washington revealed another obstacle to curbing inordinate probate fees: judicial indifference. In theory, probate judges are supposed to review requested fees on behalf of heirs on the basis of a detailed listing of hours spent, which the law requires be appended to the fee request. Yet of 74 fee applications surveyed, only one contained any such supporting data. There was no evidence of any complaint of these breaches of the law by any probate judge. Indeed, some fee requests that *exceeded* the statutory ceiling slid through without judicial protest.

That spirit of largess in the dispensing of generous probate fees finds vivid illustration in the experience of one Manhattan psychiatrist who, after testifying before a "sheriff's jury" (then part of the probate court) as to the mental competence of a very wealthy but senile gentleman, submitted a bill for three hours of his time, at his regular hourly rate. He promptly received a call from the old gentleman's attorney:

"This is an inadequate bill."

"A *what?*"

"An inadequate bill. You are supposed to be a distinguished expert. With this bill you won't be taken seriously."

Soon thereafter the psychiatrist received a check for three times the amount he had asked for.

A model Uniform Probate Code (UPC) enacted in some states supposedly eliminates the statutory basis for percentage probate fees; yet so deeply ingrained is the practice that even in those few states that have adopted the UPC, many lawyers persist in doing business the old way. In Colorado, for example, more than three years after the adoption of the UPC, one attorney suspected that many of his brethren "have been claiming fees under old percentage schedules without saying so." One such was Greeley, Colorado, attorney William P. Southard, who in 1976 saw fit to charge $42,000 for the admittedly "routine" probating of the million-dollar estate of Austin M. Painter.

The task required attorney Southard to make but a single court appearance: at the hearing to set his fee.*

Two other Colorado lawyers, in quite separate experiments, demonstrated the irrationality of the percentage method of reckoning probate fees. One tested the practice by probating a case for a close friend using the ordinary hourly-rate basis of billing. He discovered that, even by charging for every *minute* of time connected with the case at his normal rate, his fee came out to half the going percentage rate in his state.

The other lawyer set out to prove how reasonable probate rates were, but unwittingly proved the opposite. In 1966, Denver banking attorney Richard B. Bauer, feeling that lawyers were being unfairly criticized for overcharging, conducted a painstaking state-by-state survey of the going rates for probating a $100,000 estate. Presumably that was a task of reasonably uniform difficulty everywhere in the United States. Yet, Mr. Bauer's study revealed that, even in adjacent states, the fees varied wildly: in Georgia, the charge was $1,800, while in neighboring Alabama it was $5,000. In Delaware, the same work cost $2,000, while across the river in New Jersey, the standard fee was two and a half times as much.

Lawyers commonly offer three main arguments for reckoning probate fees on percentage rather than a time basis. First, they say they are justified in charging more for larger estates because their "responsibility" is greater. On that basis, they should charge twice as much for negotiat-

---

*In spite of the change in the Colorado law, the probate judge at that hearing found the $42,000 fee entirely appropriate. Both the legal fee and the $39,337 "executor's fee" charged by the First National Bank of Greeley would have stood but for a legal objection filed by one of Mr. Painter's beneficiaries. When a Colorado court, dissatisfied with the fees, sent the matter back for further consideration, attorney Southard suddenly produced time records that he had failed to furnish in the first contest over the matter, and the lower-court judge approved a fee almost as high as the original one. At this writing (December 1979), the matter is still on appeal.

ing and drafting a $500,000 contract as for a $250,000 contract. But they don't.

Second, some lawyers with modest small-town practices defend the percentage method of reckoning probate fees on the ground that an hourly charge for the smallest estates would result in a fee disproportionate to the wealth involved, and that the comparatively ample fees they receive from the larger estates allow them to handle the smaller ones for a reasonable charge. But if the modest estates are in fact money losers for lawyers, isn't that an argument for simplifying probate so as to allow the heirs to do the work, as commonly happens in England?

Finally, some lawyers argue that it is unduly burdensome for them to keep detailed time records as the basis for computing probate fees. Probate reformer David Scull scoffs at this. At the Washington, D.C., law firm with which he formerly did probate work, it was standard for attorneys to keep track of, and bill for, each six *minutes* of their working time.

As with most high-priced services, the burden of large probate fees falls heaviest on those with the most modest means. One study of probate in Minnesota showed that for an estate of under $10,000, one dollar in every seven went to pay probate expenses rather than to the heirs. It likewise showed that on estates of $15,000 to $25,000, probate fees averaged $2,200 while funeral expenses were just $780.

The high fees charged by American lawyers are only part of the explanation for why probate here costs up to one hundred times more than in England. The core of the difference lies in the fact that the British have recognized that for the vast majority of people—those leaving modest-sized estates in a comparatively simple will, typically to spouse and/or children—probate is (or can be) a comparatively simple and largely lawyerless procedure, easily and competently manageable by a family member or close friend.

The key to reform lies in two essential features:

• Simplified procedures: eliminating the need for court approval of every step along the probate road (the typical arrangement in America) and, instead, permitting judges to appoint a relative or close friend to handle the mechanics of probate (collecting financial information, paying bills, filing the tax return, and so on).

• Easily available help to facilitate do-it-yourself probate—with court staffs answering questions just as Internal Revenue personnel routinely do for taxpayers with their Form 1040s.

America lags behind the British largely because the Organized Bar here has looked with a glassy eye at self-help probate. On the matter of probate simplification, the American Bar Association has moved with glacial speed. First tackling the subject in 1941, the ABA labored on and off for nearly thirty years—and then the "simplified" measure it produced (a model Uniform Probate Code, or UPC) ran to 278 pages. There was, buried in that verbiage, the skeleton of a simpler probate system, and where it was adopted, probate costs fell by as much as 30 percent. But that was only a small fraction of the economies typically enjoyed in Britain.

Even that partial reform has enjoyed scant favor among lawyer-dominated legislatures. The ABA gave its formal blessing to the UPC but evidently little more than that, for in 1979, thirteen years after the Uniform Probate Code first emerged, only eleven states had adopted it,* in many instances in watered-down form.

As a result, probate in most states is still freighted with intimidating jargon (why must the widow/executor be called *administratrix cum testamento annexo* instead of just *administrator?*), requiring cumbersome court supervision (typically involving some nine separate court appearances) and long delays in carrying out the wishes of the deceased. In Minneapolis, the average probate time

*This excludes three states which, while failing to enact the UPC, are thought to have achieved many of its purposes through amendments to their probate laws.

even for small estates was about a year and four months, and nearly a third of the wills had not been fully probated after two years' time.

It is hard to imagine anyone questioning the proposition that the publicly paid staffs of probate courts should give unstinting help to the members of the public who pay their salaries. Can you imagine, for example, Congress enacting a law prohibiting Internal Revenue personnel from helping taxpayers wrestle with their Form 1040s? Yet, incredibly enough, precisely such a law bars the probate clerks in Prince Georges County, Maryland, from assisting the public (even though frequenters of that courthouse say the clerks routinely help *lawyers* fill out the necessary forms). Lawyer support for that law showed itself clearly when it came up for a vote in the legislative delegation in neighboring Montgomery County: every lawyer-member of the delegation supported it.

Similarly, lawyer-legislators in Wisconsin succeeded in crippling a probate-simplification bill by insisting on a provision specifying that court clerks are *not* obliged to help citizens with their probate problems. They could hardly have fashioned a more effective way of keeping the public in the grip of professionals, as Mrs. Helen Nelson of Milwaukee discovered when she sought the clerks' help in probating her husband's simple, two-page will. In other places in Wisconsin, such as Madison, the probate-court staff willingly helped heirs wishing to handle probate on their own and large numbers were able to do so successfully. But in Milwaukee, the clerks' attitude was entirely different. According to the *Milwaukee Journal*, Mrs. Nelson found herself confronted with what she termed "a series of blank walls": none of the do-it-yourself pamphlets prepared by the state and by the local bar association was available, and the clerks declined to help her in filling out the necessary forms, saying hers were "legal questions." Frustrated, Mrs. Nelson engaged an attorney who, at the cost of $50 an hour, ran up a bill of

$2,700 (much of it, she said, correcting his own errors and redoing previous work).

Few outside the legal profession would disagree with the observation of Wisconsin probate reformer Walter Heiden that "estates should be left to loved ones, not attorneys." In practice, it doesn't often work that way.

5

Buying a Home?
Legal Bills Ahead

In the fall of 1976, a year after the Supreme Court had outlawed uniform-fee schedules for lawyers, but several months before the Court was to pave the way for lawyer competition through advertising, I bought a house in western Connecticut and, as is customary in the East, engaged a local attorney. I expected to pay him as I had paid other lawyers—based on the time he devoted to the matter. Since it was a routine transaction, I was astonished to receive a bill for $750. I called the attorney and asked how much of his time the matter had required. "Oh, a couple, three hours, I suppose. But you see," he explained, "the fee isn't based on the work. It's a percentage of the purchase price of the house."

Then he added, *"And you won't find a lawyer in the state who will do it for less."*

That last remark impressed me as much as the percentage basis for the fee which, as already noted, meant that the fee on a $100,000 house would be twice that for a $50,000 home, even if the amount of time required is the same for both. That is not what one would expect if there were true competition among lawyers, and I wondered: was there nowhere in Connecticut a young attorney, struggling to meet the overhead, who would be eager to handle real estate matters more economically? My lawyer evidently thought not.

Three years passed, during which the Supreme Court struck down the long-standing ban against lawyer advertising. By 1979, it might have been assumed that the arms-locked circle in the legal fraternity would have weakened and the cost of home transfers would have fallen. I didn't know how wrong that assumption was until I came across the transcript of a hearing on real estate lawyers' fees held in Martinsburg, West Virginia, by the attorney general of that state* in January 1979—nearly four years after uniform fee schedules had been outlawed and nearly two years after the advent of lawyer advertising.

When Suzanne Offutt, a speech pathologist in Martinsburg, West Virginia, contracted to buy a house in nearby Berkeley Springs in the fall of 1978, the Citizens National Bank of Berkeley Springs was delighted to lend her the money, provided she hired an attorney to certify she was getting legal "title" to the house and land. That seemed reasonable to Ms. Offutt, especially since she had an attorney friend who would do the job for little or nothing. That was not satisfactory, however, to Citizens National. Even though Ms. Offutt would be paying the fee, the attorney had to be one designated by the bank. Ms. Offutt felt this was an "infringement of my rights," but since she had already signed the purchase contract and couldn't buy the house without the loan, she was stuck.

The lawyer chosen by Citizens National was Mr. Samuel Trump, Esquire. His fee (Ms. Offutt was told) would be about $160. At the attorney general's hearing, several things were revealed.

First, the $160 fee was not arrived at by happenstance. It was reckoned by a formula: one percent of the first $15,000 of purchase price, and one-half of one percent of everything over $15,000. That happened to be identical to the formula used by the Martinsburg firm of Martin & Seiberg and by attorney Henry Morrow of Martinsburg. A coincidence? Not according to what George W. Ponton, Jr., executive vice-president of People's National Bank, testified: "I think it's pretty much of a foregone conclu-

---

*The hearing was on a proposed regulation forbidding lending institutions from designating the lawyer to handle the legal work on the home for which a mortgage was needed.

sion," he said, "for most of the [lawyers] in Berkeley County that they probably have sort of a rate schedule, as maybe someone would call it." Mr. Ponton wasn't sure that the schedule had been printed, "but I'm sure that they [the lawyers] are aware of what other attorneys charge."

A common rate schedule in use in late 1978? Wasn't this equivalent to the minimum-fee schedules the Supreme Court had outlawed more than three years earlier? If so, the attorneys of Berkeley County, West Virginia, were honoring the Court's ruling with a wink.

Although Ms. Offutt had no way of knowing it at the time, Citizens National Bank's choice of Samuel Trump to handle the title certification was neither random nor wholly unbiased. Mr. Trump was a member of the firm of Avey, Steptoe, Perry and VanMetre, and Guy R. Avey, Jr.—the Avey of Avey, Steptoe—was chairman of the board of Citizens National. His partner, John Lee VanMetre, was vice-chairman.

Nor was that the only relationship the firm had with a local bank. Mr. Robert Steptoe, another senior partner, was chairman of the board of People's National Bank of Martinsburg. As it happened, all of the title-examination work on home loans by People's National was performed by the firm of Avey, Steptoe, Perry and VanMetre.

All told, in 1977, the firm derived $121,062 in legal fees solely from their title-examination work for the two banks.

Attorney Henry Morrow, one of those using the percentage formula for calculating his fee, saw nothing inappropriate in basing his fee on the purchase price rather than on the work he devoted to the matter. "Time," he testified, "has nothing to do with it. If I can go over here in the circuit court of Berkeley County and knock out a million-dollar suit in ten minutes' work, I'm not going to charge for ten minutes' work. I'm going to charge for my professional know-how in getting the job done."

Morrow even described circumstances in which the title-searching task might be virtually nil (if, for example, he were to do all the research and certify title to an entire housing development, in which case guaranteeing title to each house-lot on that tract would require *no* additional research). Would he, in that situation, give the individual home buyers a price break on his fee? Not on your life, Morrow responded: "I see no reason why the second, third, or fourth [purchasers] should get the benefit of my services free when that information is exclusively in my possession."

There was another, more basic, question it may not have occurred to Suzanne Offutt to ask: was title certification really so complicated as to require the services of a full-fledged lawyer? Attorney Clarence E. Martin, Jr. assured the attorney general's hearing that it was.* But Martinsburg lawyer Jerome Radosh found "some cause for grin and chuckle," hearing "an eminent attorney such as [State] Senator Martin with his white hair and forty years of practice . . . explaining the need for this great expertise in examining title," since Radosh has seen the title-examining room at the courthouse filled, "day after day, year after year and summer after summer," not with seasoned attorneys, but with "the greenest, youngest, newest law students."

The attorney general heard even more dramatic evidence that fixing legal ownership to a plot of land need not be as expensive as Berkeley County lawyers made it. Just across the Potomac River, in Hagerstown, Maryland, the cost is *half* what it is in neighboring Martinsburg. Why? Because the job there is done not by lawyers, or

*It may not have been solely Mr. Martin's white hair or his experience that accounted for his firm getting all of the $31,360 of legal fees on the 1977 home loans of the Merchants and Farmers Bank. Mr. Martin was chairman of the board and a "major stockholder in that bank."

even law students, but by specialty firms with computer-
ized records and the latest methods of automation.

The two-to-one variation in the price of title searches, as
between Martinsburg and nearby Hagerstown, is mild
when compared with the nearly *nine*-to-one discrepancy
revealed in a 1972 government study, the latest nationwide study of its kind to be made. In buying a $20,000
home, North Dakota residents had to pay an average of
only $56 and Nebraska residents $66 to solve the "title
problem," while New Jersey home buyers, on a house of
the same price, had to pay an average of $413 and New
York residents $480 *for essentially the same service.* (Can
you imagine paying nine times as much for, say, a Chevy
or Ford in New York as in North Dakota?)

Even in adjacent states, there were large disparities.
The New York costs were four times what they were in
nearby New Hampshire; and on the West Coast, Californians paid more than twice as much ($404) as home buy-
ers in Oregon.

Are home titles really nine times harder to establish in
New York than in North Dakota, or four times more questionable than in nearby New Hampshire? Or is it that the
risk of bad-title claims is in fact extremely remote—and
that the whole title-search task is being represented as far
more mysterious and complex than it need be?

A clue may lie in the frequency with which title-insurance companies have to pay out on contested-ownership
claims. For every $1 they take in on insurance premiums,
they have traditionally paid out an average of 3 cents.
When the figure rose to 9.7 cents in 1975, the year was
reported as a "bleak" one for the industry—but as one law
professor observed, that still leaves "the question of what
happens to the remaining 90.3 percent." As to that, he
said, "the data submitted [by the industry] leave us com-
pletely in the dark."

As the West Virginia hearing indicates, transferring ownership of a home or plot of land in America is enormously

expensive. The latest available figures (for 1975) indicate that homes with a total value of between $100 and $120 *billion* change hands every year, and the sheer cost of establishing indisputable ownership of those homes—the aspect that lawyers are most involved in—runs to well over *a billion dollars a year.* (One study put the national average at one percent of purchase price, but in some cases it runs as high as four percent—that is, $2,000 on a $50,000 home, just to establish legal title.)

Need home transfers be so cumbersome and expensive? After all, in buying and selling even so expensive an item as an automobile, the transfer of ownership is effected with the stroke of a pen: seller merely signs over to buyer a state-recognized title certificate and the deed is done. Such potential legal complications as loans and tax liens outstanding at the time of sale are merely noted on the title certificate.

In many countries the sale of land and buildings is handled essentially in the same simple way, that is, through governmentally registered title certificates.* America is comparatively backward, in this respect, for here the only way (in theory at least) to establish iron-clad certainty is to trace the chain of ownership of a plot of land all the way back to the original grant from the sovereign (that is, the government), perhaps back to Revolutionary days. In reality, the search only goes back to the last sale of the property (in a fast-moving real estate market that may not be more than a year or two). But the point is that no matter what the extent or difficulty of the search, the *fee* is almost always the same. The *reductio ad absurdum* came when newly elected Maryland Congressman Michael D. Barnes, seeking a new loan on his own house in order to pay off his campaign debts, was forced to pay a

*Even though land ownership *can* be far more complex than owning a car (there can be restrictions, covenants, so-called easements, and rights-of-way, etc.), there is no inherent reason those can't be noted on the title certificate.

brand new title search fee *on a home that he, and only he, had owned since the last title search.*

In many localities, title searching is made more costly by antiquated land record-keeping services. Even in such circumstances, though, title searches do not necessarily require the expertise of highly paid lawyers. *The Washington Post* has described how, in the Washington area in the early seventies, many lawyers would pick up free-lance nonlawyers hanging around courthouses, pay them $30 to $50 to consult the land records, and then charge their clients as much as a $400 title-search fee.

In Bowling Green, Ohio (1970 population 21,760), lawyers' title-search work has been done by college-age nonlawyers. It took all of two weeks for one such, Matthew Valencic, to be initiated into the mysteries by the outgoing "expert"—a college dropout quitting to go on the road with a rock band. Valencic recalls going to the courthouse "with a fistful of titles to search," a task usually accomplished at the rate of five to ten searches in twenty to thirty minutes. At his pay rate ($3.25 an hour), the cost to the attorney of each title search—even throwing in ten minutes for typing up the results—amounted to something under $1. All that remained was for the attorney to sign the title certificate—and bill the client $60.

After a month on the job, Valencic figures he had become so expert, "I could have started my own business—except that I'd have been sued for the unauthorized practice of law."

And so he probably would. Threats of price-cutting competition are likely to stir the Organized Bar into action. In March 1979, *Business Week* reported that in at least four states where title companies offered, free, to fill in standard real estate forms for which attorneys had often charged $50 per document, local bar associations had brought lawsuits charging the companies with the "unauthorized practice of law."

For most families, buying a home is likely to be both the fulfillment of a dream and by far the largest single purchase of a lifetime—an event freighted with anxiety. (One study placed it "not far" below a divorce or the death of a spouse as a "life stress event.")

The setting is ripe for consumer exploitation. The unversed buyer is a Daniel surrounded by lions—hardened, experienced specialists: broker, developer, lawyer, lender, title insurer, and occasionally a contractor, appraiser, or surveyor looking on. Because these specialists often deal with one another constantly, it is a tight circle, and in 1972 *The Washington Post* provided an unusual behind-the-scenes picture of the network. Lawyers, for example, would steer clients to a favored title-insurance firm, which would show its gratitude by sharing the insurance premium with the attorney—twenty-seven percent of it, on the average. It was, bluntly, a kickback, explicitly forbidden by the lawyers' Canons of Ethics when done without the client's knowledge and consent. Yet, the *Post* reported, home buyers were "seldom consulted."

According to the *Post,* some lawyers even went so far as to tack on a percentage bonus to the land surveyor's fee. One Maryland real estate attorney was getting $8,000 a year from that source alone.

The Washington, D.C., area was no exception. A 1972 government report (by the Department of Housing and by the Veterans Administration) stated that what little competition existed in the home-conveyancing industry found expression in "an elaborate system of referral fees, kickbacks, rebates, commissions and the like" which "rarely inure to the benefit of the homebuyer and generally increase total settlement costs."

In 1974, a new Congressional statute supposedly outlawed kickbacks in the conveyancing industry. But five years later, *The Washington Post* reported that imaginative real estate lawyers had found a way to circumvent the law—by forming their own title companies "to which they refer their [clients] and extracting 'corporate dividends' (which smell a lot like the kickbacks prohibited under the 1974 legislation) for their referrals." Apparently, too, a number of lawyers did not even bother to go through such a camouflage, for, early in 1979, a Department of Housing and Urban Development (HUD) official said that HUD was receiving complaints about kickbacks "by the hundreds."

6

The Lawyers' Monopoly

Reviewing the evidence—and in particular some of the things that lawyers have been able to do at the expense of consumers—the question arises: *how do they get away with it?*

How, for example, do they get away with charging for probate and for home sales on a percentage basis that has nothing to do with the work they do or the costs they incur?

How have they gotten away with saddling us with probate fees up to one hundred times what the British pay?

How can they charge lawyers' rates for work (like real estate title searches) that is easily—and often—done by nonlawyers?

How can an attorney like Henry Morrow assert that although he can accomplish legal tasks with little or no work (as with title searches on housing developments), he has not the slightest intention of passing on the savings to his clients?

Those are practices that clearly would not survive if the lawyers in question (or the legal profession in general) were obliged to face free-market competitive pressures.

Just as clearly, those lawyers behave as if they are unafraid of price-cutting competition, either from within the profession (for example, from struggling young lawyers eager for business) or from outside it.

What's the explanation?

The answer lies in the Lawyers' Monopoly—and in its unique nature and powers.

51

We start with the fact that no one can engage in the practice of law without a license—the license, in this case, consisting of admission to the bar.

That's not unique: many other trades and professions require licenses. Electricians, for example. Or architects. But their licenses are issued by the state, not by a trade association of architects or electricians.

Lawyers are different. The power to issue or withhold *their* licenses—and, more importantly, the power to write the rules lawyers must follow—is vested, for all practical purposes, not in publicly elected or appointed city or state officials but in the lawyers' *private* trade organizations: the bar associations, national, state, and local.*

But the unique advantages of the legal profession don't end there. Even though the rule-writing power is privately held, the resulting rules typically become embodied in and have the force of state law, which gives lawyers the best of both worlds. They write their own rules—and then get the state to enforce them. For example, when the Virginia Bar Association instigated a legal action to prevent the Surety Title Company from selling title insurance directly to Virginia homeowners, and to require the company to sell through lawyers (at an added cost of nearly $500 on a $60,000 house), the bar association did not have to pay one cent to pursue the case. Instead, that burden was assumed by the state attorney general. The ironic result: not only were Virginians obliged to pay needlessly high title-insurance premiums; they also had to foot the bill for being forced to do so.

According to former Justice Department official Joseph Sims, who made a sweeping survey of state practices while with the department, here is the way the power of the state is used to give teeth to the rules written by private bar associations: "Rules of the [legal] profession are typically initiated, debated and approved by the bar

---

*The extent to which bar associations make their regulatory authority felt among lawyers varies greatly from one locality to another.

association, and then ratified (many times without separate hearings or discussion) by a state supreme court . . . made up of lawyers."

So automatic is court rubber-stamping of bar rules, Sims says, that when the American Bar Association changes its regulations and a state bar group follows suit, "the rules of the [state] court are [modified] automatically."

The Lawyers' Monopoly exerts its dominion over attorneys even before they are sworn at the bar. Indeed, you might say the Organized Bar exercises control on a womb-to-tomb basis. Its prenatal influence may be seen in the detailed constraints the Bar imposes on American law schools. In order to receive American Bar Association blessing—a practical "must" in legal education—law schools must conform to thirty-three tightly printed pages of ABA regulations, even prescribing the office space that must be furnished to faculty members—and ABA inspection teams make periodic check-up visits to see that the rules are being obeyed. As described in Chapters 15 and 16, the Organized Bar also oversees two other prerequisites to becoming a lawyer: the bar examination and the determination that candidates for the profession are possessed of the requisite "character and fitness."

Consider the sanctions that can be brought against lawyers who transgress bar rules: they risk being suspended from practice or permanently disbarred. Either way, they are deprived of their means of earning a livelihood—a fearsome punishment. But here, too, the same rubber-stamp process obtains. Miscreant lawyers are hailed before bar association disciplinary agencies, and whatever punishment the Bar recommends the state is almost sure to carry out.

Over the decades, the bar succeeded in stifling any price-cutting competition from within the profession by means of two rules: one forbidding price-cutting by lawyers, the other banning all lawyer advertising and in-person solicitation of clients—so as to deprive any maverick attorney who might invent a better (or cheaper) mousetrap from telling the world how to beat a path to his door. Although both rules have, in recent years, been voided by the U.S. Supreme Court, their past operation is worth relating here, in part because the Court acted only over the prostrate body of a recalcitrant Organized Bar and in part because those two rules exemplify so clearly both the public-be-damned attitude of the Bar and its ability to impose that attitude on a helpless public.

That damn-the-public outlook was nowhere more manifest than in the Bar's decades-old rule forbidding attorneys to charge fees lower than those prescribed by state and local bar associations. To give their clients a break by charging less was deemed *unethical,* and violators were subject to disciplinary action. The Bar's rationale for this rule was that with untrammeled price competition, lawyers scrambling to meet the low prices of competitors would be tempted to cut corners, devote insufficient time to clients' cases, and render inferior legal advice.

The rule was nothing if not audacious. If any other industry had done what the lawyers did—that is, published minimum rates and threatened to discipline those who violated them—they would clearly have been violating the antitrust laws, as at least one lawyer openly admitted in the ABA's official magazine. In 1971, the legal publication *Case and Comment* had found it "astonishing" that "the bar has failed to recognize that the minimum fee schedules constitute price-fixing and are in direct violation of the Federal antitrust laws." But that did not seem to faze the legal profession. Bar leaders asserted that lawyers, being a learned profession and not engaged in mere commerce, were beyond the reach of antitrust laws. Sometimes, they even *boasted* of their price-fixing practices. Here is the ex-president of the Idaho Bar Association, addressing his brethren at an open meeting of the American Bar Association in the mid-sixties: "We have eight lawyers in the entire county. *We have an understanding among ourselves* that these obvious [price] shoppers get nowhere . . .

It works very well for us. I would suggest that if your local bar gets along well, you get together and discuss it openly and frankly..." [Emphasis added]

One New Jersey bar association issued a rule saying that "competitive bidding" by lawyers wishing to do work for the school board was "disapproved." In upstate New York, the Monroe County Bar Association, in issuing its minimum fee schedule, warned that "the lawyer who cuts fees encourages the shopping type of client *whose main consideration is to acquire maximum services at the minimum price.*" [Emphasis added] No such client presumption was to be encouraged.

The American Bar Association's *Lawyers' Practice Manual* adroitly suggested that client dissatisfaction could be avoided and the fee schedules made palatable with proper packaging. The manual recommended that the schedule be "presented in an attractive folder, preferably evidencing a degree of dignity and substance." A "black leather cover with gold lettering" was "more desirable" than a "plain, though neat, paper cover."

The threat of bar disciplinary action was apparently highly effective in preventing lawyers from undercutting one another, for in 1971, when Lewis Goldfarb sought legal help in the buying of a home from thirty-six lawyers in Fairfax, Virginia, not one of the nineteen who responded would quote a fee one penny below the local bar association fee schedule. Goldfarb brought an antitrust lawsuit against the bar practice, and in mid-1975, the U.S. Supreme Court unanimously declared the practice a "classic illustration of price-fixing" and illegal under the antitrust laws.

That ruling did not, however, bring about an instant blossoming of competition among lawyers; nor could it. For even if a struggling young attorney had decided to attract clients by lowering fees, he or she had no way of communicating that fact to the public—because of another long-standing rule of the American Bar Association prohibiting lawyers from advertising. That rule was predicated on a strikingly low appraisal of lawyers and what they might do if unrestrained. One District of Columbia bar report envisaged attorneys resorting to tasteless billboard advertising supplemented by balloons, bumper stickers, and even sky-writing airplanes!

The antiadvertising rule was also based on a condescending view of the consuming public who, the Bar assumed, was unequipped to spot deceptive lawyer advertising and would be made prey to needless legal expenses once lured into an attorney's office by offers of cut-rate service. Whatever validity there might be in their argument, it applies as well to unscrupulous advertising by auto and TV repair shops, home-improvement contractors, and others who have historically exploited ill-informed consumers. Yet the answer there has been to ban only the advertising that is misleading or deceptive, rather than the blanket prohibition the Bar imposed on its members.

The Bar also claimed that the cost of attorney advertising would simply be passed on to clients and would raise rather than lower fees. Plausible, but contrary to experience in, say, the eyeglass industry where, according to a 1977 Senate Small Business Committee report, glasses cost 25 to 40 percent more in states that prohibited or limited eyeglass advertising than in states that permitted it.

Many believed that the antiadvertising rule, like the minimum-fee schedules, was a clear-cut violation of the antitrust laws, although the Department of Justice failed to take any prosecutorial action.* Here again the power the Organized Bar held over its members evidenced itself: no attorney could exercise what he believed to be his legal right—and advertise—without exposing himself to bar disciplinary action and the possible loss of his livelihood. So it was an act of considerable courage when, on Wash-

*The department did, belatedly, file a "friend-of-the-court" brief in the private action described in these paragraphs.

ington's birthday in 1974, John Bates and Van O'Steen, two young attorneys in Phoenix, Arizona, purchased a dignified newspaper advertisement. Predictably, the bar association brought an action against them and a bar committee recommended a six-month suspension from practice. That action (with a reduced suspension) was upheld by the Arizona Supreme Court. But Bates and O'Steen carried their cause to the U.S. Supreme Court where, in June 1977, after more than three years of expensive legal skirmishing, they won vindication. The Court held that the antiadvertising rule violated lawyers' First Amendment right of free speech.

Even then, bar resistance to lawyer advertising continued. The American Bar Association turned aside a simple new rule that would have permitted all but misleading advertising in favor of a negatively worded rule forbidding all but certain enumerated types of advertising. Various state bar groups (which are free to follow the ABA's lead or not, as they choose) moved cautiously to adopt *any* new rule, leaving would-be lawyer advertisers in the uncomfortable position of never knowing when they might overstep an invisible boundary and face disciplinary charges. Indeed, that is precisely what happened to two Long Island lawyers who, having found newspaper ads unproductive, experimented with direct-mail advertising only to find themselves charged with "over-reaching." Little wonder, then, that a 1978 American Bar Association survey showed that only 3 percent of lawyers surveyed were advertising, with the other 97 percent clinging to practice as usual.

Perhaps more important than the legal profession's capacity to curb competition within its own ranks is its power to stifle outside competition. That emanates from the most singular privilege enjoyed by the Lawyers' Monopoly: the power not only to keep out competition, but also to define the size and the boundaries of its own sacred turf. That is, if the Lawyers' Monopoly decrees that filling in the blanks on a standard, preprinted home purchase

contract constitutes "the practice of law," then a real estate broker who performs that normally routine function
is guilty of "the unauthorized practice of law" (UPL)—and
the Bar enforces its monopoly by causing that broker to
be charged with what, in many states, is a criminal
offense.

Note that what lies inside the Bar's private preserve is,
in effect, determined by the Bar itself*—hardly a disinter-
ested group, which brings up another interesting point.
Pause for a moment and examine the phrase, *"unauthorized* practice of law." It fairly vibrates with connotations
of illicitness, of a defiance of society's rules. Then ask,
unauthorized *by whom?* By the Constitution? By an act
of Congress or of some other popularly elected legislature? By *any* public official? No, none of the above. UPL
is simply that which the American Bar Association or,
more often, a state or local bar group asserts to be "the
practice of law" and therefore "unauthorized" if performed by a non-lawyer.

Observe, too, that the offense lies in the unauthorized,
rather than in the incompetent or inadequate, practice of
law. UPL actions can be (and have been) brought against
work—planning or probating a will, for example—performed by full-fledged lawyers—say, a bank's salaried attorney for one of the bank's customers. To a nonlawyer,
this is most puzzling: it is quite acceptable for, say, Lawyer X, as a member of a law firm, to write or probate a will,
but let X move to the employ of the bank and undertake
the identical tasks and he suddenly becomes guilty of
unauthorized practice. Why? Isn't he as qualified as he
was before?

One bar answer to that question is that Lawyer X now
owes his allegiance to the bank rather than to the cus-
tomer/client for whom he is preparing the will. That argument may have merit if the bank's interests conflict

---

*In the last analysis, the disposition of the UPL charge is in the hands
of the courts, rather than the Bar. But normally the courts support the
Bar.

with the customer's, but that is a danger covered by the bar rules regarding conflicts of interest.

The Bar's UPL objections reached a height of illogic in the late seventies, when the Florida Bar Association leveled unauthorized practice charges against, and sought to close down, a legal clinic manned entirely by lawyers simply because it was *owned* by laymen. As usual, the only complaint came not from the clinic's customers but from the bar association. And, as usual, the matter was put in the hands of an ex-lawyer (a circuit-court judge) who, unsurprisingly, recommended to the Supreme Court that the clinic be terminated because there was no evident effort "to balance the Code of Professional Responsibility against profit motives." But as Sandra DeMent, head of a consumerist legal services project in Washington observed, "The fact is that the profit motive is what operates law firms."

The Bar's purported purpose in prosecuting nonlawyers who offer legal services is to assure "competence." An undeniably worthy objective—diluted, however, by the explicit section of the Canons of Ethics allowing a layman to represent himself, no matter how ignorant of legal rules and procedures.

You would think, too, that if the Bar's real concern were for the protection of the public against malpractice, most (or at least some) of the UPL actions would originate from *public* complaints of being ill-served by laymen helping with uncontested divorces, real estate transactions, and similar matters. But as you examine one UPL action after another, you find that the complaint originated not from a dissatisfied customer who suffered from erroneous advice, but from a local bar association.

A typical example is the UPL action brought in 1978 by the Florida Bar Association against Rosemary Furman, a former legal secretary, who was charging just fifty dollars —about one-tenth the going rate among Florida lawyers —to help divorce-seeking Floridians fill out the necessary forms and conduct themselves appropriately at the abbreviated courthouse proceedings. At the time the UPL action was brought, Mrs. Furman had helped hundreds of customers without receiving a single complaint. Indeed, as the Florida Supreme Court noted in its opinion in the case, the Bar itself did not even "contend . . . that [Mrs. Furman's] customers suffered any harm as a result of the services rendered . . ." But that did not prevent the Florida Bar from bringing criminal charges against her. At this writing (December 1979) the decision of the Florida Supreme Court holding Mrs. Furman in contempt of court and ordering her to cease her divorce service is on appeal to the U.S. Supreme Court.

The core of the UPL evil lies in the power of the private bar—a clearly self-interested group—to decide for the consuming public from whom and at what price it must purchase its legal services. That power was not diminished during the 1970's and, as the Furman episode illustrates, it continues to affect the public. Were it not for the threat of unauthorized practice prosecutions, residents of eastern states could buy and sell homes through real estate brokers and title companies (as is the prevalent practice in the Midwest and the West) without the need to pay high-priced lawyers. Would-be venturers in the business world wishing to incorporate themselves could buy that service directly from specialty companies such as the U.S. Corporation Company rather than having to deal through attorneys and pay a huge markup. Banks would be free to lure customers, not with offers of free toasters or clock-radios but by offering to write or probate wills, free of charge or for a fraction of what lawyers now charge.

All of those possibilities are foreclosed because of the continued power of the Bar to post no-trespassing signs where they serve the Bar's interests.

The legal profession has also, at times, sought to protect its members from yet another source of competition: the clients themselves, handling their own legal problems without the help of a lawyer. In the past, for instance, the Bar looked askance at self-help books and kits containing the necessary legal forms as well as step-by-step instructions for the lawyerless resolution of such matters as uncontested divorces, bankruptcy, and the probating of wills. The most celebrated example was the Bar's efforts to prevent the publication of Norman F. Dacey's self-help book, *How to Avoid Probate!,* during the course of which there was an effort to have Dacey jailed for contempt of court. Ultimately the anti-Dacey efforts were thwarted by court rulings and his book sold in the millions.

A few years later, on the other side of the country, California attorney Charles Sherman's self-help divorce book attracted scant attention until the head of the Sacramento Bar Association denounced the book on the steps of the Capitol Building before newsmen and TV cameras. Thereupon sales spurted and Charles Sherman found himself suspended from practice by the California Bar Association.*

Dacey and Sherman were ahead of their time. Recently, self-help books and kits have proliferated and "how to" books are now to be found in most bookstores. Yet there remain factors inhibiting self-help resolution of legal problems. There is, for example, the slowness of the courts and the Bar to make legal procedures simpler and more uniform. Where the rules vary from locality to locality, self-help books become prohibitively cumbersome and expensive. In New York, for instance, the divorce rules differ from one county to another, and even among the five boroughs of New York City itself.

The retention of required court appearances in such increasingly uncontested matters as divorces adds to costs and to public dependence on lawyers. Few courts—even those such as Small Claims and Family courts, widely used by the general public—provide personnel to answer citizens' questions, as the Internal Revenue Service furnishes

---

*The Bar offered to lift the suspension if Sherman would submit periodic affidavits swearing that he had read through and was abiding by the lawyers' Canons of Ethics. Sherman found this unacceptably akin to requiring an errant schoolboy to write penitent sentences on the blackboard.

to help people with their tax returns. In at least one instance, noted elsewhere (page 40), the law actually forbade court personnel from aiding the public in the probating of wills.

The Bar and its allies also propagate the notion that the law is a mystical and complex subject beyond the grasp of the layman. "[T]he ordinary man is incapable [of] know[ing] the principles of law," and is "ineffective in the presentation of his claims," states an article cited approvingly in the ABA's Code of Professional Responsibility. A "public service" advertisement by the Illinois Bar Association stated categorically that *"No person* should *ever* apply or interpret *any* law without consulting his attorney." [Emphasis added]

The danger of lay error exists, of course; but lawyers, too, can make mistakes, and the case of Marion Strong of Dobbs Ferry, New York, suggests that the Illinois Bar's blanket injunction was overly broad. Mrs. Strong, making $5,000 a year as a part-time secretary, was unable to afford the $750 quoted by local attorneys to obtain her divorce. Using a self-help book, she undertook to represent herself, braved the initial hostility of the court clerk, filed all the needed forms and, after a time, was notified of the date for her court appearance. This is her account of the scene at the courthouse.

> Three lawyers were there with their clients ... When they heard I didn't have a lawyer, they were appalled. They said, "Good luck, lady, you'll never get your divorce." I felt defeated, and I thought, well, I probably won't get it, but I'm not going to give up. Then—I couldn't believe it—all three [lawyered] divorces were denied because one paper or another was missing. [Shaking her head] Lawyers just like to make it look complicated.

While the three lawyer-handled divorces were denied, Mrs. Strong's went through without a hitch. The total cost to her: $59—$4 for the forms (purchased at the local sta-

tioners), $5 to pay a college student to serve the complaint
on her husband; and $50 in court and filing fees.

The public's dependence on lawyers is also fostered by
the complex language in which the law is typically
couched. Even a universally-applicable law like the Internal Revenue Code is unapproachable by the layman: a
single sentence, one hundred words in length, contains
sixteen cross-references to other sections of that law. A
so-called "tax reform" bill enacted in 1976, supposedly
aimed at reducing inheritance taxes, was labeled by one
expert "another attorney relief act," and aptly so: a 1977
American Bar Association seminar on that law heard a
"conservative estimate" that it would generate some $4
billion in legal fees from Americans obliged by the new
law to rewrite their wills. Robert C. Brown, executive
director of the Tax Foundation, observed that "some people will spend more money to get their will redrawn than
their estates will pay in death taxes."

Laymen are also intimidated by the impenetrable language in which standard-form warranties, leases, and contracts are often expressed, replete with "hereinafters"
and "Parties of the First Part" and "undersigneds," etc.
(Some law experts say the wordiness of legal documents
stems at least in part from the one-time practice of British
lawyers of charging by the word.) Some might suspect
that this verbal obfuscation is deliberately aimed at preserving the public's need to use lawyers, and indeed some
American attorneys of Revolutionary days complained
that the English legal scholar, Blackstone, in his *Commen-
taries,* had "so simplified . . . and so clearly explained the
principles of law that the same amount of knowledge,
which had cost them many years to collect, might be
obtained in a short time."

Few attorneys, however, would openly endorse such an
attitude. A more typical justification for clinging to ar-
chaic verbiage is that courts have, over time, subjected it
to detailed interpretation, and that the substitution of
new and simpler language would trigger a new wave of

litigation. Those very arguments were used to try to dissuade Citibank in New York from simplifying its loan agreement; but after protracted battling with their lawyers, the bank succeeded. One provision, formerly 348 words long, was reduced to just 31 words, and the contrast between old and new dramatizes not only the impenetrability of traditional language (I defy you to read through the old version), but the degree to which it can, given the determination, be simplified:

OLD LOAN AGREEMENT
(348 Words)

In the event of default in the payment of this or any other Obligation or the performance or observance of any term or covenant contained herein or in any note or other contract or agreement evidencing or relating to any Obligation or any Collateral on the Borrower's part to be performed or observed; or the undersigned Borrower shall die; or any of the undersigned become insolvent or make an assignment for the benefit of creditors; or a petition shall be filed by or against any of the undersigned under any provision of the Bankruptcy Act; or any money, securities or property of the undersigned now or hereafter on deposit with or in the possession or under the control of the Bank shall be attached or become subject to distraint proceedings or any order or process of any court; or the Bank shall deem itself to be insecure, then and in any such event, the

Bank shall have the right (at its option), without demand or notice of any kind, to declare all or any part of the Obligations to be immediately due and payable, whereupon such Obligations shall become and be immediately due and payable, and the Bank shall have the right to exercise all the rights and remedies available to a secured party upon default under the Uniform Commercial Code (the "Code") in effect in New York at the time, and such other rights and remedies as may otherwise be provided by law. Each of the undersigned agrees (for purposes of the "Code") that written notice of any proposed sale of, or of the Bank's election to retain, Collateral mailed to the undersigned Borrower (who is hereby appointed agent of each of the undersigned for such purpose) by first class mail, postage prepaid, at the address of the undersigned Borrower indicated below three business days prior to such sale or election shall be deemed reasonable notification thereof. The remedies of the Bank hereunder are cumulative and may be exercised concurrently or separately. If any provision of this paragraph shall conflict with any remedial provision contained in any security agreement or collateral receipt covering any Collateral, the provisions of such security agreement or collaterial receipt shall control.

*NEW LOAN
AGREEMENT*
(31 words)

"Default: I'll* be in default:
1. If I don't pay an installment on time; or
2. If any other creditor tries by legal process to take any money of mine in your possession.

*The words "I, me, mine, my" refer to the borrower and the words "you, your, yours" refer to the bank.

In April 1979, two years after the new provision took effect, Citicorp Vice President Cal Felsenfeld, who spearheaded the reform, said that the lawyers' fears had proved unfounded: the change had resulted in "no litigation, and we've lost no money as a result."

In part spurred by the Citibank experience, New York State legislator Peter Sullivan steered through that state's legislature a Plain English Law. It requires that all leases and contracts involving less than $50,000 and involving a consumer as a party must be written in a "clear and coherent manner using words with common everyday meanings." The law passed over the opposition of many Bar spokesmen, who predicted a "flood of litigation." As of late 1979, a year after the new law took effect, that prediction had not materialized.

If, in fending off competition from laymen, the Bar's true goal is the best service to the public, it would not invoke the unauthorized practice weapon when non-lawyers provide better service (and more cheaply) than lawyers. Yet the Arkansas Bar sought to prevent the handling of home purchases by real estate brokers even though, as the Supreme Court of that state found, the brokers were able to accomplish the task in less time and with fewer errors than attorneys.

In such cases, the exclusion of non-lawyers seems to fly in the face of good Free Enterprise principles. The legal teacher and philosopher Karl Llewellyn put it this way: "If laymen can do some jobs better or more cheaply and rapidly than lawyers . . . can a lawyers' monopoly—by law —stand up?"

Canon 3 of the lawyers' Code of Professional Responsibility takes a different view. It proclaims the duty of a lawyer "to assist in preventing the unauthorized practice of law."

Is the proper translation of that Canon, "Lawyer, protect the public"? Or is it, "Lawyer, protect thy turf"?

7

How Lawyers Are
Accountable to No One

That the legal profession is a state-approved monopoly—
with the state both adopting and enforcing its rules—is
clearly advantageous for lawyers. But what does the public get in return?

Not much, especially compared with other state-sanc-
tioned monopolies, such as public utilities. They, in exchange for their monopoly status, are obliged to serve the
public convenience and necessity, including providing
nondiscriminatory service to all comers. No such obligation is laid upon lawyers, who may (and ordinarily do)
freely turn aside clients they don't want, leaving (by their
own admission) a large portion of the public lawyerless or
inadequately served.

Moreover, utilities are subject to scrutiny and control
by a publicly appointed body, a public utilities commission, that is supposed to watch over them and make sure
they serve the public properly.

But who watches over the lawyers? To whom are they
accountable?

For the most part, *lawyers* watch over lawyers.

If you have a grievance or complaint against an attorney, since there is no governmental lawyers' public-ser-
vice commission, the only place to complain is to the local
bar association, which is almost sure to be peopled *and
governed* exclusively by lawyers.

No one argues that lawyers, being familiar with the
peculiarities of their own profession, should be entirely
excluded from its regulation. But should they be the *sole*

regulators? Is it right, for example, that any complaint you may have against your attorney will be weighed solely by his fellow lawyers? They are hardly the most objective or demanding tribunal, as illustrated by the following case study of what happens when a lawyer breaks the law or the profession's own Canons of Ethics.

I have referred to *The Washington Post* 1972 disclosures that lawyers throughout the Washington area were paying kickbacks and other hidden fees to developers, lenders, real estate brokers, and builders in widespread violations of the legal profession's Canons of Ethics. But none of the principal enforcers of the Canons—the bar associations in the Washington area—took any action, either before or after the *Post*'s disclosures.

In this case, there was a second disciplinary avenue. The attorney general of Virginia was asked whether certain of these kickback practices violated state law. He ruled that they did.

And yet no one was prosecuted.

Why not? Virginia's assistant attorney general, G. J. Markow, furnished an explanation: "We would not take any action to prosecute *until the bar asks us to.*" [Emphasis added]

Kickbacks by Washington-area attorneys were trifling compared with the wholesale and clear-cut violation of the antitrust laws by the Organized Bar and the entire legal profession that went unprosecuted for decades. Even while the American Bar Association rule against lawyer price-cutting (via the minimum-fee schedules) was in effect, it was believed to be an outright violation of federal antimonopoly laws. In fact, late in 1971, nearly four years before the U.S. Supreme Court unanimously confirmed that view, Assistant Attorney General Richard McLaren, the government official in charge of enforcing the antitrust laws, observed, "I don't think there is too much question . . . that there is a *per se* violation" in the minimum-fee schedules.

Yet no attorney general of the United States ever made a move to bring his own profession into line with the law.

In theory, at least, the regulation of lawyer conduct is ultimately up to the members of the judiciary. They are, of course, drawn from the legal ranks, and many of them return to those ranks after they resign or retire from public service. It is to be expected, therefore, that they would feel a kinship with their professional brethren. To illustrate, the justices of the U.S. Supreme Court, in the course of striking down the long-standing American Bar Association prohibition against lawyer advertising, were moved to "commend the spirit of public service with which the profession of law is practiced and to which it is dedicated," and then to add, "The present members of this Court, licensed attorneys all, *could not feel otherwise.*" [Emphasis added]

Other judges have offered similar evidence that they may not be the most unbiased or exacting overseers.

Example: A New York State judge told an attorney appearing before him: "Oh, you're a member of one of those prepaid [legal services] plans. You're stealing business from the private bar. I'm a member of the New York Trial Lawyers' Association, and *we* don't like it." [Emphasis added]

Example: In the course of a hearing on the propriety of lawyers' fees charged in a certain case, the mention of the going rate charged by lawyers in New York City prompted the judge, federal district court Judge Joseph P. Willson, to observe to the New York attorneys before him: "I don't blame you fellows at all. Get all you can."

Lawyers have also enjoyed unusual freedom from another potential watchdog: the American press. For example, when Mark Green, a Ralph Nader lieutenant, set about writing an article on the American Bar Association, he fully expected, considering the ABA's size and influence, to find an abundance of literature on it. He was amazed at the dearth of articles on the ABA published prior to 1973.

Much of lawyers' work, highly technical and not the stuff of which headlines are made, tends to go wholly unscrutinized, as the New Jersey-based Center for Analysis of Public Issues discovered in 1971. Center investigators discovered that local officials in New Jersey had "complained for a long time that attorneys often charge unconscionable fees for legal work on [municipal] bond issues," fees for which local taxpayers must foot the bill. No reporters had pursued the story, and when the Center published its own seventy-one-page report on the subject, it attracted scant press attention.

While newspapers frequently develop reporters expert in particular fields such as medicine and science, there has, until recently, been a paucity of reportorial expertise about the inner workings of the legal profession—as distinct from the customary coverage of Supreme Court decisions and other judicial rulings. In the late seventies, *The New York Times* and *The Washington Post* scored journalistic "firsts" by assigning full-time reporters to "the legal beat." Yet in the case of the *Times*, there was at least one indication that the newspaper did not have much zest for legal muckraking. When Ralph Nader and Mark Green wrote an article for that paper's Sunday *Magazine* in 1977 sharply critical of the large Wall Street law firms, the *Times* placed its legal affairs reporter, Tom Goldstein, more in the role of an apologist than of journalistic watchdog, by assigning him the last-minute task of eliciting comments from leaders of the corporate bar and of writing what amounted to a rebuttal to the Nader-Green article, which appeared side-by-side with it in an unusual, if not unprecedented, procedure for that magazine.

The most effective check-rein on the legal profession, potentially, are the members of state and national legislatures, for there are numerous ways legal help could be made cheaper and more widely available by means of new laws (for example, laws simplifying probate and home-transfer procedures). But there's a hitch: in almost all legislatures, the single most prominently represented profession is the legal profession. In 1979, half of the members of the U.S. House of Representatives and sixty-five percent of the U.S. Senate were lawyers.

Those figures understate the influence of attorneys in the legislative process, for even in legislatures in which they are not as numerous as in the U.S. Congress, lawyers almost invariably dominate the judiciary committees, through which virtually all legal reform laws must pass before being considered by the full House and Senate. (In the Congress, for example, every member of the House and Senate judiciary committees is an attorney.)

Maryland legislator and legal reformer David Scull discovered the importance of lawyer-legislators when he put forward a probate-reform bill that required the approval of his fellow county legislators. The four lawyer-members of the delegation voted against the reform. It was defeated, four to three.

Clearly, the Lawyers' Monopoly enjoys a degree of freedom that finds few parallels. The existence of such publicly unaccountable power would be troublesome in an industry of peripheral importance to society (say, the sporting goods industry). But granting lawyers a monopoly that is not merely state sanctioned, but state enforced and state protected, is quite another matter since, as Karl Llewellyn has observed, "Only through lawyers can the layman win in fact the rights the law purports to give him."

If the price of sporting goods becomes excessive, most people can get along without a set of golf clubs, a tennis racquet, or skis. But when, through the abuse of monopoly power, the price of legal help rises out of reach, many are obliged to do without "the rights the law purports to give" —in short, to do without justice.

8

Writing the Rules:
By Lawyers, for Lawyers

In the ongoing debate about who the legal profession is *really* interested in serving (the well-being of lawyers and their rich clients, say the Bar's detractors; the public interest and the cause of justice, says the Bar), the American Bar Association itself provides us with some of the most significant clues, through its Code of Professional Responsibility, embodying the so-called Canons of Ethics.*

Canons of *Ethics,* they are called. But as you scrutinize them and learn what they permit or encourage as opposed to what they forbid, you are repeatedly astonished that the word *ethics* should be associated with the Canons. For example:

Item: On the matter of fees, the Canons frown upon those that are *"clearly* excessive." By implication, a fee that is only moderately excessive enjoys the ethical blessing of the bar.†

Item: Kickbacks to lawyers who refer their home-buying clients to favored title insurance companies have tra-

---

*As noted in the Preface, and for reasons set forth there, this book deals with the existing Code, and does not attempt to take into account the changes suggested on January 30, 1980, by an ABA Commission of Evaluation of Professional Standards.

†As noted earlier, the Code used to be far worse on this matter of fees, making it "unethical" for a lawyer to give a client a break by charging less than the minimum fees prescribed by the local bar association. It would presumably still be that way if the United States Supreme Court had not struck down that Canon of "Ethics" in 1975 as a clear case of "price fixing" and violative of the antitrust laws.

ditionally been permissible under the Canons.* By contrast, the canons have, in the name of protecting clients against unscrupulous ambulance-chasing lawyers, historically deemed it unethical for an attorney to go out and advise a person, however impoverished and defenseless, that his or her rights are being violated and then accept a fee (even $1) for helping that person vindicate those rights.

Item: Under the Canons of "Ethics," the use of a "trade name," such as "The Legal Clinic of . . ." rather than the traditional "The Law Offices of . . ." has historically been regarded as unethical because it might mislead the public.† Yet the canons take pains to assert it is *not* misleading for large corporate law firms to list, in their firm names, partners long-since deceased (for example, the Wall Street firm of Dewey, Ballantine, etc., memorializes the late Thomas E. Dewey, indefatigable Republican presidential candidate of the 1940's).

The "ethical" spirit of the Canons is perhaps best captured in its provisions on fees. Beyond the fact, already noted, that only *"clearly* excessive" fees are forbidden, there is the question of who decides what is exorbitant and on what basis. That judgment is not made by an independent arbiter. A fee is "clearly excessive" only if deemed so by "a lawyer of ordinary prudence"—that is, by a brother at the Bar.

Moreover, the yardstick by which this prudent lawyer must judge his fellow attorney is most rubbery. It consists of various "factors to be considered"—including such unquantifiable measures as the "experience, reputation, and ability" of the fee charger; the "nature and length of the

---

*Technically, the Canons required attorneys to advise clients about the "commissions" they are receiving, but it is well known that this obligation is honored in the breach.

†As noted on page 90, the California State Bar Association sought to invoke that rule to suspend from practice two Los Angeles lawyers who opened a legal clinic and charged a fraction of traditional Los Angeles fees.

professional relationship" between lawyer and client; and the "fee customarily charged in the locality."

Then, after weighing the matter on that amorphous scale, only if the "prudent lawyer" is "left with a definite and firm conviction" that the fee is "clearly excessive" can his fellow attorney be called to task. Any doubts, that is, must, under the "ethical" rules, be resolved in favor of lawyer and against client.

It is understandable, then, that the instances of lawyers being disciplined for overcharging are rare in the extreme. It is likewise unsurprising that no bar sensibilities were offended by former Attorney General Richard Kleindienst's receiving $250,000 for just five hours' "work" in procuring a large insurance contract from the Teamsters Pension Fund, where Kleindienst had particularly close connections (p. 141); by lawyers collecting fees of up to $1,000 an hour for probating wills (by reckoning their charges as a percentage of the estate rather than based on time spent); by attorneys charging $500 to $1,-200 for a routine uncontested divorce even where the bulk of the work—the filling in of standard forms—is done by low-paid secretaries rather than the attorneys themselves; or by lawyers double-billing for their time while on air trips (an attorney, while en route from New York to San Francisco to take care of a matter for IBM, uses the airborne hours to work on a General Motors case—and bills both IBM *and* General Motors at up to $200 to $250 an hour). When I expressed shock about this practice to one attorney, he shrugged and said that when he works on, say, a legislative matter affecting eleven of his clients, he bills all eleven at his regular hourly rate of $125, which nets him $1,375 an hour.

Notwithstanding the Canons' proclamation of the lawyers' "duty to make legal counsel available," the eight factors for judging the propriety of a fee conspicuously *omit* the client's income and his or her ability to pay the fee—with one exception. One group is singled out for compassion: "brother lawyer[s] or a member of [their] immediate family"—to whom, the Canons say, "long-standing tradition" warrants "special consideration." Other than that favored group, however, ability to pay is not a factor.* After all, as the Canons note, "adequate compensation is necessary in order to enable the lawyer to serve his client effectively and to preserve the integrity of the profession."

Another clue to whom the legal profession is primarily interested in serving lies in a systematic double standard that permeates the Canons: one for the bar elite and their wealthy corporate and family clients and quite another for the small general practitioners and the more "average" clients they serve.

Let us return to the Code's regulations on lawyer advertising. The pre-Supreme Court bar prohibition against commercial advertising by lawyers appeared, on the surface, to be absolute: "A lawyer *shall not* publicize himself," said the Canons, via media advertising or "other means of commercial publicity." Period. [Emphasis added]

But there were exceptions. The Canons make it ethical for a lawyer to purchase commercial ads in a "reputable law list (or) legal directory." What makes such a list or directory "reputable"? Any that are "certified by the American Bar Association" are "conclusively established" to be "reputable." Among those enjoying an ABA pedigree are four separate directories of insurance specialists and at least two listing lawyers for banks and several listing firms doing general corporate work.

The upshot has been that members of the general public trying to find a lawyer experienced in handling their

---

*There is one instance where the Code recognizes that "a person of moderate means may be unable to pay a reasonable fee" and exhorts "every lawyer" to "find time to participate in serving the disadvantaged." But those words, unlike the eight formally set out factors, are contained in what is called the "aspirational" portion of the Code, and every lawyer knows that failure to heed the words cannot result in any disciplinary action.

particular problem—be it divorce, bankruptcy, or consumer law—traditionally had no choice but to flounder through the unmarked sea of names in the Yellow Pages, since lawyers could not advertise their specialties either there or in classified newspaper ads.

Judging from the findings of the ABA's research arm, the American Bar Foundation, the advertising ban had a telling effect. Seventy-nine percent of those interviewed by the ABF agreed that "a lot of people do not go to lawyers because they have no way of knowing which lawyer is competent to handle their particular problem."

By contrast, business clients—merchants trying to collect a small bill, for instance—had no difficulty locating a debt-collection specialist, for there are at least six distinct directories of such lawyers that enjoy ABA "certification."

A principal justification for the historic ban on lawyer advertising was the Bar's desire to avoid the appearance of being a "mere money-getting trade," rather than the "learned profession" the ABA insists it is. But that has not prevented the American Bar Association from bestowing its blessing on a publication known as *The Attorneys' Register,* although its self-proclaimed "primary purpose" is "securing SUBSTANTIAL legal business for our listees" [capitalization theirs]—not business from among the general public, but from the "careful selection of banks and trust companies, important industrial corporations, insurance companies, financing institutions and the like," to whom the *Register* is circulated, free of charge. "Ambulance chasing may be reprehensible," remarked Hofstra law professor Monroe Freedman, "but corporation-chasing carries an ABA seal of approval."

A similar dual standard applies to the restrictions on in-person solicitation of legal business—expressed in a long-standing rule that lawyers giving "unsolicited" advice to a layman "shall not" accept employment resulting from that advice. Once again, "shall not"; an apparently flat rule.

But the next words are "except that"—and there follow neatly worded escape hatches through which lawyers for the well-endowed maneuver effortlessly. For example, the solicitation ban does not apply to contacts with a "close friend"—just the sort of person one is likely to encounter on the cocktail-party circuit or at the country club.

The usefulness of the country club as a client-getter is confirmed, according to Professor Freedman, by the fact that "lawyers have been known to take tax deductions" for club dues and fees as "ordinary and necessary business expenses," and by the instance of one "prominent Federal judge" who "resigned from several exclusive clubs upon going on the Bench, explaining to friends that he no longer needed to attract clients."

A cocktail-party solicitation might go like this: "Gee, Fred, if that's what's going on, you really ought to talk to my partner, Bob, who is one of the country's leading experts on exactly that problem. He saved one of our clients a million dollars last year just on that point alone." That is no hypothetical remark, but an amalgam of *actual* exchanges observed by lawyer Jethro Lieberman, author of *Crisis at the Bar,* a book on legal ethics. Lieberman observes that such "remarks violate the [ethical] Code in half a dozen ways and yet they are all too typical."

While the Bar winks at in-person solicitation in the locker room or over a martini, the rule is likely to be more strictly enforced against in-person advice to the indigent and powerless. Thus, in the summer of 1973, attorney Edna Primus told a group of welfare mothers that their legal rights may have been violated when they were sterilized as a condition of receiving continued Medicaid treatment. Later, when advised that one of the women, Mary Etta Williams, wished to bring a lawsuit against the doctor, attorney Primus wrote her to say that the American Civil Liberties Union would pay for the suit, and to suggest a conference with Ms. Williams "to explain what is involved."

Attorney Primus never, in fact, represented Ms. Williams, because while she was waiting one day to have the doctor see her critically ill child, the doctor's attorney persuaded Ms. Williams to sign a legal release, without explaining to her that this foreclosed a lawsuit. One might have thought the parties would have been content to end the matter there. Not the South Carolina Bar Association. After the passage of more than a year, Ms. Primus suddenly found herself charged, and then convicted, by the State Disciplinary Board, of "soliciting" employment by Ms. Williams. While the United States Supreme Court later overturned the action, it was no thanks to the South Carolina Bar Association, which, in this most benign example of "solicitation"—an attorney for a nonprofit organization advising a group of poorly informed women about their legal rights—filed a stiff legal brief against Ms. Primus.

In one rule in particular, the Canons come unequivocally to the aid of the well-heeled litigant to the disadvantage of the less prosperous. The Canons forbid hiring expert witnesses on a contingent-fee basis (that is, with the expert's fee dependent on the outcome of the case and the amount, if any, recovered by the client). Lawyers, of course, are permitted to serve on that basis, and since that enables unmoneyed clients to bring lawsuits without the burden of an up-front retainer fee, it is regarded as one of the equalizing features of the American legal system. And yet, although expert witnesses can be almost as crucial as attorneys in bringing and winning lawsuits, the Canons preclude the contingent-fee method of paying them.

That very rule may have made a win-or-lose difference in a recent legal action that could have meant substantially reduced prices for automobile buyers. One venturesome businessman devised the notion of rounding up car orders from a number of individuals, purchasing cars directly from General Motors so as to obtain the fleet-discount basis (routinely given car-rental companies and other volume buyers) and thus be able to sell the cars at prices lower than GM dealers normally charge. He soon found himself stymied by GM's refusal to sell him cars, and engaged an attorney (on a contingent-fee basis) to bring an antitrust lawsuit. The lawyer, however, could not prove to a court's satisfaction that GM's policy was unreasonable and illegal without enlisting the testimony of qualified experts in auto sales practices. He and his client lacked the $40,000 to $50,000 such experts charge in a case of this size and complexity, challenging, as it did, the long-standing practices of the entire auto industry. But they were barred by the Canons from using an expert willing to testify on a contingent-fee basis. So the lawsuit failed, and car buyers were denied the bargains this inventive business arrangement might have brought them.

The rule operates in a decidedly one-sided manner. General Motors, with annual before-tax profits of more than $6 billion, could hire as many experts as it wished in order to defend its restrictive practice of selling cars only through its own franchised dealers. So can well-fixed corporations defending themselves against, say, allegations of patent or copyright infringement, or against claims of injury as a result of defective products.

In defense of its one-sided rule, the bar argues that witnesses whose fees hinge on the outcome of a case may succumb to the temptation to exaggerate or even perjure themselves. The Bar fails to explain how that very temptation fails to affect the testimony of other classes of witnesses who have a direct stake in the outcome of a case (for example, the plaintiff, defendant, or their heirs or relatives) or, for that matter, experts who may be regular or repeat witnesses for certain corporations or even on permanent retainer (a salarylike arrangement) with a given company. Clearly, tepid or ineffective testimony would have an adverse effect (either short- or long-run) on any of those witnesses. Yet the Bar seems to consider them a superior breed, above temptation, for the Canons present no barrier to their appearance in a court case.

There is an apparent duality, too, in the kinds of ethical questions that excite the Organized Bar. Here are some that have:

• Should an attorney be permitted to use blue paper, rather than white, for his business cards? (Answer: He should not. As in tennis, all whites.)

• Should an attorney be permitted to print a calendar on the back of his business card? (Answer: He should not, lest that promote "repeated use and indiscriminate distribution" of the cards.)

• Must a law firm's stationery make clear which of the lawyers listed are partners and which mere "associates" of the firm? (Answer: The American Bar Association says no; the Association of the Bar of the City of New York, in a lengthy opinion issued in 1977, said yes.)

By contrast, though, the Organized Bar declined to bestir itself to halt lawyers taking hidden kickbacks from title-insurance companies to whom they steer their home-buying clients, even when urged to do so. For example, in 1972, the ABA's Board of Governors adopted a resolution declaring kickbacks reprehensible and urging their abolition. Ordinarily, that Board's word is Gospel within the ABA, but in this case, the Association's Ethics Committee, six months later, ignored that resolution and issued a formal opinion holding kickbacks ethically acceptable if disclosed to clients. But it is common knowledge that lawyers commonly fail to comply with that requirement. (See page 49.)

In New York, lawyer-author Jethro Lieberman made a point of urging the state bar association to declare kickbacks unethical. A member of that association's real-estate panel told Lieberman that his group was fully aware of the practice, but that "for political reasons," they would not move on this "touchy" matter, and the association itself failed to act. It remained for the New York legislature—and later the U.S. Congress—to outlaw the kickbacks practice.*

---

*As noted earlier, notwithstanding the federal law, the Department of

Even as recently as 1979, some lawyers viewed the Canons as unduly restrictive of certain profitable practices. In June of that year, New York University law professor Stephen Gillers reported an effort by the American Trial Lawyers Association, the California State Bar, and "other lawyer groups" to write into the Canons something Gillers said "might be called 'the right to get paid for no work.' " Those groups, Gillers said, sought to alter the rule that now prohibits attorneys who refer a client to another lawyer, but do no work on the case, from taking a referral fee—which often amounts to as much as a third of what the client pays. Gillers was struck by the arguments advanced in favor of the change. First, said the proponents, the referral-fee practice is so rampant that the rules might as well be realistic and validate it.* Gillers feels that if the fee-splitting is wrong, the answer is to police rather than sanction it.

Secondly, bar groups argued that referral fees are needed to assure that a client will get the best-equipped lawyer to handle his case, for without the fee, an attorney may keep the case even though he many not feel competent to handle it. To Gillers, that amounts to "a form of blackmail unworthy of the profession," for it amounts to saying to clients, "You must pay us if you want us to tell you honestly whether you have the right lawyer to handle your problem."

Finally, lawyers argued that the referral fee does not come out of the client's pocket—that the receiving attorney will charge the same amount whether he gets the case directly or by referral. Not so, says Gillers: he personally encountered a case where an attorney, Lawyer A, unable to take care of a proffered case, accompanied the client to the office of Lawyer B, who quoted a price for

---

Housing and Urban Development continues to receive complaints of kickbacks "by the hundreds."

*Gillers confirmed the prevalence of the practice: it is so commonplace, he says, that lawyers often receive a referral-fee check even when no such fee was ever discussed.

handling the matter. But when Lawyer A said he was related to the client and not interested in a referral fee, Lawyer B immediately reduced the fee quotation by one-third—the exact amount he assumed he would have had to pay Lawyer A.

In addition to the double standard in the enforcement as well as the wording of the Code of Professional Responsibility there are built-in contradictions within it as it now stands. The existing Code proclaims, for example, the "duty" of lawyers both "to make legal counsel available" and "to assist in improving the legal system." And yet, as noted previously, the Bar has consistently used the Canons to block reforms that could make legal help more available to more people at lower prices. For years, "ethical" rules forbade price competition among lawyers, via the minimum-fee schedules and the ban against lawyer advertising (pages 54-7); "ethical" rules against "unauthorized practice of law" have denied the public the option of solving their legal problems by themselves or with low-cost lay help. "Ethical" rules have formed the principal inhibitors of the growth of legal clinics and of group and prepaid legal plans, potentially the most economical means of providing lawyer services.

To Charles Dickens, who developed a lively antipathy to lawyers during his days as a court stenographer, such seeming contradictions about lawyers and the law were not difficult to understand. Dickens set it out in *Bleak House* this way:

> The one great principle of the . . . law is, to make business for itself. . . . Viewed in this light, it becomes a coherent scheme . . .

9

Lawyers as Their Own Policemen

According to the latest available statistics, if you have a gripe about your lawyer and take it to your local bar association, chances are at least nine out of ten that your complaint will be dismissed out of hand, *without anyone even looking into the facts.*

What's more, the chances of a lawyer against whom a complaint has been lodged being publicly disciplined are less than two out of a hundred.

You may find it hard to believe that 90 percent of client complaints are utterly groundless—and that lawyer behavior is more than 98 percent pure. Yet that is the only logical conclusion—*if* you assume that the Bar's disciplinary machinery is functioning properly and judging lawyer behavior correctly.

Most people, including many lawyers, don't think it is. In fact, a blue-ribbon panel of lawyers headed by former Supreme Court Justice Tom C. Clark, after an eighteen-month study of the disciplinary system, came to the striking conclusion that it was nothing short of "scandalous." "With few exceptions," the Clark panel found, "the prevailing attitude of lawyers toward disciplinary enforcement ranges from apathy to outright hostility. Disciplinary action is practically non-existent in many jurisdictions."

That harsh conclusion was based on findings such as these:

• Lawyers disbarred in one community continued to practice in another.

83

• In addition to failing to report infractions by their colleagues, lawyers refused to appear at disciplinary hearings. On the contrary, they even used their influence to "stymie" the proceedings.

• Lawyers convicted of serious crimes were allowed to continue practicing until their final appeal was exhausted (often three or four *years*). As a result, lawyers convicted of stealing clients' funds continued to handle the monies of others; lawyers convicted of suborning perjury continued to try cases; and attorneys convicted of filing fraudulent tax returns went on preparing other clients' returns.

One might have expected so scathing an indictment to stir the Organized Bar to a flurry of reform activity. Not so.

• Four years after the Clark Report, Justice Clark himself is reported to have said that "no progress has been made to amount to anything," and former Stanford dean Bayless Manning (a man not given to hyperbole) observed that "the impact of the Clark Report has been like that of a feather dropped into a well."

• Two years later (that is, *six* years post-Clark) a special committee examining the grievance system of the New York City Bar Association found that in virtually every offense category the severity of disciplinary actions imposed was greater during the five years *preceding* the Clark Report than during the five years following.

• Also in 1976, a nationwide study by the American Bar Foundation—the most up-to-date such survey extant—concluded that "on a nationwide basis, the record of reform in the five years since the Clark Report has, at best, been uneven" and that "in many jurisdictions there have been no significant changes."

In January 1978, eight years after the Clark Report, the American Bar Association announced that out of the 450,-000 lawyers in the United States, 124 (about 25/100 of one percent) had been disbarred in 1977, and a total of 503—about one-tenth of one percent—had received some sort of public punishment.

The paucity of bar discipline has a simple explanation: client complaints are, with few exceptions, considered and disposed of *entirely by fellow lawyers,* who make up the grievance committees of state and local bar associations.

The American Bar Foundation's most up-to-date study (covering 1974) reported the consequences of self-regulation in four jurisdictions—California, Michigan, Illinois, and New York City. The results showed that between 91 and 97 percent of all client complaints were dismissed by bar associations *without any investigation.* In California, where over 97 percent of complaints were not examined, nearly 99 percent were either dismissed or resulted in a *private* reprimand the public knew nothing about. Only two-tenths of one percent of the complaints resulted in disbarment.*

Compounding the lawyers-only nature of the disciplinary machinery is the secrecy in which most of the proceedings are shrouded. The case of Washington lawyer Joel I. Keiler illustrates this. Keiler represented a Miami company in a dispute with the local Teamsters Union. The union agreed to arbitrate and asked Keiler to pick an arbitrator from Miami. Instead, Keiler secretly recruited one of his Washington partners to serve, going to great lengths (including remailing the partner's report from a phony address to give it a Miami postmark) to conceal the partner's relationship to Keiler. Not surprisingly, the "arbitrator" sided with Keiler's client.

It was only by happenstance that this blatant violation of the Canons of Ethics came to official attention (Keiler's adversaries in a later case learned of it and reported it to the bar). There ensued a *closed-door* hearing by a lawyers-only panel and, despite the flagrancy of the lawyers' improprieties, the outcome was a *private* letter of reprimand to the pair. If the affair had ended there, the public would never have been any the wiser and clients would

*The figures are almost identical for the other three jurisdictions surveyed.

have gone on hiring Keiler, ignorant of his questionable conduct. And it *would* have ended there had Keiler not appealed to the District of Columbia Bar Association (in an effort to get even the private letter withdrawn). Only when forced to it did the bar recommend disciplinary action. Even then, the proposed punishment was a thirty-day suspension from practice.

Bar associations can only *recommend* the disciplinary action to be taken. The final word must come from a judge, himself a former member of the bar, thus squaring the circle of the lawyers-only process. In lawyer Keiler's case, the court approved the brief thirty-day suspension proposed by the bar association.

In a more celebrated instance, however, that same court, taking pity on one of the most prominent members of the bar, saw fit to reduce substantially the bar's recommendation. After former Attorney General Richard Kleindienst pleaded guilty to having lied under oath to a committee of the United States Senate,* the District of Columbia Bar Association recommended a one-year suspension. The court shortened the period to just thirty days. (Despite the gravity of Kleindienst's lie, his home-state bar association in Arizona was content merely to censure the former attorney general, without so much as a day's suspension from practice.)

---

*That Kleindienst told the committee an outright and deliberate lie is unquestionable. Asked at his Senate confirmation hearing whether anyone at the White House had pressured him regarding pending antitrust proceedings against International Telephone and Telegraph (ITT), Kleindienst told the committee flatly, "I was not interfered with by anybody at the White House. I was not importuned. I was not pressured. I was not directed. I did not have conferences with respect to what I should or should not do." The truth, as later revealed by the Nixon White House tapes, was that only six weeks earlier President Nixon had personally called Kleindienst and said, ". . . I want something clearly understood. . . . The ITT thing—stay the hell out of it. Is that clear? That's an order. . . . The order is to leave the goddam thing alone."

Many bar associations have perfected a refined technique for shunting aside client complaints: they refuse to consider (or even investigate) "fee disputes"—on the ground that those are purely private disagreements between lawyer and client—and then throw a broad variety of complaints into that category. Here are two instances the New York City Bar Association classed as fee disagreements and dismissed, without bothering to investigate either the merits of the complaints *or* the prior history of grievances against the lawyer in question:

● *Complaint Number 1:* A client gave a lawyer $1,500 as bail to get him released from jail; the lawyer failed to use funds for that purpose and client remained in jail. The lawyer also allegedly deliberately delayed client's criminal case for the sole purpose of making several court appearances and increasing his fee. Later investigation disclosed that the lawyer had been the subject of "numerous" prior complaints and had been admonished three times by the bar association.

● *Complaint Number 2:* The client in a recently completed divorce action complained that, among other things, his lawyer (1) was withholding finds belonging to client; (2) refused to return documents belonging to client; (3) breached the confidential lawyer-client relationship to detriment of client; (4) refused to give client a written statement about what fee was to be and lied to client in oral statement about prospective fee. Within three days, the bar association advised the client that the subjects of the complaint were not within the association's jurisdiction. However, had the bar association questioned the attorney or reviewed the record of previous complaints against him, it would have learned not only of a series of complaints received *but of two bar association letters of admonition* to the lawyer.

In the preceding chapter, I noted the double standard in the *writing* of the rules for the legal profession: one for the bar elite and their prosperous clients; quite another for the rank-and-file of lawyers with more modest clients.

The same duality prevails in the *enforcement* of those rules, in at least three distinct areas:

• Aggressive bar initiatives against lawyers who threaten the status quo in the legal profession as opposed to bar passivity toward Establishment lawyers.

• Harsh treatment of political mavericks and "boat-rockers" contrasted with mild treatment of mainstream attorneys.

• The allocation of scarce bar disciplinary personnel to pursue and punish comparatively mild rule violations by rank-and-file attorneys while permitting the bar elite to go unpunished.

On the question of whether bar groups should take an active or passive role in matters disciplinary, the favored posture (as the Clark panel found) is that of the ostrich: unless a rule violation is the subject of a formal complaint, it is treated as if it simply does not exist. That attitude is vividly illustrated by the case of Hoyt Augustus Moore, whose name adorns the eminent Wall Street firm of Cravath, Swaine & Moore. In the early 1930's, Moore was counsel to the Bethlehem Steel Company, whose desired takeover of a small (and bankrupt) fabricator of wire rope ran into opposition from federal Judge Albert W. Johnson. Judge Johnson got word to Moore through associates that in return for a payment of $250,000, he would withdraw his objections and see to it that Bethlehem got its way. Far from reporting this solicitation of a bribe to the U.S. Attorney, Moore, who considered the amount "not excessive and not objectionable to him," saw to it that the payments were made—*an act he later openly admitted to a committee of the U.S. House of Representatives.*

Bribing a federal judge is a felony as well as an effort to corrupt the administration of justice. It is hard to imagine an act that would be of greater concern to the Bar's disciplinary authorities. Yet for fourteen years after Moore's open admission of that crime,* the Grievance Committee

---

*The admission was made in 1945, after the statute of limitations had expired, thus protecting Moore from prosecution.

of the New York City Bar Association did nothing and Hoyt Augustus Moore continued his highly prosperous practice of the law until his death, in 1959, at the age of eighty-eight.

Even more striking is the fact that in Pennsylvania Judge Johnson's local bar association not only failed to take any disciplinary action against the judge,* it honored him by electing him its president.

The Bar's passive tolerance of Hoyt Moore (whose stratospheric fees offered no competitive threat to other Manhattan lawyers) stands in stark contrast to the Dallas Bar Association's attitude toward three young lawyers who in 1977 opened a legal "clinic," charging fees substantially lower than the Dallas norm. The trio had barely opened their doors when they received an intimidating letter advising them that "the Grievance Committee . . . is, by this letter, *initiating* an investigation into your activities . . ." [Emphasis added]

Likewise, in California the state bar association initiated charges of "dishonesty, corruption, and moral turpitude" against attorney Phyllis Eliasberg, manager of a chain of offices offering Californians help in obtaining uncontested divorces at a fraction of the customary rate. And in Manhattan, where the grievance committee of the bar association had sat silent for fourteen years in the case of Hoyt Moore, the legal clinic of Jacoby & Meyers had not yet opened for business when it received a spontaneous telephone inquiry from bar disciplinary officials checking to make sure that the new bargain-rate clinic was adhering to the letter of bar rules.

Lawyers whose political views and types of practice are out of the mainstream of the profession are favorite targets of bar disciplinary actions. Some examples:

---

*Judge Johnson resigned, and was indicted for bribery and conspiracy, but was acquitted because his coconspirators refused to testify.

• *The lawyer:* Daniel T. Taylor III of Kentucky, frequent defender of blacks and civil rights activists. *Alleged offense:* accusing the judge in a highly charged murder trial of calling him a "dirty son-of-a-bitch." *Bar-recommended punishment:* suspension from practice (that is, denial of Taylor's means of livelihood) for *five years*.*

• *The lawyer:* Philip Hirschkop of Virginia, cofounder of the Virginia Civil Liberties Union, instrumental in striking down Virginia's law against interracial marriages and bringing about widespread prison reform. *Alleged offense:* telling newsmen that his clients (a liberal prison administrator and others) were "the good guys." *Bar-recommended punishment:* disbarment.†

• *The lawyer:* Lennox Hinds of New Jersey, head of the National Conference of Black Lawyers (NCBL). *Alleged offense:* criticizing the conduct of the judge in the trial of a controversial black woman.‡ The Middlesex County Bar Association filed a formal complaint against Hinds. At this writing (December 1979), Hinds's case is pending in a federal court in New Jersey.

Compare the five-year suspension recommended for Daniel Taylor and the disbarment effort against Philip Hirschkop with the Bar's kindlier treatment of other attorneys.

• *The lawyer:* George E. Spater, board chairman of American Airlines. *The offense:* admitted *knowingly* violating federal law by arranging an illegal $55,000 corporate contribution to the Nixon campaign. *Bar disciplinary*

---

*A court reduced the suspension to six months.
†Hirschkop was subjected to a full-dress disciplinary hearing and exonerated.
‡A noteworthy aspect of this case is that while Hinds voiced his criticism in January 1977, and the trial ended in a conviction in March, the local bar association remained silent about the affair for eight months, bringing its charges against Hinds only after the NCBL threatened to bring the black woman's trial and conviction to the attention of the United Nations Committee on Human Rights.

action: a public "admonition." Ordinarily, Mr. Spater's felonious behavior* would have called for automatic disbarment.

• *The lawyer:* Orin E. Atkins of Kentucky, board chairman of Ashland Oil Company. *The offense:* pleaded guilty to arranging illegal corporate contributions to the Nixon campaign. *Bar disciplinary action:* none.

• *The lawyer:* Harry S. Dent of South Carolina, White House counsel under President Nixon and manager of the "Townhouse" operation that received most of the illegal corporate campaign contributions for the 1972 Nixon re-election campaign. *The offense:* pleaded guilty to various Federal campaign law violations. *Bar disciplinary action:* none.

The Clark Report concluded that a basic and pervasive cause of lax lawyer discipline was the financial starvation of bar disciplinary committees and staffs. The Clark panel found that seventeen states had no specific budgetary allowance for their grievance and discipline activities. Five years later, the American Bar Foundation discovered that while there had been increases in disciplinary budgets, they were highly selective. Half the jurisdictions had either not raised their allocations at all or had increased them just enough to compensate for inflation.

The resulting scarcity of disciplinary personnel obliges bar groups to be highly selective in the cases they choose to investigate and prosecute as opposed to those they elect to let pass. From the New York City area, for example, here are some cases that local bar associations considered important enough to warrant using scarce personnel for a full-dress disciplinary proceeding, not just in the Bar's own committees, but all the way through the courts:

---

*While American Airlines was fined for the offense, the Watergate Special Prosecutor elected not to bring charges against Mr. Spater personally.

- *Lawyer:* Carl M. Field. *Alleged offense:* furnishing an insurance company an incorrect date of theft of a $5,000 boat given him by his father-in-law, after having forgotten to mail in the filled-out insurance application. *Recommended punishment:* suspension from practice for one year, which the court approved.

- *Lawyer:* Matthew Newman. *Alleged offense:* drafting and mailing to clients, while suffering an emotional disorder, a spurious judicial opinion—a charge the Bar elected to prosecute through to the courts even though the clients were so satisfied with the outcome of the case in question and with lawyer Newman's general deportment that they had recently retained him to represent them in another matter. *Recommended punishment:* suspension from practice for two years—affirmed by the court.

- *Lawyers:* Anonymous & Anonymous.* *Alleged offense:* displaying a sign, LAW OFFICES—ACCOUNTANTS —INSURANCE—REAL ESTATE, which, the bar charged, involved using those ancillary services as "feeders" (that is, to attract clients) for their law business—a charge that the Bar persisted in pushing even after the attorneys agreed to remove the signs. (Court dismissed the Bar's action.)

While New York bar associations were occupying themselves with such matters, the following highly publicized events were taking place:

- *November 1976:* The New York State Commission of Investigation alleged that Special Prosecutor Maurice Nadjari and an associate had given "contradictory and evasive testimony under oath" and had leaked information to the press that had "improperly tarnished" the reputation of several public officials. The commission recommended that the bar take disciplinary action.

*Their names were withheld in the court proceedings, which were entitled "In Re Anonymous."

• *May 1977:* Marion J. Epley III, a senior partner in the large Wall Street firm of White & Case, was suspended from practice before the Securities and Exchange Commission because of charges that Mr. Epley had permitted a large merger agreement to be completed even though he knew before the papers were signed that the accountants had expressed misgivings about the financial figures that underlay the transaction—misgivings he failed to disclose to the signatory parties.*

• *September 1978:* Mahlon F. Perkins, Jr., a senior partner in the 187-lawyer Wall Street firm of Donovan Leisure, pleaded guilty to lying under oath when he said he had destroyed certain documents that his adversary in a huge antitrust lawsuit was seeking. Mr. Perkins's concealment of the documents was considered a significant factor in the $81.5 million verdict against his client.

• *September 1978:* In the course of Perkins's prosecution, it became known that his lie had been known at the time by his junior associate, Joseph Fortenberry. Although an unambiguous provision of the Canons of Ethics explicitly obliged Fortenberry to report Perkins's lie to the court, he remained silent.†

• *Fall 1978:* City investigators alleged that William A. Shea, a senior partner in one of New York's most politically influential law firms (Shea Stadium, home of the New York Mets, is named after Mr. Shea), had "not been totally candid" with them about the theft of funds from his firm by Peter P. Smith III, a former associate who had been

---

*While there is heated controversy over the significance of the doubts raised by the accountants, the key company in the transaction was later shown to be in far worse condition than had previously been suspected; its stock plummeted after the merger and the purchasers lost millions.

†According to Steven Brill, writing in *Esquire,* notwithstanding Fortenberry's explicit violation of the Code of Professional Responsibility, the Donovan firm not only "kept him on" but went "out of their way with signs ranging from work assignments to lunch invitations to show that they hold him blameless."

named to a high city post. The investigators considered Shea's behavior sufficiently grave to refer the matter to the Bar Association Grievance Committee for action.

On February 17, 1979, *The New York Times* reported: *"So far, there has been no public discipline of any of these men."**

The nub of the problem, said *The New York Times,* was that "right now, lawyers are the only professionals in the state who play a predominant role in disciplining their fellow professionals." Even the $840,000 of public funds provided by the State of New York for lawyer discipline had been handed over to the privately run New York City Bar Association, which, the *Times* said, "has been able to hire and dismiss" all the employees responsible for carrying through disciplinary actions.

Some city judges, the *Times* added, were considering putting those employees on state rather than private payrolls, but "several bar association officials view this move as an unacceptable threat to their independence."

The *Times* 1979 report was published three years after the New York City Bar Association had studied its own grievance procedures and rendered what the *Times* called a "devastating assessment." Despite the passage of those three years, the *Times* reported there was a backlog of 2,000 unresolved grievance cases; city judges expressed "dismay" at the slow pace of the Bar's disciplinary work;

---

*Although Mahlon Perkins was sentenced to a month in prison and resigned from his law firm, the bar association never initiated any disciplinary action against him. That task fell to the United States Attorney, who said that Mr. Perkins's action was tantamount to a felony, which would, under bar rules, result in his automatic disbarment. However, the court (manned, as usual, entirely by ex-lawyers) saw "mitigating circumstances" in Mr. Perkins's case—including his "unblemished" record as a lawyer, his service with the Office of Strategic Services during World War II, as well as his service to his suburban community of Cos Cob, Connecticut. Accordingly, the court concluded, although his "dereliction" was "serious," the punishment of "severe censure" rather than disbarment was "condign to the dereliction."

and even bar officials (who declined to be named) felt the situation "had not improved."

Notably, all those deficiencies remained even though for more than a year nonlawyers had made up one-fourth of the New York City Bar Association's Grievance Committee.

Clearly lawyers, knowledgeable about their own profession and its demands, should play some role in the disciplinary process. The question is, How much of a role? The findings of the Clark panel and others have exposed the frailties of placing the matter entirely in lawyers' hands. Is the presence of a *minority* of laymen sufficient? Lawyer Martin Garbus and law professor Joel Seligman conclude that while that is helpful (in Michigan, it resulted in a *quadrupling* of public disciplinary actions in a three-year period), it is an inadequate response to the problem. They recommend, instead, "the creation of an agency independent of the state and local bar associations, composed of a minority of lawyers and a majority of laymen, to establish and enforce standards of [lawyer] integrity and competence."

As Messrs. Garbus and Seligman observe: "Lawyers have proven utterly incapable of disciplining each other. . . . [T]he general impulse is to protect a brother—even a knavish one—rather than protect the public."

10

Legal Clinics: The Bar Fends Off the Future

How has the Organized Bar used its unique powers to write its own rules and to set the conditions under which the public can purchase legal help? To bring down the cost of that help? To make it easier for people to find the lawyer they need?

Or the opposite? Those are questions to which this and the following two chapters are addressed.

In Denver, where the traditional bar association *minimum* fee for "simple" divorces was $430 (and many lawyers charged more), the legal "clinic" of Sarney, Trattler and Waitkus charges $125—*and makes money.*

In Philadelphia, where filing personal bankruptcy has always carried a $500 to $600 price tag, Mitchell Miller and his Bankruptcy Clinic, Inc., charge $300—and make money.

In New Orleans, the "clinic" of Allison and Perrone handles divorces for less than half the going rate ($175 instead of $400), and they're far speedier than conventional law firms, pushing a divorce through the courts in six weeks, rather than the usual six months.

In New York and Los Angeles, where it has traditionally cost from $150 to several hundred dollars to get a simple will drawn, the "clinic" of Jacoby & Meyers charges $45.

The story is the same in city after city: legal "clinics"— a new kind of law firm (or, more accurately, a new way of practicing law)—are able to charge a fraction of the old going rate, and still operate at a profit.

How do they do it?

The answer is astonishingly simple: merely by dropping nineteenth-century attitudes and bringing the practice of law into the twentieth century.

"The legal profession today is where the automobile was before Henry Ford was born," says Leonard J. Schwartz, a young Columbus, Ohio, attorney. That very perception lay behind the invention of the first legal clinic in 1972 by two young Los Angeles attorneys, Stephen Meyers and Leonard Jacoby. Both had been heavily involved in consumer causes and had seen the extent to which conventional practitioners had priced themselves out of reach of middle-income families, largely because most lawyers acted as if the assembly line had never been invented. Even standard tasks, such as drawing simple wills, would usually be individually handcrafted by a highly trained (and highly paid) attorney, who would spend inordinate time taking information from the client, recording it on a yellow pad, then often drafting the will from scratch, necessitating high secretarial costs. Little wonder that the simplest wills typically cost several hundred dollars. If automobiles were produced in that fashion (hand-made and assembled by high-paid master mechanics) even the lowliest subcompacts would cost tens of thousands of dollars.

Jacoby and Meyers were convinced that by applying Henry Ford's twin lessons—efficient production (resulting in lower costs and prices) plus high volume—they could reach a vast untapped market for legal help. Achieving the first goal meant introducing Ford's assembly-line principles: developing streamlined systems, forms and checklists for handling commonly experienced legal problems (divorces, wills, and so on) speedily and efficiently; using modern-day technology (computers and high-speed typing machines); and relying heavily on paralegals to minimize the use of expensive lawyers and thus cut costs.

A client desiring a simple will, for instance, would furnish the needed information on a carefully designed questionnaire and would then be interviewed by a paralegal, who could help narrow and clarify the legal issues that could then be resolved in a brief conference with the attorney. Then, guided by the attorney's advice, a computer would select the appropriate legal language to carry out the client's wishes and would actuate a high-speed typewriter that would spit out an error-free will at several times the speed of even the fastest typist, stopping at the proper points for the insertion of heirs' names and other information. The cost: not the hundreds of dollars conventional attorneys often charged, but just $45!

Just as the Ford assembly line's success depended on a mass market and low unit costs, so with the legal clinics. Jacoby and Meyers proposed simple new innovations to broaden the potential clientele: storefront walk-in offices as conveniently located as the neighborhood branch bank; weekend and evening office hours tailored for working people; credit-card charging (one expert has observed that legal help is about the only "big-ticket" item that is still generally sold on a cash-only basis); and an inexpensive initial consultation fee (half an hour with a lawyer is typically available for $15 to $20). Gone, too, would be the uncertainty about how much it would cost to solve a legal problem ("It'll depend, madam, on how many hours I have to put into this."). The clinic prices would be fixed and—even more unheard of in the legal profession—posted in the waiting room.

Such adaptations to customer needs, rudimentary and routine in almost every other industry, are noteworthy (and astonishing) only because of the legal profession's failure to adopt them decades ago.

With those principles in mind, in the fall of 1972, Stephen Meyers and Leonard Jacoby opened the nation's first legal clinic in two neighborhood offices in northwest Los Angeles, offering a limited menu (divorces, bankruptcies, and the like) at prices far below the going rate in Los Angeles. To launch their new venture, they had the tradi-

tional open-house party, to which they invited their jour-
nalist friends and, of course, answered their questions
about the clinic. Their departure from traditional law
practice made good copy, and the Legal Clinic of Jacoby
& Meyers soon found itself the object first of local newspaper and TV coverage and then of articles in the national
news weeklies.

It was not long before they heard from the California
State Bar Association. 1972 was the year in which the
American Bar Association conceded that the legal profession was failing to reach or adequately serve "the middle
seventy percent of the population"; the Bar might therefore have found reason to welcome an innovation aimed
at closing the acknowledged gap.

Not so. Far from congratulating Meyers and Jacoby, the
Bar launched a disciplinary proceeding against them—
one that threatened their suspension from practice. The
Bar's charges were harshly worded: the two lawyers had
behaved dishonestly, in a "corrupt" manner, and were
guilty of "moral turpitude."

What had the pair done to warrant such charges? Had
they absconded with clients' funds or given bad legal advice that had gotten clients into trouble? No; the Bar was
incensed over quite different matters. For one thing,
rather than use the traditional phrase "law offices of" they
had used "the legal clinic of"—a trade name that violated
bar rules and might, according to the Bar, mislead the
public. An ironic charge, inasmuch as bar rules explicitly
permit law firms to use the names of eminent but long-
dead partners. That, apparently, is not misleading.

Secondly, the Bar charged that Jacoby and Meyers had
violated the then-existing rules against lawyer advertising
by responding to newsmen's questions at their open
house and thereafter. That, too, seemed an unusual
charge: lawyers routinely respond to journalists' questions; Meyers recalls that a Los Angeles magazine had
only recently published a long article about the city's most
prestigious attorneys for which (the reporter was later to
testify in Meyers's disciplinary proceeding) senior part-

ners gave unreserved cooperation.

Meyers and Jacoby were curious about the origin of the Bar's disciplinary action. Was it because of complaints from dissatisfied clients? No: the complaints had all come from lawyers, forty of the clinic's competitors. Jacoby and Meyers had friends visit the forty, posing as clients seeking help with an uncontested divorce. All but three quoted a fee of $500. The new clinic was then offering the same service for $100.

Considering that Jacoby and Meyers were but two among some thirty thousand lawyers then practicing in California, the state bar association poured an astonishing amount of energy into the case against them: there were twenty-one separate days of hearings over a fourteen-month period; two full-dress hearings before the entire board of governors of the state bar association; a massive 210-page brief to the California Supreme Court. Ultimately, after five wearying and expensive years, Jacoby and Meyers triumphed: California's highest court ordered the charges against them dismissed, criticizing the bar association for the "triviality" of its principal complaint.

It was clear that Stephen Meyers and Leonard Jacoby has spawned a good idea. After the splurge of publicity that followed their initial opening, even before their court victory, lawyers in city after city began experimenting with the clinic idea. But also, in city after city, they found themselves confronted with menacing growls from local bar associations. In Denver, for example, three young attorneys opened shop in one of the city's historic old mansions. A visitor on a historic-house tour picked up their fee schedule and soon the trio received a three-page "informal complaint" from the local bar association's grievance committee, asking for a wealth of information, some of it personal, such as how much each person at the clinic was being paid. The lawyers produced a ninety-page response. Not a word from the grievance committee—only disquieting silence, leaving the lawyers wondering when —or whether—the Bar would drop the other shoe.

In Austin, Texas, the Legal Clinic of Russell and Mahlab was tied up for a year and a half in a dispute with the local bar association over their use of third-year law students. In New Orleans, the Clinic of Allison and Perrone was charged with improper solicitation of clients when they sought to make a group-service agreement with a local union.

As late as February 1979—two years after Jacoby and Meyers had won their pivotal court victory—the *National Law Journal* reported that persisting bar association actions against fledgling clinics was having a "chilling effect" on clinic business. In Hartford, Connecticut, the local grievance committee sued the Law Clinic of Trantolo & Trantolo for mailing a brochure with their "dramatically reduced" fee schedule to twenty-five local real estate agents, even though the Supreme Court had by then approved of lawyer advertising. In Rhode Island, the state bar association brought ethics charges against clinic operator Ira Schreiber on the "trade-name" charge similar to that the California Supreme Court had found "trivial." Schreiber requested a speedy hearing of the issue because, he said, the accusation had "had a chilling effect on business. The public has the impression the bar association hasn't placed its imprimatur on the idea of legal clinics." His request was denied.

Individual attorneys and bar leaders have also voiced concern or disdain at the clinics' efforts to mass-produce legal services and provide them to a mass market. Los Angeles Bar leader Joseph H. Cummins likens clinicians who reach the general public via advertising to "rug peddlers and used car salesmen." Delaware bar leader John M. Bader told *The New York Times* he doubted that low-cost legal service could "take into account the special needs of each client."

As in any large new experimental movement, there have been a few bad apples, but the overall experience with clinics has been favorable. A major seller of lawyer malpractice insurance has had no reason to charge higher rates to clinics than to other lawyers; none of the clinics interviewed in 1978 by the *National Law Journal* had been subjected to a single such suit.

The difficulty of tailoring legal work to the "special needs of each client" is an often-voiced justification of the conventional hand-crafted mode of law practice. Advocates of the clinic approach concede that some legal matters do not lend themselves to standardized treatment, but they contend that many, if not most, of the problems most often experienced by middle-income families—divorces, adoptions, and bankruptcies—fall into sufficiently standardized patterns as not to require individual tailoring. One clinic advocate put it this way: "There's no doubt that a custom-made, hand-tailored suit would fit some better than a mass-produced one. But at five hundred dollars a suit, how many people can afford to buy one? What the clinic tries to do—and what the Bar seems opposed to—is to give people a choice they can afford."

Clinic proponents insist that, far from offering their clients a second-class choice, clinics can, with their meticulously prepared check lists, forms, and the experience they gain from specializing in limited fields of the law, turn out better work in their field than can many general practitioners. "Nothing is left to memory, nothing is left to chance," says Ronald Sharrow, a founder of a highly successful clinic in Baltimore.

The assertion of superior clinic service received independent reinforcement from a year-long comparative study conducted by University of Miami law professor Timothy J. Muris, who in August 1978 told an American Bar Association panel that clients in Los Angeles gave the clinic of Jacoby & Meyers higher marks than conventional practitioners on promptness, honest dealing, explaining matters, keeping clients informed of progress, and "being fair and reasonable" as to fees. Seeking an objective measurement of the work done, Muris compared child-support payments won by mothers in divorce cases. He found that clinic clients won, on the average, $38 more per month than those served by traditional firms.

The Muris study concluded: "Our evidence conclusively rejects the proposition that firms charging lower prices will necessarily produce lower quality services."

As the 1970's neared their end, legal clinics had become a fixture (the ABA itself had sponsored one in Philadelphia), and, according to a 1979 *National Law Journal* report, "when a clinic opens up, legal fees in the surrounding business community sink." Nevertheless, as with any new form of business, many clinicians found the going shaky (more than one-fourth of those surveyed in mid-1977 had gone under by early 1979), and the future growth of the clinic movement is uncertain. Will bar association opposition persist? Can the lack of business know-how among many lawyers be overcome? Most important, how will clinics be financed, particularly in their starting years? Where will they get the capital for the expensive mass advertising that seems essential to success? The ABA's Philadelphia clinic, for example, failed in large part because of too little advertising too late, in the view of Gary C. Huckaby, chairman of a special ABA committee on legal-services delivery. Conversely, an intensive TV campaign by Jacoby & Meyers, launched as soon as the Supreme Court lifted the ban on lawyer advertising, produced dramatic results. In the five *years* preceding the Supreme Court ruling, Jacoby & Meyers, without advertising, had grown to a six-office, Los Angeles-only operation; but in the succeeding eighteen *months,* spurred by the TV ads, the firm mushroomed to twenty-four offices throughout California.

By January 1979, they were sufficiently encouraged to venture cross-country and to open eleven offices in the New York City area, backed by a massive $500,000 TV campaign.* By August, the firm was anticipating handling

---

*Even before they opened their doors for clients, they received a disquieting call from the New York City Bar Association—reputed to be one of the nation's most progressive—checking on details of the new venture to make sure it complied to the letter of bar rules.

50,000 clients during the course of 1979.

The success of H & R Block in exploiting a highly advertised brand name in the tax-advice field gives Jacoby & Meyers the hope of expanding nationwide. "We want to be like Sears," said Jacoby, "a place where you know you'll get quality goods at reasonable prices."

But attracting the capital needed to become an H & R Block or a Sears (both conduct multimillion-dollar ad campaigns each year) is the precise point where special bar-imposed restrictions are most likely to inhibit the growth of low-cost clinics. The Block brothers were free to attract investment capital from any source; Jacoby & Meyers cannot because of bar rules that forbid investments in legal-service ventures, by both wealthy laymen and by cash-rich corporations. As noted, as of late 1979, the Florida Bar Association was seeking to close down a nine-office legal clinic solely because it was owned by nonlawyers.

"Based on our success so far," says Stephen Meyers, "I'm positive we could soon be operating in neighborhoods all over the country—*if* we had the capital. But unlike other new ventures, we can't go out in the market and raise it. It's too bad. We could really lower legal fees in this country."

II

The Bar's Battle Against Legal Insurance

Legal clinics like Jacoby & Meyers have brought about a singular advance by handling divorces for $125 (rather than $500 to $750) and simple wills for $45 (instead of $200 and over) and personal bankruptcies for $375 (about half the old going rate).

But what about a package offering the divorce *plus* the will, *plus* the bankruptcy—all for $26 a year? Now *that's* real cost reduction.

That package is not a pipe dream. It is available today in New York City, where 80,000 members of the Municipal Employees Union (District 37) have each contributed $26 a year to a common pool and have hired enough full-time staff attorneys to handle virtually all the legal problems not just of the union members but of their immediate families as well.

The District 37 plan has another advantage over the legal clinic. You may recall that when, during the course of my 1979 telephone survey, I took to Jacoby & Meyers my friend's problem that seemed insoluble without bringing a lawsuit (the "lemon" car the dealer refused to exchange), they told me they could only handle the case by charging so much per hour for whatever lawyer time went into the suit—and therefore couldn't quote me a flat fee, as they do for divorces and other standard legal tasks. Well, Mrs. Nancy Katz of Ocean Parkway, Brooklyn, a District 37 member, had precisely that problem (with a Buick whose faulty brakes caused it to swerve into oncoming traffic, despite repeated efforts to repair it). In her case, one of the union's staff attorneys *did* initiate a lawsuit and *did* pursue it to a happy conclusion, even when the dealer brought in General Motors and *its* high-priced lawyers. It was all done as part of the $26-a-year dues.

That case alone ended up consuming twenty hours of attorney's time—the fee for which Mrs. Katz could never have afforded had she been acting alone. She would have had to forget any thought of a lawsuit, live with the dangerous "lemon" car, and swallow the injustice.

But Mrs. Katz wasn't alone. She had, in effect, 80,000 allies, each contributing $26 a year. In 1978, their contributions made it possible for her to bring her lawsuit and avert an injustice. In another year, her $26 would help solve her neighbor's legal problem, and so forth—the modern legal equivalent, in a sense, of an old-fashioned barn-raising.

So there's more than cost saving involved here. There's a vital principle: groups of people banding together to buy their legal help and sharing (or spreading) the risks. It's hardly a new principle: it's at the heart of any insurance plan—group medical plans, for instance. Yet it's a principle the Organized Bar has stubbornly resisted. In consequence, at the end of the 1970's, there were only a few District 37-type plans in the nation.

The Bar's chief weapon for shooting down group legal plans has been the exercise of its special power to write rules that forbid lawyers from taking part in group plans. As far back as the 1920's, when the automobile was coming into vogue and burgeoning auto clubs offered members free legal help with driving-related offenses, the American Bar Association declared it "unethical" for attorneys to participate in any such arrangement. The matter remained largely dormant until the 1960's, when the Bar felt strongly enough to take the issue to the U.S. Supreme Court on four separate occasions, unfazed by being slapped down each time. In the early sixties, the Virginia Bar Association sought, on "ethical" grounds, to prevent the NAACP from hiring lawyers to defend the civil rights of individual black Virginia citizens and then, a year later, sought to prohibit a union not from hiring but from merely *recommending* lawyers to its members to help with their workmen's compensation claims. But the Supreme Court flatly declared that group protection of individual rights "cannot be condemned as a threat to legal ethics."

If the Court was trying to speak to the Bar, the Bar was evidently not listening, for in 1967 it was back on the firing line. The arrangement that aroused the ire of the Illinois Bar Association was the United Mineworkers Union paying a $12,000 annual retainer to an attorney who spent a fraction of his time* helping union members file work-injury claims. In a three-year period, he succeeded in winning benefits of more than $3 million for injured miners who, if they had individually hired private attorneys, would have had to pay legal fees of $500,000 to $1 million. As it was, the total three-year legal cost, paid by the union, came to $36,000.

In objecting to this, the Bar argued it was only looking out for the miners' interests (protecting them from a lawyer who owed his allegiance to the union rather than to individual members). Significantly, though, there was no complaint from the workers. Once again the Court repudiated the Bar.

Still the Bar persisted, bringing yet another case to the Court in 1971—the fourth time in eight years it had raised the same basic issue, in slightly varying forms. Law professor Prebe Stolz, commenting on that decision in an ABA publication, *Unauthorized Practice News,* noted the Court's "rather impatient tone" and observed, "Evidently the Court is getting weary of telling the Bar something it should have understood long ago."

Did the American Bar Association respond to these four court rebuffs by "giving up and leading in the search for new ways to deliver legal services"? asked New York Uni-

---

*The attorney, in addition to being a state senator, had an active private practice of his own.

versity law professor Stephen Gillers. "Absolutely not."
This battle, he said, concerned something far more important to the Bar than professional obligations. "It concern[ed] money."

The Bar's old guard carried on its opposition, with new
rules designed to prevent lawyers from taking part in
group legal plans the Bar found unpalatable. (How would
anyone feel if the American *Medical* Association barred
a doctor from taking part in a health insurance program?)

The crucial new dividing line for the Bar was between
so-called *open*-panel plans—open, that is, to any lawyer
wishing to participate—and *closed*-panel plans, confined
to attorneys chosen by the sponsoring organization (the
labor union or credit union). Experience in the medical
field has shown how pivotal that distinction can be. With
closed plans, the sponsoring group can attach conditions
as to fees charged or, better still, it can hire its own salaried doctors (as District 37 did with lawyers)—achieving
cost controls that aren't possible in plans open to all physi-
cians. The result is that closed-panel prepaid medical costs
are markedly less than with open-panel fee-for-service
plans. One authoritative comparison found the former 29
percent less costly than a commercial medical insurance
plan and 46 percent less costly than Blue Cross.

The medical model's potential for cutting professional
fees was not lost on bar leaders, and in 1974, when the
issue came before the American Bar Association meeting
in Houston, the ABA adopted a new "ethical" rule making
it far more difficult for lawyers to participate in closed
plans than in open plans. But was this a question of ethics
or of profits? Insurance executive William B. Pugh, Jr.,
whose company wanted to test the group-legal-plan market, was skeptical. First, he noted, the "ethical" objections
to closed-panel plans did not emanate from the ABA's
Ethics Committee (indeed, that body recommended a
rule treating open and closed plans identically) but from
the ABA's General Practice Section—the very attorneys
who, Pugh said, "by and large would be affected ad-
versely" by the rise of group-practice plans. Mr. Pugh also

found it noteworthy that the ABA had never raised any ethical objections to the closed-panel plans under which insurance companies had routinely funneled profitable business to ABA members.* Finally, Pugh noted that under the new Houston rule, closed-panel plans the Bar found ethically objectionable when marketed by insurance companies suddenly became acceptable when controlled by local bar associations.

Other ABA critics have observed that while the bar, in protesting closed-panel plans, laments their denial to clients of a free choice of lawyers, that is a disadvantage the ABA seems to find acceptable for the very poor. After all, the Legal Services program (which the ABA warmly endorses) is a rigidly closed-panel arrangement: the poor must take the Legal Services lawyer offered them or do without.

The Houston rule stirred widespread protest and the ABA meeting in Chicago six months later softened the rule a bit. But it remains a dampener rather than an encourager to lawyers interested in group-practice arrangements. For example, the Chicago rule begins with the dissuasive words "A lawyer shall *not*" participate in any group plan that fails to meet a long list of detailed ABA requirements. The implication: attorneys venturing into this uncharted field do so at their own risk, and if a bar association should deem their particular plan out of bounds, they stand to be disciplined. In such an untried arena, there are bound to be many ambiguities and uncertainties. For example, one group plan for BankAmericard holders, sponsored and operated by the Kansas City Bar Association, received the blessing of that bar group. On the other hand, an identical plan—identical, that is, except for its lack of bar sponsorship and control—was disapproved by the Cleveland Bar Association.

Moreover, the ABA's adoption of even the Chicago

---

*This was done under arrangements giving the insurance company, rather than the insured, the power to choose counsel.

rule's mild improvements was only advisory to the various state bar associations, and a survey made three years after the Chicago meeting showed that only eight states had adopted the Chicago rule intact. By contrast, twenty-three states had failed to approve either the Houston *or* the Chicago rule, retaining old regulations that virtually rule out attorney participation in any meaningful group-practice plan.*

If the District 37 plan could apply the risk-spreading insurance principle so as to produce broad-scale legal help for $26 a year merely by drawing on 80,000 members of one union in a single city, think of the benefits that could flow if legal insurance plans could draw on a *nationwide* market such as, say, all members of the steelworkers or autoworkers union, or even all BankAmericard holders. Such broad-scale group plans might be marketed by major national insurance companies or, alternatively, they might be marketed and operated through a nation-wide network of franchised law offices, operating in the manner of H & R Block.

But operations of that magnitude require considerable start-up capital, and a combination of restrictive state insurance laws plus confining bar association rules have created a catch-22 situation: those with the necessary capital are by and large forbidden to engage in the practice of law; and those able to practice law are cut off from the sources of needed capital. As noted, bar rules preclude infusions of capital by corporations as well as by laymen with business, marketing, and advertising skills that most lawyers lack. Moreover, insurance companies, which have both the capital and the sales forces to market widespread

---

*The revised Code of Professional Responsibility proposed in January 1980 by an ABA panel (see page x) appears to eliminate the restrictions in the present Code against group and prepaid legal plans, however, the proposal is subject to change before the ABA considers it in February 1981. Moreover, as noted above, even if approved by the ABA, the action would be only advisory, and could be modified or ignored by the state bar associations, as with the Houston and Chicago rules.

group legal plans, often find themselves stymied by state laws, enacted at the instance of bar groups, forbidding them to market cost-efficient closed-panel plans.*

In 1977, a decade after the U.S. Supreme Court's pivotal upholding of group legal plans in the United Mineworkers case, lawyer-author Jethro Lieberman, the legal affairs writer for *Business Week* magazine, wrote that the Court's 1967 ruling in that case should have set the stage for a "radical reorganization of the delivery of legal services in the United States"—that is, for a vast expansion of the group legal plans of the sort upheld by the Court. Congress had done its part to make such a revolution possible, passing three separate laws to facilitate such plans.† Yet, Lieberman found, a decade after the mineworkers decision, the reorganization had barely begun— a "tribute," he felt, to "the Bar's ethical insensibilities."

*In addition to such laws, insurance companies are frustrated by the fact that Congress, in 1946, delegated the regulation of the insurance industry to the fifty states, and naturally, the laws vary from state to state. That inhibits companies desiring to market a single legal-insurance package to some nationwide group, because any given plan is bound to run afoul of some state laws. Moreover, in some states where the insurance law makes no mention of legal-insurance plans (for example, New York), regulators have taken the position that such insurance cannot be sold until the legislature specifically authorizes it.

†Those were: (1) a provision of the Employee Retirement Income Security Act (ERISA)—the pension reform law enacted in 1974; (2) an amendment to the Taft-Hartley labor law making it legal for unions to bargain for (and to strike for failure to win) group legal plans; and (3) a 1976 change in the federal tax laws granting employer contributions to legal service plans the same tax-free status that other employer-paid fringe benefits enjoy.

12

No on No-Fault: Adding Insult to Injury

Here are some essential features of two alternative plans for insuring the victims of automobile accidents. Which system seems preferable?

Feature	Plan A	Plan B*
Percentage of persons killed or seriously injured in auto accidents who are compensated by auto insurance	45%[1]**	100%[8]
Percentage of direct accident losses*** recovered by persons seriously injured in auto accidents	16%[2]	100%[3]
Percentage of each insurance-premium dollar returned in benefits to accident victims	44%[4]	70–75%[5]
Percentage of each insurance-premium dollar paid to lawyers	23%[6]	0%[7]

*Plan B is a "pure no-fault" plan involving (a) unlimited benefits (that is, full recovery of medical expenses and wages lost); and (b) an absolute ban on lawsuits to recover more than those direct losses. No state in the U.S. has adopted such a "pure" no-fault plan (all of them permit lawsuits for "pain and suffering" under certain circum-

stances). The pure no-fault plan is selected here to illustrate the principles of no-fault and the benefits those principles can bring. As discussed in the text, there is a
trade-off involved in no-fault because of the diminished
right to bring private lawsuits.

**Sources for statistics in this table may be found in the
Notes and Sources section.

***Medical expenses and wage losses

If you prefer Plan B, you are in diametric disagreement
with the official position of the American Bar Association
and the more vigorous stance of the Association of Trial
Lawyers of America (ATLA). They (especially ATLA) not
only prefer Plan A, they lobby for it, electioneer for it, and
sometimes even assess the members of local chapters for
political contributions to candidates favoring it. In short,
they are dead serious about standing between the public
and Plan B.

Why? Because Plan B largely bypasses lawyers while
Plan A nets members of the legal profession *in excess of
a billion dollars in fees every year.*

Plan B is, of course, no-fault auto insurance (we're
speaking here solely of insurance against injuries to people, and not against damage to the automobiles involved).
Under a no-fault arrangement, all auto accident victims
are fully and promptly compensated for their direct losses
—their medical expenses and their wage losses—regardless of who, if anyone, was "at fault" in the accident.

Plan A is the present "fault" system in effect in most
states under which, in order to collect from an insurance
company, accident victims have to prove two things: that
someone else who carried insurance was "at fault" in the
accident and that they themselves were *not* at fault. If it
can't be established who was at fault, no one collects.
Even worse, if you're in a single-car crash (say, for example, your car skids on slippery pavement and rams into a
tree), you won't collect a dime from your auto liability
insurance. Reason: no one was "at fault." In other words,

under a "fault" system, when you buy bodily injury auto insurance, you aren't buying a penny of protection for yourself—only for other people you may be responsible for injuring. If you are hurt in an accident, the only way you can collect is from the other person's insurance company—*if* there is "another person" and *if* it can be established that other person was "at fault."

Those many complex conditions explain why, by actual experience, less than half of those seriously injured in auto crashes get compensated from auto liability insurance. It is often more like a roulette game than an insurance plan. Would we think it sensible to be compensated if our house burned down only if it could be proved that someone was "at fault" for the fire? "Fault" auto insurance makes just as little sense.

Why, then, would anyone prefer Plan A—and why does ATLA support it so vigorously? Because under Plan A, you maintain the right—which you give up under pure no-fault plans—to sue for damages *beyond* your medical expenses and wage loss, and to be paid for what the law calls "pain and suffering." Such lawsuits are generally brought by trial lawyers who will represent you for no advance fee, provided you pay them a portion (usually one-fourth to one-third) of whatever damages you are awarded by the court.

If you are very "lucky," you (and your lawyer) may win a great deal of money. I say "lucky" because by and large the only way you can receive a large damage award is if you have been seriously—perhaps permanently—injured or disfigured. In that event, no amount of money will erase the scars or make you walk again. The same cannot be said of your lawyer, who is likely to walk, briskly and uninjured, out of the courtroom—probably directly to his bank.

Indeed, one of the gravest indictments of the "fault" system is the immense diversion of dollars away from the injured and into the pockets of various go-betweens. Under "fault" insurance only 44 cents of every dollar paid in insurance premiums find their way back to the victims.

The other 56 cents goes, in part, to insurance company expenses and profit—but also, in considerable part, to the lawyers. Their "take" is colossal: it has been estimated at $1.8 *billion* every year.

On the other hand, under effective no-fault systems, between 70 and 75 cents* out of each premium dollar— nearly twice as much as under "fault" insurance—goes to the people who really need the help: the injured victims.

In practice, the "fault" insurance roulette game is played with a wheel that is cruelly "fixed"—fixed so as to favor those with the smallest injuries while shortchanging the most grievously injured. Studies have shown that the least injured (those with less than $500 in medical expense and wage loss) end up recovering, on the average, *four and a half times their actual loss.†* By contrast, a U.S. government study found that those with direct damages of more than $25,000 recover an average of just five cents on the dollar—ironic, because it means that the most seriously injured, who suffer the greatest pain, end up getting no compensation for their "pain and suffering."

The roulette wheel is also fixed against poor families. The same government study showed that when the tug-of-war with the insurance companies is over, families with under $5,000 income emerged with just 38 cents for each dollar of loss while those with incomes over $10,000 got 61 cents. The reason for this discrepancy, given to the Senate Commerce Committee by ex-insurance company attorney John J. O'Brien, is not pretty. O'Brien told the senators that the "fault" system "favors the affluent and mitigates against the poor [because] the individual injured in an auto accident who is living from paycheck to

*Data submitted to Congress in 1977 by New York State Insurance Commissioner Thomas A. Harnett revealed that nearly 75 cents of each premium dollar in his state was going to accident victims.
†The excess comes because insurance companies are willing to settle comparatively small claims for several times the direct cost in order to avoid the expense of litigating the claim.

paycheck *is a soft touch for the experienced* [*insurance*] *adjuster."* [Emphasis added]

Even for those who, with an attorney's help, do win a pot of gold, there's a hitch: not a penny comes in while the victim is hospitalized and inundated with bills; such money as is finally awarded arrives only after years of negotiating and/or court trial—a delay that can be critical if permanent injury can be avoided only by embarking promptly on often expensive rehabilitation. But how is a person to finance such a program while injured and out of work?

To compound the injustice, no one except the victim has any incentive to provide prompt rehabilitation funds. The insurance company that has to foot the bill certainly does not; and at least one person who has dealt extensively with auto victims and their attorneys has observed that personal-injury lawyers are often not eager to see their clients regain robust health and thus become less sympathetic figures in the courtroom. Dr. Bernard F. Finneson, a leading neurosurgeon with twenty years in practice, told a committee of the House of Representatives: ". . . [O]ftentimes the doctor who . . . wants the symptoms to subside as quickly as possible *is working counter to the desires of the attorney* who . . . may feel it is his job to ask the patient, 'Are you sure that you still don't have any symptoms?' . . . In many cases management of this sort can only tend to prolong symptoms." [Emphasis added]

Those legal authorities who voice concern over the litigation explosion and the overloading of court dockets should, logically, be at the forefront of the no-fault crusade.

As things now stand, auto accident cases are probably *the* greatest single cause of clogged calendars, and they soak up astonishing amounts of scarce judicial resources. New Jersey Chief Justice Joseph Weintraub has estimated that 51 percent of noncriminal cases arise from auto accidents—and, more alarmingly, that auto cases occupy eighty percent of all the civil (that is, noncriminal) court trial *time.*

The experience in Massachusetts shows the dramatic extent to which the advent of no-fault can declog the courts. Between 1970 (the last year of "fault" auto insurance) and 1975, when no-fault had been in effect for three years, motor vehicle tort cases in the state's district courts plummeted from nearly 34,000 to just over 4,000. Their proportion of all court cases dropped from about 35 to about 6 percent at the district-court level, and from 66 percent to 25 percent at the superior-court (appellate) level.

Chief Justice Warren Burger has also said in speeches that unless auto accident cases are removed from the courts, judges and juries will not be able to handle important civil and criminal cases demanding attention. Yet a search of the Chief Justice's speeches disclosed no explicit advocacy of no-fault insurance.

With such powerful arguments of fairness, economy, and clearing of court congestion on its side, the fact that no-fault auto insurance has been adopted in only a handful of states is a tribute to the heels-dug-in opposition and the political clout of the Organized Bar in general and the Association of Trial Lawyers of America (ATLA) in particular.

No-fault was first adopted in Massachusetts in 1970. Even in that first legislative battle, the hand of ATLA was present, although disguised in a highly deceptive manner. Soon after the Massachusetts House had passed a no-fault bill, a spate of full-page anti-no-fault newspaper ads appeared around the state, ostensibly paid for by the Teamsters Union. It was later revealed, though, that the ads were paid for not by the Teamsters but by the state's trial lawyers.

In other states, trial lawyers moved to head off no-fault bills. The Texas trial bar dunned each of its members $10 a month for a political fund supporting no-fault opponents. The El Paso Trial Lawyers' newsletter proudly reported that the fund was "responsible" for the nomination of six of the eight candidates it had backed for the State Senate.

The Texas political tithing program quickly spread to Ohio and Illinois. In both states, trial lawyers predicted that no-fault would never pass. As of late 1979, they have proven correct. Neither state has no-fault—Ohio has enacted no such law; the no-fault measure passed in Illinois was voided by the courts and has not been replaced.

Where they could not defeat no-fault outright, trial attorneys have contrived to cripple the legislation so as to make the resulting system costly and unworkable, and give no-fault a bad name. For example, the only way of paying *all* accident victims their direct costs without sending insurance costs through the roof is to do away with (or at least severely curb) the right to sue for "pain and suffering"—in other words, an either-or trade-off. In eight states, the no-fault laws are "both-and" rather than "either-or"—that is, they provide limited no-fault benefits with no diminution of the right to sue for "pain and suffering." (Some wags have called those "yes-fault" laws.) In other states, the trade-off has been all but eliminated by adroit loopholes inserted into the no-fault law, often at the behest of the trial bar, which trial attorneys have then exploited to their advantage. For instance, one such loophole authorized lawsuits by anyone incurring medical expenses of, say, $200 or $500—and in at least two states, lawyers were discovered teaming up with doctors, hospitals, and clinics to boost medical bills over the magic threshold. Senator Frank Moss of Utah charged that New York state lawyers actually circulated a letter that "encourages accident victims to seek larger medical expenses" so as to push them over the $500 cutoff mark. The senator said the letter also offered a carrot to doctors to go along with the higher charges: attorneys offered, without charge, to collect the doctors' fees from the insurance company. In Miami, a doctor indicted for conspiring with a lawyer to defraud an insurance company was the proud owner of a boat he named *Whiplash*.

Trial-lawyer efforts to halt or cripple no-fault bills have paid off. Not a single state has enacted a no-fault bill since 1975 (largely because the battleground shifted to the federal level, as described below). And of the fifteen states that have passed some form of no-fault, in all but four, no-fault benefit levels are so low as to cause public dissatisfaction and only two of the fifteen have what experts consider adequate barriers against private lawsuits.

The resulting prevalence of "yes-fault" states has achieved a side objective: it has prevented meaningful comparisons of the costs of "fault" versus *true* no-fault insurance, and thus thwarted the contention that no-fault can reduce auto insurance rates.

Nonetheless, one study conducted for the American Insurance Association offers evidence of the dramatic savings an effective no-fault system can bring to auto insurance buyers. The study compared what happened to liability insurance rates between 1972 and 1975 in three states: Michigan (a no-fault state); Maryland (a "yes-fault" state that provides some no-fault benefits but retains the right to bring private lawsuits); and Washington (which, having passed no new law, remains a "fault" state):

	WASHING-TON (A "fault" state)	MARY-LAND (A "both-and" state)	MICH-IGAN (A no-fault state)
Change in Liability Insurance Costs, 1972–75			
Dollar change (no inflation adjustment)	up 56.7%	up 72.6%	up 1.5%
Change adjusted for inflation	up 29.4%	up 42.5%	*down* 16.1%

The Michigan performance is the more impressive considering that state pays the most generous no-fault benefits—unlimited reimbursement of medical expenses, for example. But in one sense, the savings there are not surprising—in fact, they offer the most persuasive evidence on behalf of the no-fault principle, for Michigan has combined its generous benefit payments with the most effective curbs on private lawsuits. In short, the no-fault trade-off helps everyone—except the trial lawyers.

The no-fault *principle* is not new in America: it has been applied to job-related injuries, via the Workmen's Compensation laws, since around the turn of the century. But nearly forty years elapsed between the first and the last state's adoption of Workmen's Compensation, and in order to avoid a comparable delay, no-fault proponents sought enactment of a congressional bill prescribing federal minimum no-fault standards for all the states.

To the surprise of the Association of Trial Lawyers of America, such a bill passed the Senate in 1974 by a vote of 53 to 45 although it died when the House failed to act on it. ATLA reacted quickly. Political fundraising was diverted from the state to the national arena. By 1976, a new "Attorneys' Congressional Campaign Trust" had amassed $400,000. Evidently, the funds were put to effective use, for when a no-fault measure came up in the Senate in 1976, it was defeated, 45 to 49. Eleven senators who had supported no-fault in 1974 had had a change of heart. Five of them were up for reelection in 1976. All received large campaign contributions from ATLA's "Campaign Trust." Four of them received gifts of $5,000, the fifth $2,500.

Since then, the Trust has raised more than a million dollars and has distributed funds lavishly in pivotal congressional campaigns. In 1978, when the no-fault bill was due for a crucial vote in a House Committee, no-fault advocates had high hopes of winning one of the "swing" members of the committee, Congressman Douglas Walgren of Pennsylvania, but his vote went the other way (the bill was defeated by a slim, two-vote margin). That fall, Congressman Walgren was graced with a trial-lawyer contribution of $5,000—a gift of conspicuous generosity in a race for the House of Representatives.

Joining ATLA in opposing federal no-fault legislation has been the American Bar Association. But the ABA's objectivity is open to some question. In 1972, a special ABA committee was named to consider whether to reverse the association's long-standing opposition to no-fault. All ten members of that committee were attorneys who had engaged in and collected fees from auto negligence cases, the very kind that would be curtailed if no-fault insurance were to become widespread. As of late 1979, the ABA has remained opposed to no-fault.

Trial lawyers view no-fault auto insurance as the tip of the iceberg and, according to the *New York Law Journal,* foresee further fights "to prevent the no-fault concept from creeping into the areas of products liability, aviation and medical malpractice, among others." And why shouldn't it, asks law Professor Jeffrey O'Connell, co-inventor of no-fault auto insurance? If no-fault has reduced delays and middlemen's "take" in workmen's compensation and can do so in auto insurance, why not expand it to those other fields? Indeed, New Zealand in 1974 enacted a comprehensive no-fault law that covers accidents of all kinds—even skiing accidents—and, from early accounts, it is working well—at least for the general public.

Given the intense political opposition of ATLA, however, any such sweeping no-fault plan must at the moment be considered utopian for the United States. Congress has yet to adopt the no-fault principle for automobile accident insurance.

Not all trial lawyers are opposed to no-fault. One of the most conspicuous exceptions is attorney Benjamin Marcus of Muskegon, Michigan—notable because he was the first president and cofounder of ATLA. On June 28, 1971, attorney Marcus wrote Senator Philip A. Hart of Michigan, then the Senate's leading no-fault champion:

> [I am] convinced that No Fault is the only way out of the wasteful, irrelevant, burdensome and exasperating procedure now employed . . . [I] feel it is probable that when the dust has all cleared, No Fault will be conceded by all to be substantially speedier, less wasteful and more fair than our present system.

13

Stacking the Deck for the "Haves"

I have previously described the extent to which lawyers sell their talents to the well-to-do. But the imbalance in equity that produces is compounded by the legal system itself and by the ways in which that system tends, from the very outset of a legal controversy, to stack the deck against certain kinds of litigants—usually, the have-nots.

To illuminate how this works, I have chosen two real-life situations. One is a dispute that was resolved in court. The other involves an out-of-court settlement which is by far the more prevalent way of deciding legal controversies, yet just as much a part of the legal system.

Case Number 1: John Harris of Brooklyn, New York, is served with an official notice of eviction for nonpayment of rent.* Technically, his landlord is correct: Harris has not paid the rent for three months—because there has been no hot water for nearly four months; the roof leaks; rats are unwanted visitors; and the plaster walls are crumbling. Harris doesn't see why he should pay when the landlord hasn't lived up to his part of the bargain.

Fair or not, the eviction notice has arrived. Harris, new in Brooklyn, hires a lawyer his neighbor has vaguely heard of: Leon Goodman, two years out of law school and hungry for clients, who agrees to the $150 fee Harris says is all he can afford. This is Goodman's first eviction case and

*The Harris case is a composite, drawn from a number of actual cases that have come before the Brooklyn Housing Court.

123

he knows little landlord-tenant law. At that fee, he can't afford much time for research, but from his quick cram course he concludes the lack of hot water legally justified Harris's withholding of rent. But there also appears to be a basis for Harris to counterclaim for a *refund* of past rent: the roof leak and crumbling plaster violate housing laws. Goodman duly files a counterclaim.

On trial day, Harris and Goodman find the case has been assigned to Judge George Holtzman, formerly a lawyer for landlords and still, himself, a multibuilding landlord.

Goodman's legal adversary is to be Jerome Kurt, *the* landlord lawyer in Brooklyn (he handles some ten thousand cases a year)—Kurt is on first-name terms with all the court clerks and knows all the ins and outs of landlord-tenant law by heart. No book research is needed.

Harris's case is called. Goodman, aware that juries are far more sympathetic to tenants than are most judges, moves for a jury trial. Lawyer Kurt is quickly on his feet: the motion is not in order. Why? Because John Harris waived his right to a jury trial when he signed his lease.

This is news to Harris, who naturally had not read the fine print in the landlord's preprinted lease. More remarkable, the jury-waiver clause also takes attorney Goodman by surprise. Harris has long since misplaced his copy of the lease and Goodman has been unable to obtain one from the landlord. Lawyer Kurt shows them the clause, tucked away in Paragraph Seven, and Goodman's crucial motion fails. Harris's fate will be decided not by a jury of his peers, but by Judge (and landlord) Holtzman.

Now Lawyer Kurt moves to dismiss Harris's counterclaim for back rent. On what grounds, Goodman demands? The lease; again the lease. Paragraph Seven also contains a provision precluding Harris's right to all counterclaims.

With the case now reduced to the claim that housing-code violations legally justified rent withholding, Goodman puts Harris on the stand to describe the apartment's condition. But when it comes Lawyer Kurt's turn to question, he asks if Harris can produce any official city inspection reports alleging code violations. Harris looks hopelessly at his lawyer; but Goodman, in his inexperience, had not thought to obtain such reports.

Well, does Harris have any photographs? Again the inexperienced Goodman shakes his head.

The case has been reduced to Harris's word against the landlord's, Acme Realty. On the stand, an Acme vice-president admits the hot water is "temporarily" out, but denies any of the other conditions. Also, unlike Harris, he produces all the legally required documents (rent receipts, deed to the building, and so forth).

The trial is over; the judge decides that Harris must pay the back rent, but that Acme must take "immediate steps" to restore hot water. Next case.

The court clerk suggests that Goodman and Harris wait while the judge's order is prepared and signed. They move to a rear bench while the next case begins.

It proves strikingly similar to their own (an eviction sought for unpaid back rent). Jerome Kurt again represents the landlord, but now the tenant is represented by James Connor, a lawyer from the government-supported Neighborhood Legal Services office, who has handled a great many landlord-tenant cases.

Connor begins, as Goodman had, with a jury-trial motion. Kurt, as before, argues that the tenant has already signed away that right, but Connor, rather than yielding, reels off the names of court decisions holding jury-waiver clauses to be "unconscionable" and hence unenforceable. The judge, clearly familiar with Connor's litany, upholds him and, focusing on Lawyer Kurt, expresses the hope a settlement can avert a long jury trial. Kurt, painfully aware of landlords' fates in juries' hands, nods understandingly.

John Harris's anger mounts, as does Lawyer Goodman's chagrin that his cursory research failed to unearth the "unconscionability" doctrine, which Connor invokes again to overrule Lawyer Kurt and uphold the tenant's counterclaim for a rent refund. Annoyed, Kurt says that

Connor's belligerence is clouding the chances of a settlement—but Connor calmly responds that he is quite prepared for a full-dress trial in which, as His Honor and Kurt know from past experience, he will invoke every letter of court rules. It could be, he says, time-consuming. The judge sighs, having endured many Connor trials. Kurt gets the message and motions Connor to meet him outside, clearly prepared to make substantial concessions to the protesting tenant.

Case Number 2: The Universal Insurance Company, having paid $3,000 to Howard Strickland to repair his damaged but highly valuable antique table, seeks to recover its outlay by suing Mrs. David Digby for $3,000, based on the claim that she damaged the table while a summer tenant of Strickland's.

Mrs. Digby, recalling distinctly that the table was unharmed when she departed, is sure the claim is erroneous. She consults attorney Thomas Martin, who advises that because of the difficulties of proof in the case it will cost her about $3,000 to defend herself in a full court trial. That presents her with a dilemma: even if she *wins,* she's out $3,000; if she loses, she'll have lost $6,000.

Infuriated and perplexed, Mrs. Digby accepts Martin's advice to try to negotiate a settlement and offers to pay $500. But Universal's attorneys summarily reject her offer and threaten a court trial.

Mrs. Digby, assuming such a trial will cost the insurance company as much as it will cost her, wonders why Universal is willing to spend $3,000 to collect $3,000. Nonetheless, frightened by the prospect of an open court fight, she trebles her offer to $1,500. Universal grumpily accepts.

Result: Without ever having her case heard on its merits, Mrs. Digby pays Universal $1,500. Legally she doesn't owe it, but she pays it. Under all the circumstances, she figures it is the cheapest way out.

Were John Harris and Mrs. Digby treated justly by the legal system? However much "right" was on their side, might—*legal* might—was indisputably on the side of the landlord and the insurance company—and in both cases, crucial to the outcome.

What is the source of that legal might?

It springs, basically, from a fundamental distinction between two types of litigants (that is, parties to lawsuits). Acme and Universal—landlord and insurance company— are "Repeat Players" in the legal arena because, by their very nature, they are sure to be involved repeatedly in disputes of this sort. Hence, they are prepared for it.

John Harris and Mrs. Digby, by contrast, are "One-Shotters." That is, they are people who in all likelihood have never been sued before and don't expect to be involved in a lawsuit again.

The world is full of legal conflicts between Repeat Players (RPs) and One-Shotters (OSs)* between corporations (usually Repeat Players) and consumers (almost always One-Shotters); between banks (RPs) and borrowers (OSs); between landlords (RPs) and tenants (OSs).

As you can see, Repeat Players are generally haves and One-Shotters are usually have-nots. But this is not always the case. Legal Services attorney James Connor, an experienced defender of tenants, was able to flex much of the legal muscle of a Repeat Player lawyer. The central point is that by the very nature of legal battles and the way they are fought, Repeat Players have enormous leverage over One-Shotters, *leverage that is built into the legal system.* It is that inherent bias of the system, and not merely financial superiority, that explains why, in the words of Professor Marc Galanter, "the 'haves' come out ahead."

What are these built-in factors that skew the legal system in favor of Repeat Players?

*The terms and abbreviations Repeat Player (RP) and One-Shotter (OS)—as well as much of the analysis in this chapter regarding the differences between them—are the brainchild of Marc Galanter, a sociologist on the faculty of the University of Buffalo Law School. I appreciatively acknowledge my debt to Professor Galanter.

Let's begin with the matter of legal representation in which most RPs hold a dual advantage: lawyers are on hand early in the game; and, being specialists in the RP's particular field of interest, they are highly expert. In the John Harris case, for example, finding and, more importantly, paying an attorney was far easier for Acme Realty than for Harris. Indeed, Repeat Players usually don't have to go out and find lawyers: they either keep full-time lawyers on their payrolls or have an arrangement with an outside law firm (like Kurt's) to have its services always at the ready. It is inconceivable that an RP like Acme would lose a case by default (failing to appear and be represented in court). But a One-Shotter like John Harris rarely has a lawyer at hand and OSs frequently lose by default, without having their case heard on the merits. Surveys in New York City found that tenants were unrepresented in 61 percent of court contests with landlords, and in many courts, more than 90 percent of debtors lose their cases by default.

Two advantages of early and expert legal advice showed themselves in the John Harris case. Acme Realty's lawyer, with all the fine points of landlord-tenant law at his fingertips, had seen to it his client kept and produced all the needed documents. One-Shotter John Harris, not similarly forewarned, had lost his copy of the lease and his inexperienced lawyer had failed to collect vital documents.

More crucial, Harris lost his best and maybe his only chance of winning long before he set foot in the courtroom—when he signed that lease with its jury-waiver clause, with no attorney on hand to warn him of the consequences.* By contrast, Acme's preprinted lease (like that of all other sizable landlords) was carefully drafted by its lawyers, who inserted the jury-trial and counterclaim waivers solely to maximize their clients' interests. They were able to do so in part because of the landlords' supe-

---

*In a housing-short city such as Brooklyn, he would probably have had little bargaining power to protest; but that is a separate question.

rior bargaining power in a city as short of low-cost housing as Brooklyn, but also in part because they knew that most tenants would, like John Harris, sign the lease without benefit of legal advice.

Do not imagine that tenants like John Harris, untutored in the law, are the only people inveigled into signing away jury-trial rights. At least until the late 1970s, sometimes-sophisticated depositors at New York's Manufacturers Hanover Trust did the same, simply by signing the standard signature card, on the *back* of which was a densely worded 600-word contract which, in lines 34 and 35, spirited away all rights to a jury trial.*

That very Repeat Player advantage operates against you every day. Who do you suppose devised the legalese in the warranty for your car, TV, or refrigerator—and with whose interests in mind? Whose lawyer wrote the fine print on the back of the parking-lot ticket, which says the lot is held harmless for any damage done to your car while there? And whose lawyers write those pages-long insurance policies that so often prove, when misfortune strikes, to include some opaquely worded phrase in Clause 312(b)(3)(iii) that places your particular accident just a *little* outside the policy's coverage?

Repeat Players reap a variety of benefits from having expert lawyers long marinated in their special field of interest. Some of the advantages may be subtle yet crucial. For example, the assignment of John Harris's case to prolandlord Judge Holtzman was not happenstance, but the result of Lawyer Kurt's first-name acquaintanceship with the clerks of court who parcel out such cases and can be helpful to attorneys they know (and who may "remember" them at Christmas).

Specialization also brings major economies for RP lawyers and their clients. Having long ago mastered the law in his narrow field, the expert bypasses the time-consum-

---

*In the process of simplifying the language of its depositor contract, the bank recently did away with the jury-waiver provision.

ing and expensive research the generalist must undertake. The specialist also has most matters reduced to standard forms and letters ("Miss Angelo, type up a Form 43-B complaint for the Digby case"), and in some fields, especially debt collection, law firms operate with high-speed computers that spit out summonses and complaints around the clock. That explains how a law firm could easily afford to serve a full-dress court summons on the Rowan family (mentioned in the Legal Parable on page 5) over so comparatively small a matter as a $50 unpaid hospital bill.

Moreover, whereas One-Shotter attorney Goodman had to make a special time-consuming trip to the courthouse just to handle John Harris's case (which might often involve waiting for hours until that case is called), Repeat Player lawyers like Jerome Kurt, with a high volume of court cases, can often arrange to have several heard in a single day*—making the RPs' legal costs a fraction of the One-Shotters'. It's all built into the system.

In a legal battle, having the law on one's side can be pivotal. But "the law," in a court case, can be of two kinds: statutory law, enacted by legislatures, and judge-made law, of the kind invoked by Legal Services attorney James Connor when he called forth prior judicial rulings regarding the "unconscionability" of jury-waiver clauses.

Repeat Players enjoy decisive superiority over One-Shotters in shaping both kinds of law to their advantage. Their dominance in legislative lobbying is well known (I discuss that in the next chapter). They have a comparable but less-known advantage in shaping judge-made law, stemming principally from their superior ability to determine which cases do and do not become judicial precedent setters. A Repeat Player has no trouble pursuing to

*A law firm representing a Repeat Player such as, say, Universal Insurance, can station a single lawyer in court to handle any of Universal's (or other clients') cases that may come up that day—yet another economy resulting from a high-volume practice.

the hilt any case where the facts are on his side and a favorable court outcome is likely. Conversely, in cases where the facts are unfavorable, a harmful court decision can almost always be avoided by making the One-Shotter opponent a settlement offer he can't refuse. The following case will show how this works, and how cheaply it can often be achieved.

Back in the 1960's, Tracy Westen, a brilliant lawyer in Washington, D.C., resolved to challenge a practice whereby finance companies were skirting D.C. interest-rate ceilings by making loans to Washingtonians from offices located just outside D.C. boundaries, in neighboring Maryland and Virginia, where interest ceilings were higher. Westen found an impoverished D.C. citizen to act as plaintiff and filed suit. The finance company instructed its attorney to initiate the standard delaying tactics that usually wear down most One-Shotter attorneys, but when it was clear Westen was not only undaunted but intent on knocking out the whole law-avoidance device, there was a quick offer to forgive the plaintiff's outstanding debt, plus a $50 settlement bonus. Westen was, of course, obliged to present the offer to his client, who snapped it up, instantly snuffing out Westen's legal challenge. Thus, the D.C. finance companies' law-skirting scheme was saved for posterity.

The finance company enjoyed a crucial flexibility not available to Westen, since for the company this was but one of many cases, easily sacrificable to save a profitable permanent arrangement. For Westen, no such trade-off was possible: he could not ask his One-Shotter client to pass up a good bargain just to establish a new legal precedent, no matter how valuable.

The Westen example is not an isolated one. For years, auto dealers fought with manufacturers over what they felt were arbitrary terminations of their valuable franchises. In this running battle, the manufacturers could pick and choose: pursuing to the limit cases favorable to them and settling where the facts were adverse. The individual dealer, on the other hand, being more interested in a favorable outcome in his own case than in establishing a general rule helpful to all dealers, was easily bought off. "The net effect," observes Stewart Macaulay in a book about this controversy, "was to prompt a sequence of cases favorable to the manufacturers."

Not only are Repeat Players better able to shape judge-made law, they also tend to be better at taking advantage of their precedent-setting victories. News of such triumphs travels fast to others in the same RP industry, via one of the myriad trade-association newsletters and loose-leaf reporting services (for labor, patent, admiralty, tax law, for example). The extent of newsletter specialization is often remarkable: in 1978, for instance, when the federal government undertook a massive swine-flu immunization program, there quickly sprang up a *Swine Flu Claim and Litigation Reporter,* sent out to attorneys interested in filing damage claims against the government.

Lawyers for One-Shotters, on the other hand, are often handicapped by the lack of communication channels. For example, during the Vietnam war, growing numbers of Americans, wishing to avoid participating in a war they thought unjust, sought to invoke the legal rights that were theirs under Selective Service law regulations and previous draft-board rulings. But their lawyers were largely groping in the dark, since Selective Service officials had exclusive possession of the prior draft-board decisions. Moreover, if any of these lawyers did persuade a given draft board to adopt a new policy, it was likely to remain an isolated victory, there being no established way for them to communicate with other lawyers representing draftees. When a group of foundations underwrote *The Selective Service Law Reporter,* a new publication that published draft-board rulings, draftees' lawyers made instant use of it and their successes increased markedly.

No foundation need underwrite the law reporting services in, say, the patent or maritime or antitrust fields. With tens or hundreds of millions of dollars riding on a single case or government regulation, for most well-heeled Repeat Players and their lawyers, law-reporting services in those fields are a must, no matter how high the subscription price.

Let's turn, now, from court battles to the more prevalent settled-out-of-court disputes, such as Mrs. Digby's set-to with Universal Insurance. The outcome in such cases is the result of negotiations in which each party is constantly weighing the cost of holding out compared with the cost of yielding. It is precisely in that war-of-nerves process that the Repeat Players enjoy the greatest leverage over One-Shotters.

That showed itself clearly in the comparative cost calculation that prompted Mrs. Digby to pay $1,500 she was sure she didn't owe. For Mrs. Digby, staying in the litigating game meant anteing up $3,000 she would otherwise spend for, say, rent, food, or clothes. But Universal had enough predictable legal problems to warrant a staff of full-time salaried lawyers. Since those attorneys had to be paid whether or not Universal took Mrs. Digby to court, as Universal reckoned it, the *added* cost of suing Mrs. Digby was, essentially, zero.* Universal could, in effect, stay in the game without anteing up.

But that is, quite literally, only half of the advantage Universal enjoyed. The imbalance is further compounded —in fact nearly doubled—by the fact that Universal's legal expenses are tax deductible while Mrs. Digby's are not. As a result, nearly half of Universal's legal fees are, in effect, borne by the U.S. taxpayers while Mrs. Digby must carry the entire burden herself.

A concrete example will show why that is so. Suppose Universal's legal expenses in year X are $100,000, and company taxable profits after paying those costs are $1 million. If that legal outlay were not tax deductible, Universal's taxable profits would be $1.1 million rather than

---

*Therein lies the explanation for Mrs. Digby's puzzlement as to why Universal would be willing to lay out $3,000 to collect $3,000. The simple answer is: they didn't have to.

$1 million and, at the corporate tax rate of 46 percent, the firm's tax bill would be $46,000 higher. To put it another way, if Universal did not spend that $100,000 for legal fees, it would at best only keep $54,000 of it, the other $46,000 being paid out in income tax.

Because the legal fees *are* deductible, though, Universal doesn't pay the added $46,000. That, however, deprives the U.S. Treasury of the $46,000, and the rest of the U.S. taxpayers must make up the difference. In that sense, the taxpayers end up paying about half the legal expenses, not just of Universal Insurance, but of all the corporate Repeat Players in the country.

Mrs. Digby's unsought legal fees, by contrast, are not tax deductible, so she must bear one hundred percent of the burden, about twice as much, net, as Universal Insurance. It's leverage piled upon leverage.

All this gives the Repeat Players what Professor Galanter terms "credibility as a combatant," a term all poker players will readily understand. In any negotiated dispute, each side is wondering, Is he serious about going to court—or bluffing? How well can he afford a legal defeat? If he loses, will he appeal to a higher court? In all respects, the One-Shotter finds himself looking at deuces and treys —and at an RP who holds a royal flush, with more chips and lasting power, better and more expert lawyers, and so forth. Note, though, that the client's finances are not always the determining factor. Legal Services lawyer James Connor—serving in effect as a Repeat Player lawyer, albeit for an impecunious client—was able to exhibit "credibility as a combatant" in threatening an extended jury trial. He could do so only because he was an experienced Repeat Player attorney. (In addition, his employment by Legal Services, freeing him from dependence on a fee in this one case, made it clear he could afford to take the time for a jury trial, and added to his believability. But, as noted in Chapter 2, among the half-million American lawyers there are only a few thousand attorneys like James Connors-type attorneys.)

A vital factor in the legal poker game is that most Repeat Players are far better able to bear the consequences of a legal defeat than the usual One-Shotter. When John Harris lost and had to pay back rent, that was a third of his income. If Acme had lost, Harris being one of 150 or so tenants, the loss would have been a comparative pinprick.

The legal system also causes disparities in the costs of a defeat to the respective parties in, for example, the probability that a court order will actually be enforced. If John Harris didn't pay the back rent, as ordered, the landlord's lawyer would doubtless have a new eviction action instituted in short order. Enforcement against the landlord —say, to repair the leaky roof or the crumbling plaster— is not nearly as sure or swift. The One-Shotter's low-paid lawyer is less likely to follow up; and so, apparently, are city authorities. For instance, in July 1975, one New York City building was found to have 98 housing code violations, which a judge ordered corrected immediately. One year later, that same building had 111 violations. Six months after that, the number had risen to 117.

The legal system also works to spare Repeat Players the consequences of defeat in ways not applicable to One-Shotters. For example:

• In practice, penalties are usually far lighter for Repeat Players than for One-Shotters. More time has been spent in jail by violators of the Migratory Bird Act than by violators of the antitrust laws. When electric companies were convicted of illegal overcharges totaling $840 million, they were fined just $2 million, about one-half of one percent of their ill-gotten gain. And when a worker at the Delaval Turbine Company of Oakland, California, was caught in a conveyor belt and crushed to death—the *second* conveyor-belt accident at that company—the company was convicted of *wilfully* violating the occupation health and safety laws, and fined just $500 (the maximum permitted by law).

• Corporate litigants know that, in general, penalties

for wrongdoing will not be borne by the responsible executives but will come out of the corporate treasury and thus be borne by shareholders.

• In at least one instance, corporate officials took special precautions to make sure they would not be held personally liable for their actions. Gulf Oil stockholders got a court to order company executives to repay the company for political contributions illegally made from Gulf's treasury, only to find that the company had taken out insurance (at shareholder expense, naturally) to shield the officers from any such order.

• Even in small-claims court—the legal forum supposedly designed for One-Shotters—Repeat Players have enjoyed effective insulation. One study found that from one-third to one-half of the One-Shotters who won small-claims judgments against RPs were never able to collect what the court had awarded them.

By contrast, the legal system affords a One-Shotter litigant like Mrs. Digby no such protection against defeat. She knew that if she were to lose to Universal Insurance, she and she alone would have to pay the damages—which is why she paid $1,500 she was sure she didn't owe, without even having her case heard by a court of law.

The picture of the imbalances between Repeat Players and One-Shotters would not be complete without mention of two other disparities that have, in recent years, been exacerbated by decisions of the courts.

One discrepancy has been summarized in a cogent observation by the sociologist C. Wright Mills:

> It is better to take one dime from each of ten million people at the point of a corporation . . .
> . . . than $100,000 from each of ten banks at the point of a gun.
> It is also safer.

That is no theoretical speculation. It happens every day, although in hidden ways. For example, during the fifties and sixties, Pfizer and four other major drug companies were accused of illegally fixing the price of the widely-prescribed antibiotic, tetracycline, so that tens of millions of families were obliged to pay $6 to $9 per prescription, rather than $2 to $2.50, according to the charges. While the companies denied the price-fixing charges, they did, before the lawsuits went to trial, offer to pay damages amounting to $100 million in a group of cases in the East, and ultimately paid out damages in excess of $200 million.

Even with total indicated damages of those gargantuan proportions, each of the millions of tetracycline purchasers, overcharged by just a few dollars per prescription, could not possibly afford to bring a lawsuit, even if aware of the alleged price-fixing. Only by banding together and bringing a joint lawsuit (as was done) could those diffuse victims bring their case against the companies before the courts.

That banding together was made possible by a 1966 amendment to the federal court rules, which permitted just such group legal actions (called class-action lawsuits), and the drug-company suit, resulting in damage payments of about a quarter of a billion dollars, is a prime example of what those collective actions can achieve. But in recent years, as class action proponents see it, the courts have been interpreting the 1966 rule with undue strictness* thereby shutting off, in many cases, the only means of legal redress scattered One-Shotters have.

Recent court decisions have also exacerbated another disadvantage suffered by One-Shotters: the greater difficulty they experience, compared with Repeat Players, in getting their grievances heard by a court. The imbalance here is clear. It is the rare Repeat Player who does not have the resources to bring any grievance he may have before the courts and, what's more, to pursue it to the Supreme Court of the United States if he so desires. The same cannot be said of most One-Shotters, who must swal-

---

*Some of the key court decisions and their effect on class actions appear in the Notes and Sources section.

low many a complaint out of sheer lack of financial capacity to bring or carry on a lawsuit.

In recent years, under the aegis of Chief Justice Warren Burger, the U.S. Supreme Court has been aggravating that disparity by making it more and more difficult for unmoneyed One-Shotters to get federal courts to hear their grievances. The Burger Court has made it more difficult, for example, for aggrieved citizens to establish so-called legal "standing" to be heard in court. Sometimes One-Shotters found themselves in an impossible catch-22 situation. Take the dilemma of a group of poverty-stricken citizens of eastern Kentucky—in need of medical help they couldn't pay for, but turned away by a hospital that, notwithstanding its uncharitable attitude toward the poor, called itself a "charitable" institution and reaped substantial advantages from the resulting tax-deductible status. The citizens sued, claiming the law obliged the hospital to make a choice: if it wanted to retain its tax-favored "charitable" status, it had to give free treatment to people unable to pay. But the Supreme Court said that in order to show they had been "injured in fact"—and to establish legal "standing," to sue and enforce the law— the impoverished Kentuckians would have to prove that the hospital, *if* forced to the choice, would elect to treat the poor rather than give up their tax advantages. That put the plaintiffs in an impossible posture: as long as federal regulations spared the hospital from making that choice, they couldn't prove what the Court asked; yet the Court was telling them they couldn't knock down the regulations until they proved what choice the hospital would elect. With the door to the federal courthouse slammed shut, there remained no way they could get the medical attention they needed.

The Court created a similar catch-22 dilemma for a group of low-income citizens of Rochester, New York, who, seeking urgently needed low-income housing, sought to challenge the restrictive zoning ordinances that barred such housing in the suburb of Penfield. But the Court said that to prove "injury in fact" and show legal standing the protesters would have to find a housing developer generous (or foolish) enough to ignore Penfield's laws, spend the tens of thousands needed to plan a low-cost housing project and apply for permission to build it, *and then be turned down.* Without going through that expensive exercise in futility, the courthouse door was shut tight.

These and other decisions narrowing One-Shotters' access to the federal courts are technical and hence seldom discussed. Yet many legal experts regard them as more significant than other more publicized Burger Court reversals of the Warren Court policies of the fifties and sixties. Few would dispute that they add significantly to the infirmities One-Shotters suffer at the hands of the legal system.

If, as I have suggested, there are built into the legal system biases that stack the deck against certain kinds of litigants (by and large isolated and unmoneyed individuals), what role does the legal profession play—especially bearing in mind that the declared purpose of the Organized Bar* is "to promote . . . the administration of justice" and "to apply the knowledge and experience of the profession to the promotion of the public good"?

With those self-proclaimed goals as a backdrop, a question arises: does the behavior of the legal profession and its members tend to lessen the imbalances suggested in this chapter, or does it make them worse?

That is the subject of the next chapter.

*In the very first section of the American Bar Association's Constitution.

14

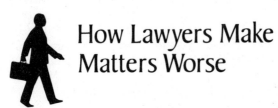

How Lawyers Make
Matters Worse

The following pages describe how certain Repeat Player lawyers frequently behave.* They do so for a variety of reasons: perhaps because the political or economic system gives them or their clients the power to behave this way; sometimes for competitive reasons (another lawyer will do it if they don't).

The object of this chapter is to set forth certain actions lawyers routinely take, for consideration against the background of certain questions:

Is this the way we *want* lawyers to behave? Do we approve of the systems—legal, political, economic—that permit or even encourage their actions?

At 10:30 P.M. on November 4, 1975, in an unusual evening session the tax-writing Ways and Means Committee of the House of Representatives approved a measure embodying a special change in the normally applicable rules for taxing stock market profits and losses. Nowhere was there any mention of the name of H. Ross Perot, the Texas tycoon said to be worth, at one time, some $300 to $500 million. Yet the measure was deftly and deliberately tailored to his particular circumstances and, what's more, in such a way as to spare him from having to pay about $15 million in taxes on a colossal stock market profit that any other citizen with a comparable gain would, under normal tax law, have had to pay.

*This behavior is not, of course, confined to lawyers.

At least two factors presumably contributed to the committee's $15 million favor to Mr. Perot. One was the $27,-000 in contributions he had, with foresight, made to the political campaigns of twelve committee members. The other was his choice of an attorney.

This was no ordinary lawyer chosen at random. Virtually all of the thousands of tax attorneys in the U.S. had the technical skill to draft the "Perot amendment." But few of them would have been as well and favorably known to the members of the committee as the man Mr. Perot chose—Sheldon Cohen, who, as former Commissioner of Internal Revenue (1965–69), had often worked with the committee and had earned a reputation for courage and independence. Any measure Sheldon Cohen brought to the group was almost surely slated for special and favorable attention.

In short, H. Ross Perot was buying something other than Mr. Cohen's skills as an attorney. He was buying (and Mr. Cohen was lending him) his reputation and, above all, that most precious of commodities in the world of power, his special *access* to the ears of the decision makers—a commodity not available to ordinary citizens.

Access to the right ear at the right moment . . . the insider's knowledge of what ear at what moment . . . a commodity that can command a handsome price.

To illustrate: in 1975, lawyer (and former attorney general of the United States) Richard Kleindienst was paid a fee of $250,000 by the Old Line Insurance Company. As Kleindienst himself later recounted, it required just five hours of his time to earn that $250,000, five hours devoted to winning an insurance contract for Old Line from the Central States Pension Fund of the Teamsters' Union. According to *The New York Times,* it was not Mr. Kleindienst's *legal* prowess that made his five hours of effort worth a quarter of a million dollars: "It appeared that Mr. Kleindienst's role resulted only from [his] long-standing friendship with Frank Fitzsimmons, the Teamster President."

As anyone who has locked horns with a government agency knows, access to bureaucratic decision makers is another highly valuable asset. After all, only one piece of paper can be at the top of that pile on an official's desk; only a few of the myriad phone calls can be answered. A bureaucrat must pick and choose, and calls from former colleagues or letters from a former boss are bound to get special treatment.

It is not surprising, therefore, that in the mid-seventies corporations involved in environmental disputes with the government flocked to a newly formed Washington law firm. It was headed by former Environmental Protection Agency (EPA) chief William D. Ruckelshaus and also included several former top EPA officials. Other Washington lawyers were expert in environmental *law,* but few knew the name of the official at EPA who most likely would make the decision on Corporation X's case—someone, moreover, likely to be a first-name acquaintance.

Ruckelshaus and his colleagues were not shy about contacting former associates: they made no fewer than 178 calls to them in their first eighteen months in practice, most of the calls coming from Ruckelshaus himself or from his former right-hand man at EPA, Gary H. Baise.

And the calls got results. One from Ruckelshaus on behalf of the Eli Lilly Company extracted a promise that EPA regional officials would meet *personally* with the Lilly officers before issuing a potentially costly antipollution directive against the company.

Could every company dealing with EPA receive such personal attention?

The Ruckelshaus firm is but one instance of the "revolving door" phenomenon, in which attorneys for government-regulated clients move back and forth from the private to the public side of the negotiating table. Peter Hutt, a partner in the prestigious Washington firm of Covington & Burling, represented clients before the Food and Drug Administration (FDA) both before and after his stint as FDA's general counsel. Prior to becoming general counsel of the Federal Energy Department, Lynn R. Coleman had been the Washington partner of John Connally's 279-lawyer Texas firm, Vinson & Elkins, which has represented twenty oil and gas companies with cases pending before the Energy Department.

Notwithstanding Canon Nine of the ABA Code ("A Lawyer Should Avoid Even the Appearance of Professional Impropriety"), none of this role-switching appears to prick the conscience of the Organized Bar—as is most vividly illustrated by the case of Frederick Crowley, Esq. On September 29, 1978, Mr. Crowley resigned as a senior trial attorney in the Navy Department General Counsel's office. Less than two weeks later, he purchased an advertisement in *The Wall Street Journal* announcing his resignation, reciting his Navy experience in dealing with "the largest claims ever filed [by a subsidiary of Litton Systems, Inc.] against the U.S. under a Gov't contract" and openly seeking "association with law firms and representation of contractors & others w/ claims against any agencies of the U.S. Government."

Wisconsin Senator William Proxmire found this "the most blatant example of the revolving door" he had ever seen. Proxmire assailed the Navy's settlement with Litton (of which Crowley boasted in his advertisement) as a "bailout" for Litton and called upon "the legal profession to determine whether such conduct is ethical." But the Bar found nothing to complain of in Crowley's ad. Indeed, although a Navy official thought that Crowley would be barred from representing the Litton company as a private practitioner, the top disciplinary official of the Washington Bar Association thought that, so long as it didn't involve the same contract case Crowley had previously handled, even that would be perfectly acceptable.

A frequent requisite for lawyers entering and exiting government service through the "revolving door" is flexibility of conviction.

Imagine that you are an attorney in the U.S. Treasury

Department, duty-bound to scrutinize proposed changes in the tax law to determine whether or not they are likely to achieve their objective (that is, whether they are likely to represent an effective—rather than a wasteful—use of the taxpayers' money). Representing the taxpayers' interests, you confront a proposal called DISC,* whose purported aim is to offer a tax incentive for American companies to boost their export trade. Clearly nonsense, you conclude, for under the proposal companies can qualify for large tax concessions even if they do *nothing* to expand exports. All they need do is form a special dummy company and funnel *existing* export business through it. A waste of taxpayers' money, you conclude.

But then you walk through that revolving door and enter private practice. An old client of your law firm seeks your help in setting up a dummy corporation to take advantage of the DISC (by now enacted into law). To ascertain if your old Treasury Department fears were well founded, you ask whether the client intends to take any measures to boost his export trade (other than forming the dummy). The answer: "Are you kidding? Not a goddamn thing."

Your doubts are confirmed: you now *know* the tax break you are helping arrange will be a windfall for the client and a waste of taxpayers' money (yours included). Nonetheless, your law partners shower you with arguments to dispel your misgivings:

"Congress enacted that law, you didn't."
"It's the law of the land; what right do you have to deprive our client of his rights under it?"
"If our firm doesn't help him, someone down the street will."

There's logic in each of those arguments, but they do not alter the fact that whatever convictions you had before about the "public good" had to be put aside the minute you went through that revolving door.

*An acronym for Domestic International Sales Corporation

Long-held notions of common sense may have to be sub-limated if you are an attorney for a well-to-do Repeat Player. Suppose someone were to suggest you entrust your funds to a bank purportedly making $120 million of loans per year but operating out of one closet-sized room manned by a single bookkeeper—and a part-time one at that. Prudence and common sense would tell you not to give a second thought to so preposterous a proposition. Yet if you were an attorney for the staid Fidelity Bank of Philadelphia in the 1960's, not only would you take such a bank seriously, you would draw all the necessary legal papers to set it up. For, as of 1972, such a hole-in-the-wall did constitute the Nassau, Bahamas, "branch" of Fidelity.

Technically speaking, it was all legal. Indeed, your assignment as attorney for Fidelity was to draw the papers and oversee the "branch" operations so as to steer it carefully through nooks and crannies in the tax law. Even as you did so, though, you would be aware that the Nassau "branch" had but one real purpose: to have the profits on $120 million worth of loans treated—and taxed—as if earned in the Bahamas where, as it happens, there is no income tax.

Fidelity's Bahamas "branch" is by no means the only work of legal fiction devised by sophisticated attorneys. *Fortune* magazine reported that the Barracuda Tanker Corporation, one of several shipping companies owned by billionaire Daniel Ludwig, was created in a New York investment banking house, incorporated in Liberia (thus freeing it of many U.S. shipping and safety requirements), and housed, with "its registered headquarters in a filing cabinet," in Bermuda. *The Wall Street Journal* reported that Bermudan filing cabinets also served as headquarters for several "captive" insurance companies, created and owned by major U.S. corporations to write insurance on their own overseas activities. The profits of these "captive" companies could thus enjoy the favorable tax climate of Bermuda, similar to that of the Bahamas.

In short, these "corporations" and "branch offices" were purely paper constructions, fabricated by the best legal minds money could buy.

On November 29, 1967, the witness before the Senate Small Business Committee, which was investigating the pricing and advertising practices of major drug companies, was Dr. Leslie Lueck of the Parke-Davis Company, maker of a potent antibiotic called chloromycetin. While often effective, the drug had been shown to produce severe side effects, serious enough to warrant mention in an editorial in the *Journal of the American Medical Association* as early as 1952.

Seated beside Dr. Lueck on that November day was Lloyd N. Cutler, senior partner of one of Washington's most influential law firms and himself among the most respected and potent of lawyer-lobbyists, known as an effective advocate for the major automotive and pharmaceutical companies, both in court and in legislative corridors. But Lloyd Cutler was by no means a run-of-the-mill Washington lobbyist. Legislators were well aware that he had interwoven his private law practice with stints of distinguished civic and government service,* in addition to having dabbled in politics and political fundraising. So he brought more than average stature and respect to clients he represented at hearings such as this.

The Small Business Committee had a particular interest in Parke-Davis and chloromycetin, for although the drug's side effects caused, according to one estimate, more than six hundred deaths in the 1960's, the company

*He was, at various times, an officer of the Lawyers' Committee for Civil Rights Under Law; executive director of President Johnson's study Commission on the Causes and Prevention of Violence in America; chairman of a panel to study the Washington, D.C., riots that followed the murder of Martin Luther King. In 1979, he was first tapped to serve as coordinator of the Carter administration's presentation to Congress of the Strategic Arms Limitation Treaty (SALT II) and later named White House counsel.

had soft-pedaled those dangers in its advertisements and chloromycetin had become one of Parke-Davis's best-selling drugs ($86 million in 1960 sales, compared with $52 million in 1951).

At the November 29 hearing, the committee chairman, Wisconsin Senator Gaylord Nelson, inquired whether Dr. Lueck thought the warnings then required by the Food and Drug Administration for chloromycetin ads were justified. Yes, Dr. Lueck thought they were. And would he approve of publishing an ad without the required warnings? No, Dr. Lueck would not.

Whereupon Senator Nelson confronted Dr. Lueck with two advertisements for chloromycetin appearing in the same month's issue of *The Lancet,* a medical magazine published both in England and in America. The American version contained some 1,300 words of warning required by the FDA. *The British version of the same ad contained not one word of warning.*

Nelson pressed for an explanation. The surprised Dr. Lueck floundered.* Counsel Cutler interceded; the British ad, he said, "meets all of what they [the British] consider to be appropriate requirements." In other words, Parke-Davis obeys the law of whatever country it is selling in.

From a purely technical legal standpoint, the position voiced by Lloyd Cutler was impeccable: his client was within the letter of the law. Likewise, Parke-Davis was within the letter of the law for at least the ensuing six years, during which time it recommended chloromycetin in various unsophisticated Central and South American countries for such minor ailments as tonsilitis at the same time it was warning U.S. doctors to confine its use to such life-threatening diseases as typhoid fever. (Not until 1976, after further publicity, did Parke-Davis move to bring its

---

*Lloyd Cutler later objected that Dr. Lueck had been called to testify about a matter having nothing to do with the chloromycetin advertising and therefore was understandably unprepared to deal with this unexpected line of questioning.

overseas promotion practices in line with its U.S. guidelines.)

Later, Cutler was to argue that a lawyer should only defend positions "as to which he believes a reasoned and *responsible* argument can be made." [Emphasis added] Would he have viewed the Parke-Davis position "responsible" had it been *his* ten-year old son who died of gangrene and unstoppable bleeding, rather than the son of Dr. Albe Watkins of La Canada, California who, having been assured by a Parke-Davis salesman that the drug was "perfectly safe" and free of adverse "reactions," administered it to his son, and said later, "I might have done better had I taken a gun and shot him. At least he wouldn't have suffered."

Picture two lawyers, A (for plaintiff) and B (for defendant), locked in battle in a court of law. Lawyer A rises and says, "Your Honor, I ask that the defendant in this case waive all right to a jury trial as well as all right to enter any legal counterclaims against plaintiff." How many seconds do you suppose would elapse before Lawyer B would be on his or her feet protesting the surrendering of such rights? Can you conceive of B silently acquiescing? Of course not. Neither can Lawyer A.

But suppose there is no adversary, no Lawyer B. Suppose the same situation occurs outside a court of law—as, for example, when Lawyer A writes into the "standard" preprinted lease used by a major slum landlord (page 124) or into the "standard" printed depositor's contract used until recently by Manufacturers Hanover Trust (page 129) a clause by which tenants and depositors sign away (perhaps unwittingly) their right to jury trials and counterclaim suits? As he writes the lease or the contract, Lawyer A knows full well that, for all practical purposes, no tenant or depositor will have an attorney on hand when presented with the densely worded form to sign. Lawyer A is also likely to be well aware that in his apartment-scarce city, would-be tenants have little choice but to sign the lease, whatever it provides.

If Lawyer A should experience qualms about taking advantage of those circumstances, his colleagues at the bar can summon a variety of arguments to quiet his misgivings: "The root cause of the unfairness here is in the shortage of affordable housing—which neither you nor the legal profession created; so how can anyone fairly blame lawyers? . . . What's more, if you, Lawyer A, refrain from writing in that jury-waiver clause, that isn't going to help the housing shortage one whit . . . and if the *tenants* were somehow to get the economic whiphand, don't think *their* lawyers wouldn't try to slip some protenant clauses into leases. . . . That would be their duty—just as it's your duty now to represent the landlords 'with Zeal' . . ."

All arguments of undeniable logic, so in go the waiver-of-rights clauses.

Perfectly legal, in most localities.*

But fair?

Suppose Lawyers A and B were once again engaged in courtroom combat and it came to light that Lawyer A had secretly visited the judge and discussed the merits of the case without the knowledge or presence of Lawyer B. In such a case, B would lose no time in moving for a mistrial —and he would almost surely win, for A would have violated one of the most sacred principles of the adversary system: all of the decision maker's information about the case must be received in public and be subject to challenge by the other side. A secret approach to a courtroom judge would be, for virtually all lawyers, unthinkable.

But in politics and government, neither the protagonists nor the procedures are so fastidious. On the contrary, most lawyer-lobbyists planning a visit with a Congressman, cabinet officer, or even a lower-level bureaucrat would laugh at the thought of advising adversary parties of their intentions, much less of inviting them to be present.

The legal profession did not, of course, devise the rules

---

*In many jurisdictions, courts have struck down certain waiver-of-rights provisions in leases as being so unfair as to be "unconscionable."

governing lobbying activities, and lawyers cannot fairly be held accountable for those rules. But they are not noticeably eager to have them changed. Lobbyists—nonlawyers and lawyers alike—consistently make their pitches to government officials about decisions involving tens or hundreds of millions of dollars wholly in secret, with no one present to rebut any half-truths or overstatements of an avowedly biased presentation. In such situations, the protections of the adversary system are not operative.

An example: On May 1, 1969, the U.S. Food and Drug Administration (FDA), faced with mounting evidence that the drug Panalba (a mixture of two antibiotics) was not only ineffective but potentially harmful, with sometimes fatal side effects, informed Panalba's manufacturer, the Upjohn Company, of its intention to ban the drug from the market. Significantly, the FDA found some of the most persuasive anti-Panalba evidence in Upjohn's own files. FDA investigators unearthed no fewer than eight company reports on the drug's dangers and ineffectiveness—reports that should, by law, have been submitted to the FDA four years earlier, but that Upjohn had withheld.

The law provided procedures through which Upjohn could publicly fight the ban, but the company and its lawyers in the influential Washington firm of Covington & Burling were apparently not content to follow the public channels prescribed for the general citizenry. Instead, they sought and obtained, by unusual means, a *private* meeting with Welfare Secretary Robert Finch,* who

---

*Not every citizen, or even every corporation, can secure the ear of so ferociously busy a public official. To achieve that difficult end, the Covington lawyers enlisted the help of a fellow lawyer, Garry Brown, a partner in the law firm representing Upjohn in its headquarters town, Kalamazoo, Michigan. But Mr. Brown was more than an ordinary private attorney. He was also the Republican Congressman from Kalamazoo and therefore a person to whom Secretary Finch was obliged to accord more attention than he would to other private practitioners.

oversaw the FDA, to urge that before the ban could become effective, he order a time-consuming FDA hearing.

Evidently, the presentation the Covington attorneys
made to Finch at a May 5 meeting with Finch was potent,
for four days later he ordered the hearing Upjohn was
seeking. The Covington presentation was potent, yes; but
balanced and fair? It would seem not. By 3:00 P.M. the
same day, Finch reversed himself and withdrew the hearing order. Why? Author Mark Green reports that in the
intervening hours (according to FDA General Counsel
William Goodrich), Finch had been "enlightened about
the dangers" of Panalba that the Covington lawyers "had
omitted to mention."

There is a postscript to the Panalba story. The FDA ban
was initiated on December 24, 1968. Yet, despite the
drug's reported harmful side effects, it remained on the
market for an additional fifteen months during which
there was a protracted court battle. The delay was, in
considerable part, the result of lawyering maneuvers by
Covington & Burling on Upjohn's behalf. The company
was, of course, entirely within its legal rights; the lawyers
simply squeezed every moment's advantage accorded
them by the rules. Example: when the lawyers obtained
a delay to submit additional pro-Panalba evidence, they
took the full thirty days to do so—noteworthy in view of
the fact that the evidence consisted merely of fifty-four
already-published medical articles on Panalba.

It is estimated that during the added fifteen months
Panalba was on the market, Upjohn grossed $1.5 million
a month, or a total of $22.5 million, on the sales of Panalba.
On the other side of the ledger, by March 1970, when the
drug was finally removed from the market, the FDA estimated that nearly a million Panalba users had suffered
blood or liver disorders from the drug. Moreover, twelve
reported *deaths* were traced to Panalba.

When it comes to legal delaying maneuvers, one of the
kings (in all likelihood *the* self-proclaimed king) was the

late Bruce Bromley, Esquire, a senior partner in the gigantic Wall Street firm of Cravath, Swaine & Moore.

To Bromley, the delaying game was precisely that—a game—and not one to be in the least ashamed of. On the contrary, it was a skill to be proud of, to boast of publicly —as Bromley did in a 1958 speech to a conference of judges wrestling with the (to them) vexatious problem of the "protracted case," the gigantic lawsuit that drags on for years. Speaking as if unaware of or unfazed by the oath all lawyers swear upon their admission to the bar ("I will never . . . delay any man's cause for lucre or malice.") Bromley proclaimed his realization, "in my early days at the bar, that I could take the simplest antitrust case . . . and protract it for the defense almost to infinity."

That was no case of braggadocio. As a young attorney, Bromley said, he "resolved to make a stupendous production" out of a government antimonopoly case against Paramount Pictures—and that is precisely what he proceeded to do, dragging the case out for *fourteen years.* Four of those years resulted from Bromley's insistence that the court sit in each of sixty-two cities, to force the government to prove separately, *in each city,* the existence of the complained of block-booking practice (requiring distributors desiring any Paramount picture to take all of Paramount's output, the flops as well as the smash hits). He insisted on this even though, as he later acknowledged, "there really wasn't any dispute about the facts at all," and if the judge had asked, he would "have admitted reaily" that his client was using the all-or-nothing booking scheme and the court could have moved swiftly to rule on its legality.* But since the judge failed to foreshorten the proceeding, Bromley felt no compunction about putting on a "road show production." He seemed almost to chortle as he told his audience, "As you know, my [law] firm's meter was running all the time— every month for fourteen years." But to him that was of

---

*The U.S. Supreme Court was ultimately to rule that the scheme was "illegal *per se*" under the antitrust laws.

little moment: his client, he said "was very prosperous."

The fourteen-year delay in the movie case was far from Bromley's crowning achievement. In that same 1958 speech he described, with even greater relish, his *eighteen* years of foot-dragging in a price-fixing case against the American gypsum industry. Once again he unashamedly told his audience that if he had been "called on the carpet" and asked to "admit" that the complained of price-fixing agreements existed, "we would have done so," and the case "certainly would not have lasted eighteen years." Then he added, "I think I ought to confess that during the last part (of the eighteen years) I stirred up a fight among the co-defendants *just to keep the case going a little longer . . .*" [Emphasis added]

A game, a game, nothing but a game.*

As an indication of how Bruce Bromley's brethren regarded him and the kind of delaying tactics for which he was celebrated, on January 3, 1963, the Association of the Bar of the City of New York dedicated its Annual Twelfth Night Party to "Bruce Bromley, Esq., Michigan's Gift to the New York Trial Bar." The event was heralded with a poster depicting Mr. Bromley as a barefooted, patched-pantsed country fellow, under a scroll bearing this doggerel:

> BUST IF YOU MUST
> THIS GIANT TRUST,
> BUT LET'S TAKE
> DEPOSITIONS† FUST.

So refined (and taken for granted) has the delaying game become in fending off government antitrust charges that one junior attorney in a large Washington antitrust-specialty firm sheepishly admitted, in a dinner party conver-

---

*As in the motion picture case, the Supreme Court finally declared the price-fixing arrangement in the gypsum industry illegal.
†Depositions are pretrial interrogations of witnesses and interested parties that can frequently drag on for days.

sation, that his *sole* function in the firm was to protract court proceedings by drawing up and filing motions for extensions of time.

Lawyers for Repeat Players sometimes exploit legally permitted pretrial tactics to bludgeon hapless and penniless litigants into settling a case on ignominious terms. Former consumer attorney Philip Schrag has written of his representation of an ill-educated New York City janitor who had been cajoled into paying over a thousand dollars for a shoddy food freezer on the false promise that he would be furnished ample supplies of food at bargain prices. When Schrag sought to invalidate the purchase contract as fraudulently obtained, lawyers for the freezer company subjected the janitor and his wife to days of relentless pretrial questioning—but then used every allowable legal tactic to resist Schrag's efforts to use the same rule to question company officials.

In response to some of the episodes I have recounted, members of the legal profession would doubtless seek to deflect criticism from the attorneys in question:

• If Bruce Bromley's delaying games are to be criticized, don't blame Lawyer Bromley (many attorneys would argue); blame the judges who failed to stop him.

• If Parke-Davis's publication of a warningless advertisement for chloromycetin in that British magazine was wrong, don't hold Lawyer Lloyd Cutler accountable; blame the British Parliament for failing to require the proper warnings.

• If the jury-waiver clauses in preprinted apartment leases are one-sided, the real culprit is not the lawyers who wrote those provisions, but the big-city housing shortages that give landlords the leverage to impose such terms on tenants. Those shortages, lawyers argue, are the result of a political and economic system the legal profession did not create and cannot fairly be expected to cure.

• If the absence of an adversary attorney permitted

Covington & Burling's lawyers to make an unbalanced presentation about Panalba to Secretary Finch, they were only acting within a set of lobbying rules they didn't devise. Blame the rules, not the lawyers.

• And don't reproach the lawyers who arrange broom-closet bank branches in the Bahamas or set up dummy corporations to take advantage of the DISC law. Blame the legislators who wrote those tax laws.

All right. There is undeniable logic in each of those arguments. But the implication in all such rejoinders is that lawyers should be absolved of any accountability for what they and their clients do and for the harm it may cause others—as if they were helpless puppets, mere instruments, rather than purposeful human beings with values and with ultimate freedom of choice. If members of the legal profession thus elect to suspend their personal moral judgments, if they insist on divorcing themselves from results *they* feel to be unjust, then the public is entitled to scoff when a senior spokesman for the New York City bar, Arthur H. Schwartz, characterizes the lawyer as "a person looked upon by laymen as a person of superior standing, a person of integrity and character, a person to be trusted." And we may be forgiven for smiling at the proclamation of one president of the American Bar Association that "the bar is guided by the desire to serve the country, not itself."

Is the kind of behavior described in this chapter confined to lawyers? If not, why single out the legal profession for criticism?

Because underlying the episodes recounted here there is something special, an ethic that is unique to the legal profession, one in which lawyers find a rationale for the suspension of their own sense of what is fair and right.

That rationale is found in the profession's Canons of Ethics, embodied in the Code of Professional Responsibility. That Code places duty to client at the pinnacle of a lawyer's responsibilities, asserting that a lawyer's prime duty is to serve his clients "zealously, within the bounds of the law." For example, the Canons demand that a lawyer "should *always* act in a manner consistent with the best interests of his client." [Emphasis added] Always. A command.

But an attorney's fidelity to, say, his personal conscience, his sense of justice—that, say the Canons, is a distinctly subordinate obligation. Here is the relevant provision: ". . . when an action in the best interest of his client seems to [a lawyer] to be unjust, he *may* ask his client for *permission* to forgo such action." [Emphasis added]

"May," not "must." No duty there. And all the attorney "may" do is ask his client's permission to forgo the injustice. The client remains the ultimate decider. The attorney, it would seem, is the servant of the client's commands—with but a single, drastic alternative: to quit the client's employ.

Most lawyers would protest the notion that duty to client represents a public-be-damned attitude. On the contrary, they see duty to client and duty to public as synonymous.

That view derives from the adversary system of justice, under which, the theory goes, truth and justice are best protected by the clash of conflicting gladiators, each presenting the facts and the law in the most partisan light, each zealously pressing for every advantage that is arguably legal. Such undiluted partisanship is legitimate, the argument continues, because there exists an adversary ready and eager to blow the whistle, to cry foul, to challenge partial truths, overstatements, unfairness. The combat between opposing advocates serves the public by giving all arguments their most forceful expression.

That rationale has great persuasiveness when the adversary process is fully in force—that is, where the rules guarantee that no argument or fact may be presented without an opposing advocate present to challenge any misstatement of fact, any overstepping of rules. But, as observed earlier, suppose there is no adversary on hand to fulfill that function—as in the case of lawyer-lobbyists, or the drafters of one-sided apartment leases and bank depositors' contracts? In those instances, although the safeguards of the adversary process are absent, *the Canons of Ethics do not call upon lawyers to alter their ethical behavior.* Quite the contrary. While taking explicit note of the absence of the adversary process in legislative and administrative proceedings, the Canons require that "regardless of the nature of the proceeding, [the lawyer] has a continuing duty to advance the cause of his client within the bounds of the law." In other words, no duty of self-restraint. On the contrary, business (that is, duty to client) as usual.

The question of whether—and when—lawyers should interpose their personal moral judgments does not lend itself to facile answers. Absolute rules—of "never" or "always"—produce troublesome results.

For example, the prescription that attorneys ought *always* to judge their clients' behavior crumbles when applied to criminal or to politically unpopular defendants. One shudders at the thought of the entire bar refusing, on the grounds of moral repugnance, to defend a modern-day Sacco or Vanzetti or an accused rapist or child molester.

But does it follow that lawyers should *never* inject their own personal sense of morality, no matter how great they believe the injustice or the injury to others they see flowing from their own or their clients' behavior? Can we be comfortable with a lawyer—especially one of Lloyd Cutler's manifest sensibilities toward the public weal— defending a warningless advertisement for a demonstrably risky drug? Are we content with the cheerful abandon with which a Bruce Bromley boasts of deliberately playing the legal delaying game?

If the question "Should lawyers interject moral scruples?" is not happily answered either by an "always" or a "never," then the answer must lie in that misty region of "sometimes." The boundary line is difficult to draw, but lawyers, who often proclaim that their training qualifies them especially for that task, should welcome the challenge.

Were I an attorney confronted with that question, here are questions I would consider relevant:

• Am I called upon to defend my client against a criminal charge?

• To what extent are the safeguards of the adversary system operative?

• Is my client seeking to assert or protect a constitutional right?

• To what extent has my client sought and been denied representation by other attorneys?

• What is the likelihood of my client ending up unrepresented if I decline to serve or if I withdraw from the case?

• To what extent, in my judgment, will my client's conduct (or my own) result in injustice or the inflicting of needless injury on others?

Putting the answers on my own personal balance scale, the presence of a criminal charge, of an asserted constitutional right, and of the protections of the adversary system would all militate against injecting a personal moral judgment. So would the likelihood that but for me, the client would be unrepresented.

Conversely, I would feel entitled, if not bound, to listen to personal conscience if the matter were noncriminal; if I were operating outside the adversary system (for example, lobbying); if my client were a General Motors or an IBM and could, in my view, easily find able representation elsewhere; and most especially, if I believed that my client's conduct or my own would result in undeserved injury to others.

Those are my own criteria. Others may propose different guidelines. What is crucial, in my view, is that attorneys pause to ask those questions and consider obligations other than those to their clients.

One sentence tucked away in the Canons acknowl-

edges—or at least suggests—the existence of such an obligation. Duty to client, it says, does not lessen a lawyer's
"concurrent obligation to treat with consideration all persons involved in the legal process *and to avoid the inflic-
tion of needless harm.*" [Emphasis added] Unhappily,
that statement resides in a portion of the Canons termed
"aspirational" in nature (lawyers know that no punishment can result from their failure to adhere to it). It is not
couched in the urgent "must" terms in which duty to
client is presented. If it were, if it created an absolute
professional duty for lawyers, it might, at the least, serve
as a refuge for troubled attorneys seeking an escape from
defending "with zeal" a cause they regard as unjust.

Some attorneys will tell you they already have a moral
screening process for selecting clients, and from personal
knowledge I know there are lawyers who weigh their
practice on a moral balance scale. But are they the rule
or the exception? If they were the rule, would one-time
White House counsel John Dean have been prompted, or
even have had the occasion to ask, during the Watergate
hearings: "My God, how could so many lawyers get involved in something like this?"

Few lawyers, of course, would in public go as far as
Weymouth Kirkland, a founding member of the large
Chicago firm of Kirkland & Ellis, who is quoted by one of
his partners as saying, "A good lawyer is like a good prosti-
tute. If the price is right, you warm up to your client."
Nonetheless, is self-restraint the norm in the legal profession—or was the lawyers' ethic more nearly captured by
the hiring partner of a major Wall Street law firm who, in
extolling the challenge and excitement of a major lawsuit
to an idealistic young applicant, brought his presentation
to a climax with: "And the greatest thrill is to win when
you're *wrong!*"

15

 Who Are Lawyers
Trained to Serve?

If, as this book maintains, there is a seemingly endless supply of attorneys available (and eager) to serve corporations and the well-to-do and a dearth of lawyers both equipped and willing to help poor and middle-class clients, the question arises as to whether there is something about the way lawyers are (a) selected, (b) trained, and (c) admitted into the profession that contributes to that.

That is the question to which this and the following two chapters are addressed—examining, in turn, legal education (and the manner in which people are selected for law schools); the bar examination; and the screening of lawyers for their "moral character and fitness" to be members of the profession.

It was not so long ago that apprenticing with a practicing lawyer was the customary entry into the legal profession. No longer. Today, law *schools* are virtually the sole gateway to a career in the law.

It is thus the law schools that largely determine the kinds of people who will become lawyers; how they think about their role, how they view their responsibility to the public, and to their own sense of right and wrong.

It is important, therefore, to inquire what and whom our law schools prepare their graduates to serve. Will they learn primarily how to defend corporations and the well-to-do? Or will they be taught law that is relevant to people with modest incomes? How much concerned are most law professors with the latter?

160

Harvard law professor Robert Keeton has told of a personal experience that led him to ponder those questions. After a lecture on property law, Keeton recalls, a student approached the rostrum. Keeton expected a question about the "Doctrine of Worthier Title" or some other abstruse subject he had covered in his lecture. The student's question proved entirely different: a local garage, which had assured her it would repair her car for $50, now refused to release it unless she paid $250. What, she wanted to know, were her rights?

The question stumped Keeton. Embarrassed by his inability to help with such a commonplace problem, he put the question before several of his colleagues. Not one of those professors of the Harvard Law School—widely regarded as premier among American law schools—knew the answer.

Although that everyday problem was not evidently a standard agenda item at Harvard, the "Rule against Perpetuities" is a universal law school "must." Considerably oversimplified, that rule determines whether a person can legally leave property, say, to the surviving spouse of an as yet unborn great-grandchild—a question of considerable interest, perhaps, to a Rockefeller or a J. Paul Getty, sufficiently endowed to be able to skip over children and grandchildren and leave property to *great-*grandchildren in order to avoid large estate taxes. But for lawyers dealing with the other 99 44/100 percent of the population, the question is hardly likely to surface.

No matter; not only is the "Rule against Perpetuities" a prescribed part of every property-law course; as much as a week of classroom time may be devoted to its intricacies.

A week on the "Rule against Perpetuities." Little or no time on how to deal with exploitative merchants.

Whose law is taught in law schools?

A generation ago, the classic illustration of law schools' preoccupation with the propertied classes was a traditional textbook entitled *Creditors' Rights.* The clear implication was that *debtors* had no rights worth teaching—as startlingly one-sided as if a modern text on consumer law were entitled *Merchants' Rights.*

Surely (one would like to think) an anachronism, long since supplanted by a more even-handed treatment of the subject. Yet as recently as 1977, among the standard law school subjects listed in that year's directory of the Association of American Law Schools, right there in black and white, was "Creditors' Rights."

That same AALS directory provided some clues to the curricular priorities of law schools and their faculties. While indisputably those priorities have, in recent decades, shifted markedly in favor of consumers and the poor, even with those changes, in the academic year 1977–78 a listing of all law school faculty members and the subjects they taught showed these comparisons:

Subject	*Number of Teachers*
Corporation Law	615
Corporate Finance	517
Commercial Law	694
Consumers' Rights	162
Law and Poverty	193

How well do law schools prepare their graduates to meet the everyday problems of clients who need, say, a contract that will put "the deal" the client has made into "legal language"?

An actual incident may suggest the answer.

The scene: A gathering of law school freshmen celebrating the completion of their last exam—in contract law —and comparing notes on their first year. Suddenly one of them says, "It just dawned on me: we've just finished the *one* course on contracts we're required to take—and we've memorized hundreds of cases. But no one spent even five minutes teaching us how to *draft* a contract. If a client came to me right now and asked me to write one, I wouldn't know where to begin!"

Since lawyers often deal with people under stress (a marriage breaking up, a child in trouble with the law) a frequent client need, in addition to technical, purely legal advice, is for calm, wise counsel fulfilling the lawyer's role as "attorney and *counselor*-at law."

Doctors, too, routinely confront people under stress. Yet long before graduation, they have face-to-face contact with real patients in clinics and hospitals, after which come the years of internships and residency. Not so with the legal profession: few law schools offer the clinical experience that is routine in medical schools. Indeed, instruction in client counseling is almost unheard of. No postgraduate internship is required of lawyers. It is estimated that about two-thirds of all lawyers begin practice without *any* face-to-face dealing with clients.

The impracticality of legal education has been noted and criticized for decades, not merely by clients, but by judges and practicing attorneys. As long ago as 1921, an eight-year Carnegie Corporation study of law schools noted a "failure [to provide] practical training." In the thirties and forties, Judge Jerome Frank excoriated what he termed "library law schools" that turned out bookworms rather than qualified practitioners. In the fifties, attorney Arch Cantrall, in a controversial article in the *A.B.A. Journal,* complained of courses on corporate law that never mentioned a corporate charter and insurance courses that never showed students an insurance policy.

Yet almost sixty years after the Carnegie Report, New York University Law Dean Norman Redlich stated in 1978, that "law schools do not even pretend to graduate qualified lawyers." So narrow are the skills taught in American law schools, Dean Redlich has observed, that the typical graduate emerges prepared for just three kinds of jobs:

1. To be a law professor;
2. to be a clerk (a legal aide) to an appeals court judge;
3. to be a junior in a large law firm with a predominantly *corporate* clientele.

Although there are 227 law schools in America, and thousands of would-be lawyers beating at their doors to be admitted to them, still tens of millions of Americans are not getting the legal help they need. In theory, therefore, the full play of competitive market forces should work to bring legal education into harmony with the needs of practitioners, judges and, most important, the unserved general public. Yet it is criticized from all sides for being ill-tailored to real-world needs. Why?

The answer is that where legal education is concerned, free-market competitive forces are *not* at work. As has been pointed out, The American Bar Association exercises monopolistic control over the gateway to the legal profession, which comes about because all but five states require a law school diploma for admission to the Bar; and in four-fifths of the states, it can't be just any law school. *It must be one that enjoys the official blessing of the ABA.*

It didn't used to be that way. As recently as the 1930's, the *norm* was to learn by apprenticing in a law firm rather than by attending law school. Indeed, no state required law school attendance until 1928.

Apparently the apprenticeship method was capable of producing attorneys of the highest standards—John Jay, the first Chief Justice of the United States, and two subsequent Chief Justices, one distinguished attorney general (William Wirt), and a renowned secretary of state (Daniel Webster), not to mention United States Senator Stephen A. Douglas and his more illustrious one-time adversary Abraham Lincoln. Lest those exemplars be shrugged off as valid only for the distant past, when life and the law were simpler, I would cite one illustrious modern Supreme Court Justice, Robert Jackson (1941–54) and one contemporary president of the American Bar Association

(Robert G. Storey, 1952–53), neither of whom ever set foot in a law school.

The phasing out of the apprenticeship method of learning the law was primarily instigated by the American Bar Association, according to former Yale law professor Robert Stevens, a student of American legal education. Although the ABA urged the change in the name of "raising standards," Stevens says the change "also represented an effort on the part of many practitioners to restrict [the] numbers [of lawyers]" and, in particular, to "keep blacks and immigrant groups—especially Jews—out of the profession." One New York delegate to an ABA convention put it bluntly. There was, he said, a "need to have lawyers able to read, write and talk the English language—not Bohemian, not Gaelic, not Yiddish, but English."

While no Organized Bar leader would today even whisper such openly prejudiced words, many modern-day requirements for admission to the bar do build racial and economic fences around the legal profession. Affirmative Action and minority scholarship programs have brought about dramatic improvements in recent years: the number of black law students, for example, more than doubled between 1970 and 1977, and the number of students of Hispanic descent quintupled. Despite that progress, however, black students occupied just 4.5 percent of ABA-approved law school seats, although blacks make up about 11 percent of the population.

In part, the barriers are economic—for example, the generally prevailing requirement for four years of college plus three years of law school, resulting from the phase-out of the apprenticeship route to bar admission. That puts the price of admission to the profession in the $22,-000 to $50,000 range (not counting seven years of sacrificed job earnings). In 1976, according to the most recently available government figures, only 24 percent of teen-agers could count on getting a college degree and only 8 percent a graduate degree, largely for financial reasons.

Other ABA standards (such as the requirement that a

majority of faculty members serve full-time) act to keep
law school tuition high and beyond the financial reach of
many who may be qualified. What's more, by insisting
that no more than one-fifth of the classes at an ABA-
approved school be held at night, the Bar has effectively
slammed the door on many who are obliged to hold down
daytime jobs while studying for the law.

Thus there is no room, in the ABA scheme of things, for
a law school such as the People's College of Law (PCL) in
Los Angeles—a school that has consciously set out to make
legal education accessible to minority and Third World
students, but which does not enjoy ABA blessing. A
predominantly evening class schedule at PCL (imper-
missible by bar standards) not only suited the needs of
job-holding students, but made possible a faculty made up
entirely of practicing attorneys (also against bar rules)
willing to teach for scant pay. That, in turn, enabled PCL
to hold tuition to $415—one-eighth that charged by the
nearby University of Southern California Law School.

The American Bar Association keeps U.S. law schools
tightly pinioned, for in order to gain and keep ABA approval—a necessity in 32 states if its students are to be
permitted to take the bar exam—a law school must:

• bring itself into compliance with thirty-three closely
printed pages of ABA requirements—including such details as the office space that must be furnished faculty
members and the list of books that must be in the school's
library;

• apply to the ABA's certifying body;

• go through a period of limbolike provisional approval;

• subject itself, even after permanent accreditation, to
periodic scrutiny by ABA inspection teams;

• live constantly in the knowledge that if the school
incurs the disapproval of the ABA educational hierarchy,
it can lose its accreditation.*

---

*While that has been infrequent in recent years, law schools know that
the disaccreditation weapon can be used to potent effect. Robert

That is not an arrangement that encourages variety—or experimentation. As Northeastern law professor Joel Seligman observes in his book on legal education: "In a legal profession as large and diverse as that in the United States it is absurd that few law schools specialize in training government, legal-services or public interest attorneys; that all leading law schools employ identical four-year college—three-year law school structures; that only 2 of 162 law schools could reasonably be defined as 'clinical.' "

It is the lack of "clinical" schooling—where students are taken out of the classroom and thrust into contact with real-life clients and their problems and into courtroom-litigation programs—that many find American legal education most wanting. In contrast to medical schools where, beginning in second year, students spend increasing portions of their time in hospitals and clinics, the teaching of law takes place almost exclusively in the classroom. Indeed, prior to 1968, virtually no American law school offered *any* clinical instruction. Beginning in that year, prodded by an organization known as CLEPR* and encouraged by the infusion of some $11 million, law schools did begin to expose students to the problems of actual clients and the trial of real cases in court. While measured against the zero-based start in 1968, law schools have come a considerable way, they also seem to have far to go, for despite those millions and a decade of effort, CLEPR's pioneering president, William Pincus, said in early 1979 that two out of three law students were not being exposed to any clinical instruction.

Moreover, symptomatic of law schools' low regard for clinical courses, five out of six law schools place a ceiling on the number of such courses a student may take for

Stevens states that "the ABA deliberately drove out, by the accreditation process, particularly during the twenties and thirties, the law schools which today would have provided minority lawyers."
*An acronym for Council on Legal Education for Professional Responsibility.

credit toward graduation. No such ceiling applies to, say, the plethora of courses on corporate and commercial law.

How well do American law schools prepare their graduates to defend their clients when a courtroom battle is the only solution? For the vast majority of clients, the required skills are at the trial-court level, where all cases must begin. Only about one case in twelve is appealed to a higher court, an understandably small fraction since the cost of such appeals is out of reach for most clients.

It is ironic, then, that while most schools require students to make at least one mock-court appearance, it is at the *appeals-*court level, thus providing skills that only a handful of clients will be able to use. By contrast, a distinct minority of law schools offer, and none *requires,* trial-court experience relevant to most clients.

The law schools' failure to teach prosaic low-level courtroom skills diminishes both the inclination and the capacity of lawyers to fight the legal battles of the poor, in the view of Harvard law professor Gary Bellow. Bellow recollects his experience as a supervising attorney in the California Rural Legal Assistance (CRLA) program in the 1960s, when there was zeal aplenty among CRLA lawyers and no shortage of cases to be brought on behalf of impoverished farm workers. Yet, Bellow discovered, months went by without a single case being filed. The reason: a fear, born out of inexperience and lack of training, of doing battle in court, where mistakes are highly visible and embarrassing. Understandable, Bellow thought, among the fresh graduates on the staff. But he also found the same reticence among CRLA lawyers several years out of law school. The explanation was that since none of them had served in huge corporate law firms, where learning by apprenticeship is routine, they were as green and as apprehensive as the newly graduated attorneys— and even more embarrassed to admit it.

Convinced that in-school training for public lawyering is essential for poverty lawyers, Bellow determined to launch such a program as part of the for-credit curriculum at a major law school. It took him nearly twenty years, but he finally persuaded Harvard to inaugurate such a student program in Boston's slums. It represents a singular advance in legal education; but it is a rarity among American law schools.

If, as CLEPR's William Pincus believes, one result of clinical programs is to remind "the professional-to-be" that part of being a lawyer "is the capacity to respond on a one-to-one basis to another human being's need for help," then the lack of clinical instruction in most law schools bears directly on a concern voiced by Erwin Griswold, former dean of Harvard Law School, on the one hundred fiftieth anniversary of that prestigious institution: "For some years now, I have been concerned about the effect of our legal education on the idealism of our students. . . . They bring to this school a large measure of idealism. Do they leave with less? . . . If they do, what is the cause? *What do we do to them that makes them turn the other way?*" [Emphasis added]

Dean Griswold's fears seem confirmed by a survey of the class of 1975 at the law school of the University of California at Davis: as first-year students, 37 percent of the class foresaw themselves serving as "poverty," "public interest," or "movement" lawyers, but as seniors, three years later, the figure had dropped to 22 percent. The proportion listing their primary motivations as "alleviating social problems" or "helping individuals" dropped from 57 to 34 percent.

No one, of course, can accurately pinpoint what underlies such attitude changes. Many, though, believe that a cardinal factor is the philosophy, originally propounded by the titan American of legal education—Christopher Columbus Langdell, the first dean of Harvard Law School—that law is a "science" for which "*all* available materials" are "contained in printed books." [Emphasis added] Since most American law schools are patterned after the Langdell-Harvard model, the typical law student spends most of his or her time shuttling between classroom and library, reading, reading, reading. But reading what? Materials that portray disputes between flesh-and-blood human beings to whose problems law students can relate? Textbooks that set forth the law in a larger setting (examining, say, the income tax for its fairness and its effect on society)?

Far from it. Clinging to the Langdell model, students pore over excerpts from judges' opinions in appeals-court cases focusing, not on the human aspects of the participants or their controversy, but on an intellectual dissection of the *logical* issues therein. This prompted Dr. Bernard L. Diamond, a psychiatrist on the Berkeley Law School faculty, to comment: "Somehow, in the preoccupation with legal logic the humanity of the participants is lost."

The case that forcibly brought Dr. Diamond to that conclusion was that of Daniel M'Naughten—one of the most celebrated cases in legal history, for it contains *the* rule for measuring criminal insanity (hinging principally on the defendant's ability to distinguish "right" from "wrong"). Dr. Diamond wrote that he "became intensely curious as to what eventually happened to M'Naughten after he was convicted. Was he really insane? Or was his defense of insanity a clever scheme . . . ?" Yet, although the "legal and historical references to the case number literally in the thousands . . . a long and thorough search failed to provide the slightest clue as to what happened to the famous defendant."* It was the *rule,* the *principle,* that concerned the legal scholars; M'Naughten was reduced (as all such persons are, in law students' notes) to a mere "D"—for Defendant.

Another factor that may make law students "turn the

---

*Dr. Diamond ultimately thought to write to the British hospital to which M'Naughten was sent, and obtained copies of M'Naughten's original hospital records. "Yes, M'Naughten really was insane. He remained confined in institutions for the criminally insane until his death in 1865."

other way" is the extent to which the lessons extracted from law cases depart from students' pre-law school notions of common sense and fairness. Take the case, glancingly mentioned in the textbook, of a young boy who lost an eye when he walked into a parked Ford automobile and fell upon its nine-and-three-quarter-inch-high pointed hood ornament. There was no evidence that the ornament was placed there for any purpose other than bolstering Ford sales.

The boy's parents sued Ford, but the company won. On what ground? That the only dangers for which Ford, the manufacturer, bore legal responsibility were those arising from the car *in motion,* "the normal manner for which it [is] manufactured to be used." But since in this case the car was at rest, Ford was not legally liable.

To many a student, that outcome may seem to depart from all common-sense expectation. After all, isn't a parked car essentially as commonplace as a car in motion? And, since kids regularly play around parked cars, isn't that purely decorative gewgaw a predictable hazard whether or not the car is moving?

No such questions are presented in the typical casebook. Nor is there any assurance that issues of fairness, "right," or "wrong" will be raised by the professor. If those issues do *not* surface, there is only one lesson for the student to glean from the case of *Hatch* v. *Ford Motor Co.:* common sense or no common sense, fair or not fair, the Ford-is-not-responsible-for-pointed-hood-ornament-injuries-from-parked-cars argument won the day—the ultimate lawyer's reward.

Scott Turow, in his book *One-L,* a compelling account of his freshman year at Harvard Law School, describes the distress he and his fellow students experienced when they first encountered cases such as *Hatch* v. *Ford*—cases reaching conclusions that "had no roots in the experience, the life they [the students] had had before." It all falls under the heading of "learning to think like a lawyer"; and part of that is learning to be morally detached. "Like a good lawyer," Turow observes, "the student is expected to be able to argue both sides," expected to serve clients loyally "without making an extensive ethical scrutiny of either the clients or themselves."

The classroom curriculum is only a part of what future lawyers are taught in law school. From the moment they pass through the school's doors, they begin to learn a number of intangibles that go directly to Dean Griswold's question, "What do we do to them that makes them turn another way?"

To illustrate: from day one, students are made acutely aware that there is an overriding measure of their worth: academic grades, which boil down, essentially, to their success in pleasing Professor X or Y on a single written examination taken under artificial circumstances that will never obtain in private practice (that is, under artificial time pressures and relying wholly on memory). There are, by and large, no rewards for courtroom skills or for prowess in client counseling or for work done in neighborhood law offices serving the poor. It is grades alone that determine whether or not students win the law student's Holy Grail: a position on the Law Review, a scholarly publication edited by the students with the highest grades in most law schools, and an absolutely certain passport to a golden future. Students are constantly aware that their grades can affect their entire careers, as vividly illustrated by the case of Harvard President Derek Bok. As a freshman at Harvard Law School, Bok received a C− on a midyear practice exam which, at the time, did not count in the Law Review competition. According to law professor Joel Seligman, if it had counted, Bok would not have made Law Review, probably would not have been hired as a professor (and later dean) at Harvard Law School, and "presumably would not be president of Harvard University."

Harvard law professor Alan Stone, a psychiatrist who has specialized in studying law school stresses, sums up the typical result: "intense effort and anxiety" during the first year, leading to an "ever increasing disengagement from the formal educational process" in the second and third years—a sharp contrast, Stone notes, from the medical school experience, where the student, "during his last two years, is given increasing professional responsibility in the clinic and the ward."

The following is a summary of Scott Turow's account of what he and his fellow Harvard Law freshmen could not help learning: to work compulsively (eighty to one hundred hours a week); to eclipse all (including one's spouse) except law school; to be terrorized by the law school's Socratic method of teaching (another Langdell invention) applied, at times, with cruelty and relish by power-hungry professors; to compete savagely with one's fellow students (Turow found one of his classmates hoarding a key library book so others could not use it); to internalize the law school's grades-only value scale. There is, Turow says, a growing "madness in the atmosphere" as final exams near, with students "surreptitiously handing each other course outlines in brown paper bags," as if one or another student outline contained some success-assuring magic; all-night study sessions; always that fixation on law review, and on grades, grades, grades.

What kind of human beings, what kind of lawyers, does all this produce? Is the Socratic method, with all-powerful professors publicly humiliating students, likely to add to the humaneness with which they will later use the power that lawyers have with distraught clients? Does measuring a whole year's work by a single exam taken under unnatural time pressure make for good test-takers or good attorneys? Does the expectation that a student be able to argue both sides of any question develop lawyers with moral sensitivity, or a group of super-bright hired guns?

Another factor bearing on Dean Griswold's concern about the declining idealism among law students is the nature of the law *teachers*—who are, after all, the role models for these future attorneys. Do they offer an image of a Clarence Darrow, tilting with injustice? Do they bring to their students the benefit of practical experience in lawyering?

By and large, precisely the opposite. Many, if not most, law teachers are copies of the emphatically *non* practical model depicted by Christopher Columbus Langdell: "What qualifies a person to teach law is not experience in the work of a lawyer's office, not experience in the trial or argument of causes, not experience, in short, in using law, but experience in *learning* law." [Emphasis added]

Langdell would, no doubt, be pleased by the observations of a modern-day student of legal education, University of Michigan law professor Andrew S. Watson, who writes that law teachers "ordinarily have had little if any practice experience," having mostly "gone directly into teaching from their own academic training, with the elite having served as a clerk to a Supreme Court Justice or some other high court judge."

A random survey of a 1977 directory of full-time law teachers underscores Watson's statement. Judging by biographical information they submitted, only about one-third of them appeared to have any appreciable experience (five years or more) in the practice of law.

Moreover, by American Bar Association edict, full-time law teachers, who, also by ABA fiat, must form the core of any law school faculty, are expressly forbidden to maintain any significant outside practice—quite the opposite of medical schools, where many teachers are ongoing practitioners.

In the view of Berkeley Law School's Bernard Diamond, law teachers thus become odd role-models, for in contrast to medicine, where the student "need only imitate his teachers to guarantee his future professional success," law students "are confronted mostly with teachers who perform few, if any, lawyering tasks," their sole non-teaching occupation being "writing textbooks and Law-Review articles. This encourages the best and the brightest of the law students to do likewise."

Law schools have another immense power: being virtually the sole gateway to the profession, they determine, by their selection of students, who does and who does not get to be a lawyer. Accordingly, their criteria in making that selection profoundly affects the character of the profession.

Since there is no shortage of applicants with the *brainpower* to complete law school (overall, there are two to three applicants for every law school opening; in the more prestigious schools, as many as ten or fifteen vie for each prized slot), the schools have considerable latitude in looking for other qualities—leadership; desire to help others; ability to deal with and help people; reputation for integrity.

Unhappily, law schools exhibit, at best, a secondary interest in such traits, contenting themselves with a single, comparatively narrow aptitude: the ability to do well on examinations, both in college and on a special multiple-choice Law School Admissions Test (LSAT). Most law schools reduce their screening process to pure mechanics and numbers, with a centralized computer, which serves all ABA-approved law schools. That procedure flattens the applicant's many qualities into a single numerical index (the composite of college grades plus the LSAT score), which becomes the most important single factor in the yea-or-nay decision, with the LSAT score often making the decisive difference. For example, in 1978, New York University Law School had 573 applications from students with A− to B+ records in college. How to choose from among this cream of the academic crop? NYU leaned heavily on the LSAT, admitting only one-sixth of those with LSAT scores of 600 to 649 (on a scale of 800), but accepting three-fifths of those with LSAT scores just 50 points higher. That is a great deal of weight to place on applicants' performance on a single four-hour test, especially since:

• The designers and administrators of the LSAT, Educational Testing Service (ETS), acknowledge the test has a sixty-point error factor (that is, the applicant's "true" score may be thirty points higher or lower than the test result).

• ETS also acknowledges that above scores of 600, the test becomes "less and less meaningful."

• Candidates have been able to improve their LSAT scores by fully one hundred points, either by taking the test a second time or by enrolling in one of many commercially offered cram courses for the test.

The law schools' reliance on the LSAT also has racial overtones. Writer Steven Brill, who investigated ETS testing, found one study that showed a discrepancy of 133 points—33 percent—between the median LSAT scores of black and white male candidates.

Admittedly, such intangible qualities as leadership and motivation are extraordinarily difficult to assess. Even so, some colleges *try* to discern those traits. A few do so through personal interviews, often enlisting willing alumni to share the burden. Almost no law schools regularly conduct such interviews. Other colleges try to assess nonacademic qualities through careful weighing of recommendation letters and of the essays submitted by applicants about their life goals or college selection criteria.

It comes down, essentially, to the importance the institution attaches to the screening task. Recently Bowdoin College in Maine assigned seven full-time professionals to review 3,700 applications for admission. By contrast, Georgetown Law School, in Washington, D.C., had only two full-time admissions officers to screen 7,000 applications.

Northeastern University law professor Joel Seligman has illuminated the character of American law schools by suggesting what they might be but are not. He has done so by imagining the dean of an ideal law school welcoming incoming freshmen with these words:

> You are about to enter a profession considered noble because under the United States Constitution . . . it has an ideal of providing equal representation for all. . . . Accordingly, we expect you to spend some of your time working in a free legal clinic for the poor. This will not only be a good practical education for you, but will also illustrate your most basic ethical responsibility.*

In my view, Professor Seligman's fantasy should be carried a step further, with the hypothetical law school dean continuing his remarks in this manner:

> We consider your clinical service, not as a mere adjunct to, but an integral part of your legal education, whose successful completion, like that of your academic courses, is one of the requisites of your graduation—with one difference: your performance will be appraised, not merely by your instructors, *but also by the clients you serve.*

If such were the premises on which both students and teachers embarked on preparing future lawyers, what might be the impact?

Would there be as much disinterest in consumer law and poverty law?

Would the clinical courses aimed at the teaching of practical lawyering skills be treated as much like stepchildren?

Would more law schools begin to teach the art of client counseling? And would only 6 out of 1,700 students enter the Client Counseling Competition (as recently occurred at Harvard Law School)?

*That welcoming speech stands in sharp contrast to that with which, according to Professor Seligman, Harvard's Dean Erwin Griswold used to greet each year's incoming freshmen: "There are no glee clubs at Harvard Law School. This is a law school for lawyers who will practice law in the grand manner, [where] the essence of the preparation must be in the fundamentals: straight thinking and cliché avoidance."

Would an *appeals-*court argument be the only required exposure to courtroom skills?

Would law school graduates emerge with as little experience in negotiating, drafting documents, dealing with clients, and other workaday lawyering skills?

Would they, once in practice, deal more humanely with their clients?

I appreciate that law schools do not operate in a vacuum and that there are reasons quite separate from (and outside of) law schools that explain why deans don't make speeches of that sort and why law schools don't require service in a poverty clinic and why students do not flock to courses in consumer and poverty law even when law schools do offer them. It would be naive to expect that without a change in those external realities there will be any basic transformation in the way American lawyers are trained.

Those outside realities can be summed up in a single experience reported by Scott Turow in *One-L.* One of his fellow freshmen was faced with the choice, one summer, between two job offers: one a Legal Aid job on an Indian reservation; the other, a job with a large law firm. Legal Aid paid $80 a week; the law firm $325.

But those *are* the realities; and as a result, many see law schools more as vocational than as professional schools, focusing more on the breadwinning than on the philosophical and moral aspects of lawyering.

That view is summarized in an incident that, according to legend, took place in a Harvard Law School classroom. When a student protested what he regarded as the unfair outcome of the case under discussion, the professor is said to have replied:

"If it's justice you're interested in, go to the divinity school."

16

The Bar Exam: Protector of the Public — or the Bar?

The second of three hurdles that candidates for the Bar must surmount is the bar examination. On the face of it, it is sensible to protect the public by trying to make sure that those admitted to practice law are competent to do so and by trying to weed out those who are not.

But is the bar examination, as now structured, well tailored to that task?

I raise the question for two reasons:

First, as with other aspects of the legal profession, the examination is designed, administered, and scored by members of the profession itself. As we have seen, in other areas (for example, the writing of the Canons of Ethics), the result aids the Bar more than it serves the general public.

Second, the bar examination is shot through with illogic and inconsistencies that could lead us laymen to question its suitability as a protector of the public.

For example, as noted in the previous chapter, the American Bar Association has gone to immense trouble to assure the quality of the law schools upon whom it bestows its blessing. It has written thirty-three pages of detailed requirements; and it even sends out inspection teams periodically to see that everything is up to snuff at each school. Logically, that should lead to the supposition that graduates of those meticulously screened law schools emerge qualified to practice law.

In fact, though, the Bar in effect makes precisely the opposite assumption—namely, that virtually all law school graduates (even the top graduates of the top law schools) are *not* qualified for admission to the bar. With few exceptions, the only way they can overcome that assumption of nonqualification is to take and pass the bar examination.

There is a partial rationale for that seeming inconsistency: most law schools teach the general principles of law; very few try to teach the variations from those principles embodied in the laws of the various states. Thus, if the bar exam tested solely the applicant's familiarity with the law of his or her particular state, the inconsistency would largely disappear. Yet only part of the exam is devoted to state law; and the basic assumption of *non*qualification until the entire exam is passed would lead the layman to conclude either (a) that the Bar's elaborate law school accreditation system is largely meaningless or (b) if that's not the case, that the bar exam requirement is a waste of time and energy.

But even if we give the Bar the benefit of the doubt and assume the examination is not a fruitless exercise, that merely leads to the next inconsistency, which is this: if even the top graduate of the top law school is presumed nonqualified until he or she passes the bar exam then it follows that exam must be *essential* to protect the public from incompetent lawyers. Apparently that's not the case, for the Bar in five states* allows the graduates of ABA-approved schools located in those states to be admitted to the bar without taking the exam. If waiving the exam requirement for graduates of home-state law schools produces a markedly higher degree of lawyer incompetence in those states, it is a well-kept secret. If not, then maybe the bar exam isn't that essential after all.

Let's follow the Bar's logic down yet another path: if the examination is as valid a way of determining who is and is not qualified to practice law as the Bar seems to claim, then presumably anyone who succeeds in passing the exam, whether or not a law school graduate, is *ipso facto* qualified for admission to the bar. Wrong again. In all but

*Mississippi, Montana, South Dakota, West Virginia, and Wisconsin.

five states, it doesn't matter whether a person has read and memorized every book in the law library and is capable of getting a perfect score on the examination. In those forty-five states, without a law school diploma a person is not even permitted to *take* the exam.

Is the dual requirement—of law school *plus* the bar exam—really sensible? If so, then the five states that admit persons to the bar after "reading the law" (usually as an apprentice with a practitioner) and passing the bar exam are exposing clients to undue risks of incompetent attorneys. But one does not hear complaints of that sort from any of those states.

Since we are "one nation . . . indivisible," presumably the practice of law is not appreciably harder in one state than in another. If that's the case, and if the examination is the valid indicator of competence claimed by the Bar, then the pass-fail percentages in the various states should, logically, be reasonably uniform.

They are decidedly not. In 1977, the percentage of candidates passing the bar exam ranged from 100 percent in West Virginia, through 51 percent in California, all the way down to 25 percent in Mississippi.

There are two alternative ways of viewing those disparities. One is that the practice of law is four times as difficult in Mississippi as in West Virginia. Another is that the widely varying pass-fail rates reflect a desire on the part of state bar associations to control the number of new lawyers admitted to practice. Notably with rare exceptions, the bar examinations are scored entirely by existing *active* practitioners—no law professors or retired practitioners participate.

Is the bar exam really effective in separating qualified sheep from the unqualified goats? If so, then one might assume that those who fail the exam are not fit to practice law. But it doesn't turn out that way. Those who don't pass the exam on the first try are generally permitted to take it again a few months later and, if unsuccessful, yet again some months after that—*and ultimately, 98 percent of the candidates for the bar end up passing.* The layman is entitled to wonder whether a test that 98 percent can pass is really the reliable screening mechanism the Bar represents it to be. Alternatively, the onlooker might ask whether, if the result is to screen out only two percent of the applicants, it is legitimate and necessary to put 100 percent of law school graduates through the effort and expense.

And that effort and expense are considerable, for another irony is that, even after three years of hard study at the most prestigious of the elaborately screened law schools, the brightest graduate would not dream of taking the bar examination without enrolling in a two to three-month cram course, typically costing several hundred dollars. Beyond that cash outlay, there is the several months' income loss for those applicants whom law firms will not hire until the bar exam is satisfactorily passed.

That Bar-imposed cost is one of the many barriers that draws class and racial lines around the legal profession. It may be bearable for candidates whose families have enough savings, but it is onerous for those who can't afford the bar-review course or who are obliged to take a full-time job immediately in order to support themselves or to begin paying back debts incurred for law school tuition.

Oliver Morse, associate dean of the predominantly black Howard University Law School in Washington, says that such obstacles have confronted many Howard graduates, and he feels they may account in part for the striking discrepancies in bar exam success rates between whites and blacks.

The word *striking* accurately describes this gap, as shown by the statistics on the next page—the most recently published figures I have been able to find.

The Georgia bar exam results are especially dramatic: every one of the *white* graduates of the Yale, Harvard, and Columbia law schools passed the bar exam; but not one of the six black graduates of those same law schools

State	Time period Studied	Percentage of whites passing	Percentage of blacks passing
South Carolina	1967–72	95.4	55.6
Alabama	1966–76	70	32
Pennsylvania	1955–70	70	27
Michigan	Spring 1971	71	16
Georgia	July 1972	58.5	0

passed. This came at a time when blacks made up 27 percent of Georgia's population, but just 1.4 percent of the state's lawyers.

The bar exam also has a homogenizing effect on legal education. In recent years, more and more states have adopted, for the "national" segment of their examinations, a single multistate set of questions, and the awareness of that, both by law school administrators and by students, has tended to lessen diversity in law school curricula and teaching methods. Research by curriculum critic Jane Kelso indicates that the sameness among law schools is largely attributable to the fact that about four-fifths of the courses students take in law schools are aimed at the bar exam. Moreover, by its very nature, the bar exam, lacking in any test of nonclassroom skills, tends to discourage law schools from offering, and students from electing, "clinical" instruction.

Finally, many find the kinds of questions asked on many bar exams—coupled with an undue emphasis on memorization—to be an unrealistic measure of later competence as a practitioner. The 1978 bar exam in the District of Columbia, for example, gave candidates less than one minute to answer questions such as the following: "What is the minimum number of incorporators necessary to form a corporation in your state?" "What are the six elements of the crime of 'burglary'?"—a common-law crime that no longer exists, having long since been supplanted by the statutory crime of theft.* And in 1977, candidates for the D.C. bar exam were told that it would test them, not on a newly-passed divorce law, but on the old, admittedly out-of-date statute.

Are such questions a valid test of legal competence, or simply of brute memory? And if the latter, is that a realistic gauge, since almost no practicing lawyer would dare rely on his or her memory for such crucial (albeit detailed) matters as the number of days allowed to answer a complaint. What if their recollection was wrong and a vital deadline were allowed to pass?

Some have suggested that the bar exam would make more sense if it rested on an applicant's knowledge of where to find the answers. That could be achieved by administering the test on an "open-book" basis, with all sources available to the applicants. But that is not the way the Organized Bar chooses to run the test.

That is the crucial point. The Organized Bar administers the bar examination as it sees fit. Whatever racially discriminatory elements are embedded in the exam—as suggested by the racial differences in pass-fail rates already described—are not likely to be corrected when those who design and administer the test—the bar examiners of the various states—are as all-white as they were as recently as 1971, when Detroit Judge Edward F. Bell found that there were only four black examiners in the entire nation. Two of those were in the District of Columbia, leaving but two distributed among all the other states. Nor is the bar exam likely to attempt the admittedly difficult task of testing nonbook skills (drafting, negotiating, client counseling) so long as client groups have no voice in its design.

All of this is not to say the bar examination is wholly

---

*These short-answer questions that hinge on specific provisions of law or of court rules do not make up the whole of the bar exam. There are also essay questions aimed at testing the applicant's ability to analyze and spot legal issues from a particular set of facts, as well as testing knowledge of the law itself.

without value. New York University law dean Norman Redlich has listed some "important functions" the bar exam serves—including sparing law schools the dreary task of teaching the law of individual states; forcing students into areas of the law they might miss in law school; and giving the public confidence in the profession by holding law schools up to an independent standard of testing. But then Dean Redlich adds that even if the bar exam were fulfilling all of its positive purposes "superbly, *it would border on consumer fraud to claim that bar examinations were testing for qualifications to practice law . . .*" [Emphasis added]

17

Screening Out the Mavericks

After passing the bar exam, would-be lawyers face another hurdle: they must prove to the Bar's satisfaction that they possess "the good moral character and general fitness requisite for an attorney and counselor-at-law."

The objective is laudable; but how well tailored to that goal is the screening mechanism the Bar has devised? The sifting process can be described simply: the applicant furnishes answers to a long list of detailed and often intensely personal questions, submits letters of recommendation from independent persons, and then, typically, appears for a brief, often superficial personal interview with a member of the Bar's character and fitness committee.

The process is far simpler than the problems presented both for the Bar and the applicant. How is the Bar to define, and to measure, such amorphous qualities as "good moral character and general fitness"? And how is the applicant to prove his or her moral character, especially since the standards for doing so are nowhere set forth?

Moreover, how effective can the screening process be, since what is basically involved is an effort to peer decades into the future and predict whether a person will behave with propriety through a lifetime as an attorney. Even an intensive "full field investigation" by the well-staffed FBI cannot provide such assurance, and the Bar's character and fitness screening is, in general, cursory. Bar committees generally operate without staff and, with rare exceptions, no pretense is made at investigating or verifying the information furnished by the candidates.

186

The imperfections in the Bar's sieve are illuminated by the fact that the following attorneys breezed through the character and fitness committees without the slightest hint that they would one day be put to moral tests and be found grievously wanting:

• Former Attorney General Richard Kleindienst, who admitted having lied to a committee of the United States Senate—and in the most deliberate and flagrant manner. (See page 86.)

• Hoyt A. Moore, who openly admitted giving a $250,-000 bribe to a Federal judge. (See page 88.)

• Mahlon F. Perkins, who admitted lying to a judge about destroying certain key documents he was withholding from evidence in a major lawsuit. (See page 93.)

• Former Attorney General John Mitchell, former presidential assistants John Ehrlichman and John Dean, and several lesser government officials—who pleaded guilty to or were convicted of obstruction of justice.

• Richard M. Nixon.

Given the difficulty of the task and the casual way in which the Bar ordinarily undertakes it, it is not surprising that very little real winnowing does take place. While the Bar ordinarily guards the figures with great secretiveness, a New York City Bar Association study found that 99.9 percent of the applicants get through the screen, 95 percent without the slightest doubts raised.

All of that raises certain questions:

• If (as the bar seems to have concluded) 99.9 percent of lawyer applicants are passably pure, is there a need for the screening mechanism?

• Is the process a serious effort to measure character and predict future behavior as a lawyer?

• Are the questions asked of applicants relevant to those goals?

• And, above all, is the process administered in even-handed fashion? Or does it operate in such a way as to shunt aside or discourage the nonconformist, the deviant, the boat-rocker, leaving the legal profession more mono-lithic and conformist than it otherwise might be?

For the applicants, satisfying the Bar as to their moral character and fitness is a laborious business, given the Bar's inquisitiveness about their past. The Bar's eleven-page questionnaire requires applicants to furnish infor-mation such as the following—all supposedly designed to elicit information relevant to their "character and fitness":

• Every place of residence since birth, with the *exact* address and inclusive dates of *every* residence since en-tering high school.

• Whether the applicant has *ever* been "ticketed or summoned or arrested" for violating *"any* law, ordi-nance, traffic, or parking regulation."

• Photocopies of Selective Service Registration card* and of certificates of discharge or release from the armed services, and a certified copy of any decree of divorce or separation.

• The "full name of all persons with whom you are presently living and [their] relationship to you."

The questionnaire is at pains to warn applicants that they are responding to those detailed questions "under oath" (thus exposing them to perjury charges for erro-neous answers) and that their "failure fully and accurately to disclose any fact or information" can result in "denial of [their] application."

The New York City Bar Association study group found that even after the applicant "has performed the labori-ous task of assembling [this] detailed information about his past, virtually *no effort is made to do anything with that information."* [Emphasis added throughout the above]

---

*This was a requirement that persisted, at least in New York, after the termination of the draft.

In filling out the formidable questionnaire, the applicant is in the dark as to "the grounds on which [he or she] will be deferred or rejected," since, according to the New York study, these are "nowhere catalogued." Indeed, the Bar panel found the character committees reluctant even to divulge the figures on rejections and deferrals of applications. This, the study group said, was "not inadvertent": the character committee's secretary openly told them that revealing the rarity of rejections and deferrals "would ruin the mystique of the committee" and "might interfere with the deterrent function [of] discouraging individuals from going to law school 'if they have something to worry about.'"

The probers also discovered that, at least in the view of the character committees, behavior of the following sorts was "something to worry about:"

• Failing to live with spouse or living with a person not one's spouse, in what the committees termed a "meretricious relationship."

• Being in psychotherapy or analysis (which might require a letter from the doctor attesting the candidate as a "safe risk").

• Extreme obesity (which in one instance obliged the overweight candidate to produce an opinion from a psychiatrist that the weight problem was not due to a serious emotional difficulty).

All of the above created what were called "problem cases" regarding the applicant's "moral character and fitness" to be an attorney.

After the questionnaire has been submitted, there is a final further hurdle: a personal interview, usually with a single member of the character committee who may or may not have glanced at the information provided on the questionnaire. There are no guidelines or limits to the interview, which may last only eight to fifteen minutes. The Bar study group in New York found that the topics might include the weather, mutual acquaintances, or law schools. New York candidates gave these glimpses of questions asked:

- "How many brothers and sisters did I have? What did my parents do? How much campus unrest was there at my law school? Also, 'Did I really have no parking tickets?' "
- "Very cursory interview composed primarily of polite small talk and a few questions about past parking violations."
- "I was asked about political groups I belonged to . . . and was given a twenty minute lecture on why students should keep their mouths shut and just study while at the University and leave government to the more mature."

Perhaps the most telling experience was that of an applicant who had meticulously compiled and submitted documents on a German lawsuit in which he had been involved, only to have the interviewer concede that no one involved with the character screening could read German and that "the compilation of these documents was an empty formality." The applicant was not asked a single question either about the lawsuit or about his medical draft deferment. He *was* asked, however, "to explain in detail the circumstances surrounding my traffic ticket, my credit standing with Diners' Club, and my high school attendance record."

The superficiality of the questions and the investigative efforts of the character committees raise serious questions as to whether their prime purpose really *is* to protect clients from prospective lawyers of flawed moral character.

Skepticism about the true objective is heightened by the exceptions to the typical casualness—instances in which the character committees sift the applicant's past in excruciating detail and subject him to days of interrogation. Judging from those cases where details have come to light in court contests, one kind of candidate is particularly apt to excite the Bar's inquisitory energies: the person with nonconformist *political* views, especially views that suggest a propensity to side with the disadvantaged. Here are a few examples:

• *Rudolph Schware:* son of an immigrant, he took his first job at age nine, worked all through school, college, law school; during the depth of the Depression, he assumed an Italian "alias" to avoid anti-Semitic hiring practices; he joined the Communist Party at age 18 but resigned at age 26 when he became disillusioned by the Soviet alliance with Hitler; charges against him of recruiting for Spanish loyalist army were dropped before trial. He participated in a bitter maritime strike in San Francisco and was arrested, along with 2,000 other strikers (but never charged), for "suspicion of criminal syndicalism." He volunteered for paratrooper duty in World War II, served in New Guinea, and was honorably discharged. His good character was attested to by his rabbi, a local lawyer, the dean of his law school, all law professors who knew him, and every member save one of his law school class.

After graduation from law school, Schware was denied permission to take the bar examination by the New Mexico Bar Association. While the Bar committee called no witnesses to question his character and introduced no evidence against him, it subjected Schware to lengthy hearing and interrogation and denied him admission to the bar on the basis of (a) his use of "aliases"; (b) his arrests; (c) his membership in the Communist Party thirteen years earlier. The denial of bar membership was upheld by the New Mexico Supreme Court, obliging Schware to appeal to United States Supreme Court, which reversed the bar and ordered his admission, four years after his graduation from law school.

• *Terence Hallinan:* son of a prominent attorney who ran for President in 1952 on the Independent Progressive ticket and who was notorious for his outspoken defense of unpopular causes. Son Terence participated in a peace demonstration in London, was arrested for "blocking a footpath" to the U.S. Embassy, and fined one British pound. While helping to register black voters in Mississippi in the summer of 1963, he was arrested twice, once for "loitering" and once for "littering in a public place." He joined in picketing and sit-ins against various San Francisco business establishments that engaged in discriminatory business and hiring practices, was arrested six times on charges such as "unlawful assembly," "disturbing the peace," and "willful disobedience of court order." His good character was attested to by the judge before whom he represented himself and by the prosecutor in the case; also by his law professor, who found Hallinan a "quiet, serious, intelligent" student who, if admitted to the bar, would concentrate on representing "persons whose beliefs are unorthodox and unpopular."

After graduating from law school and passing his bar exam, Hallinan was subjected to lengthy hearings and denied admission to the bar for failing to prove his "moral character," a judgment based on acts of civil disobedience and "habitual resort to fisticuffs" (the bar cited nine fistfights, including one in which a romantic rival lay in wait for Hallinan when he escorted his date home). The thoroughness of the bar's investigation is indicated by charges of lack of candor for failing to report his having signed certain legal documents, at his father's request, in a will contest. The Board of Examiners denied Hallinan admission even while acknowledging he had established prima facie case for admission through attestations of good character by others. Hallinan fought his case all the way to California Supreme Court and ultimately won admission to the bar by court order nearly two years after graduating from law school and passing his bar exam.

• *George Anastaplo:* the son of Greek immigrants; Anastaplo grew up in a small town in southern Illinois, discontinued his education at age 18 to join the Air Force, and flew as a navigator in every theater of operations in World War II. After his discharge, he finished college and law school at the University of Chicago, emerging "well regarded" by his academic associates, by professors who had taught him, and by members of the bar who knew him. He passed the bar exam and submitted his personal history form to the Character Committee of the Bar that, according to one Supreme Court Justice, "did not contain so much as one statement of fact about [his] past life that could have, in any way, cast doubt upon his fitness for Admission to the Bar."

But in answer to a bar question about what he considered "principles underlying the Constitution," Anastaplo recited the goal of securing "Life, Liberty and the Pursuit of Happiness" and then added: "And of course, whenever the particular government in power becomes destructive of these ends, it is the right of the people to alter it or to abolish it and thereupon to establish a new government."

Whether or not the character committee recognized it as a near-verbatim paraphrase of the Declaration of Independence, Anastaplo's statement provoked extensive interrogation and questions about possible membership in a variety of organizations, including the Communist Party, the Ku Klux Klan—*and the Democratic and Republican Parties as well.* Anastaplo refused to answer all those questions out of conviction that the committee had overstepped Constitutional bounds by inquiring into political beliefs and associations. The Bar committee denied Anastaplo its approval by vote of 11–6; ten years later, the U.S. Supreme Court upheld the Bar by a single vote and ended Anastaplo's legal career—essentially for the offense of embracing the Declaration of Independence.

The record does not reveal an impartial bar concern over the past political affiliations and beliefs of bar applicants. While in the above instances the character committees exhibited acute concern over what would generally be regarded as the "leftist" views of candidates, a careful review of bar admission court cases by Harvard Law School's Professor Daniel Rosenberg failed to disclose a single instance in which admission to the legal profession was either delayed or denied because of the applicant's membership in the Ku Klux Klan, the John Birch Society, or, in any year after World War II, a candidate's past membership in the pro-Nazi German-American Bund.

Nor has the bar been uniformly insistent that members of the legal profession uphold the law of the land. For example, during his lengthy interrogation by the character committee about his acts of admitted civil disobedience, one committee member read to Terence Hallinan, with evident approval, an article in the *American Bar Association Journal* that stated: "We [lawyers] must support and protect the laws, *whether we agree with a particular [law] or not.* We cannot settle for lip service to legality. *We cannot be 'sometime' lawyers."* [Emphasis added]

Yet here is Tom P. Brady, former vice-president of the Mississippi Bar Association, speaking in the mid-fifties about the Supreme Court's school desegregation ruling— then, as now, the law of the land: ". . . if [this] constitutes disrespect or treason, then let the most be made of it. . . . A law is never paramount to mores. . . . We say to the Supreme Court and to the entire world, 'You shall not make us drink from this cup.' "

And here is George Corley Wallace, former governor of Alabama and for twenty-one years a member of the Alabama bar, proclaiming to the nation: "I draw the line in the dust . . . and I say, 'segregation now, segregation tomorrow, segregation forever.' "

So far as I have been able to discover, there was not one effort by the Organized Bar to censure, much less disbar, any attorney for calling for open defiance of the law of the land on school desegregation.

After the study panel of the New York City Bar Association had completed its 1977–1978 scrutiny of the character and fitness screening process, one of its members, Jay Topkis, found "the whole business an incredible waste of time." While Mr. Topkis thought a "theoretical case" could be made for some kind of "limited inquiry"—as to, say, whether an applicant had ever been convicted of perjury or embezzlement"—he went on to say he had "not heard it suggested that any convicted perjurer or embezzler in this century applied for admission to the Bar of this state."

Mr. Topkis concluded:

> We lawyers claim to act on the basis of evidence and real experience rather than fantasy. . . . But so far as I can see, there is no basis whatsoever in evidence and experience to warrant the further existence of the entire machinery for inquiry into character and fitness. . . . Accordingly, I would favor junking the entire present structure. . . .

18

What Should Be Done

Something is awry.

Every element of the American system of justice—the judges, the courts, prosecutors, the police—is made available, free of charge, to all citizens alike regardless of wealth or station.

Every element, that is, save one: the means of gaining access to the system. Legal help. An indispensable ingredient.* Without the assistance of an attorney, a citizen cannot, for all practical purposes, get through the courtroom door.

It is curious: few of us would tolerate placing a turnstile at the door of our courts and charging citizens for their use. And yet that is essentially what the present system does. As noted at the outset of this book, the key to the courtroom—a lawyer's help—is not freely available to all, but is on the auction block, available to the highest bidder.

More serious, it is *un*available—in the civil-law arena, at least—to those who cannot meet the price tag.

To me, that is unacceptable. It ought to be unacceptable in a democracy that claims descent from the Magna Carta, which proclaimed, "To no one will we sell . . . justice."

It ought to be unacceptable in a country whose Pledge

*Indeed, the Supreme Court, in a notable 1975 decision about the legal profession, explicitly noted that "lawyers are essential to the primary governmental function of administering justice . . ."

of Allegiance aspires to "one nation . . . indivisible, with
. . . justice for all."

It ought to be unacceptable in a country on whose Supreme Court pediment are engraved the words "Equal
justice under law."

That Supreme Court inscription speaks of *"equal* justice"—not more for the rich and less (or none) for the
poor.

The Pledge of Allegiance talks of "justice for *all"*—not
just for those able to pay for it.

There is but one way to make those words mean what
they say:

> *Place legal help on a par with all the other parts
> of the justice system. Make it equally available,
> free of charge, to all citizens alike regardless of
> wealth or station.*

It's all very well to assert that "there's only one way" to
make the Pledge of Allegiance more than empty rhetoric.
But is that, in itself, more rhetoric? Is there *really* no way
short of turning, once again, to big government to solve
the problem?

Well, the American legal profession has had two hundred years as a private, almost wholly self-regulating institution to meet its self-proclaimed goal "to make legal
counsel available." How close has it come? As we've seen,
the American Bar Association itself has acknowledged
that, after nearly two centuries, the profession fails to
reach or serve adequately the "middle seventy percent of
our population."

Thus, contrary to popular supposition, it is not just the
very poor who lack access to legal help, *but the preponderance of middle Americans as well.*

That is the acknowledged result of two hundred years
of wholly private lawyering.

Look at the problem in concrete terms:

Suppose corporation A brings a groundless debt-collection suit against unprosperous B (based, say, on a computer error that no one will admit)—an action that will, if successful, bring financial ruin to B. Under the existing legal system, whether B will be able to present *any* defense in a court of law hinges upon B's ability to hire an attorney. Should that be?

Or imagine that B has an open-and-shut legal grievance against A (the roof in B's apartment leaks and A, the landlord, while legally obliged to repair it, refuses to do so). As the legal system is now structured, if B lacks the money to hire an attorney, *the odds are he won't even have his grievance heard in court.** Should *that* be?

Nor does the present system satisfy the ethical imperatives of the legal profession itself. The very first commandment in the Code of Professional Responsibility of the American Bar Association states categorically: "A basic tenet of the professional responsibility of lawyers is that *every person in our society* should have *ready access* to the independent professional services of a lawyer of integrity and competence." [Emphasis added]

"Ready access" to a lawyer for "every person in our society." Is there any truly effective way of making that a reality short of offering free legal help to all citizens?

Is there, too, any other meaningful way of curing the root cause of most of the problems suggested in this book —namely, the concentration of wealth in the upper strata that makes millions of people unable to pay for the services of lawyers? Can we expect law schools to alter their business-oriented curricula as long as the overwhelming share of lawyering dollars lies with corporations and the well-to-do? And how else offset the basic biases against the have-not One-Shotter litigants that are built into the legal system? Indeed, free legal help for all would be *the* way of furnishing ordinary people attorneys with experience and expertise comparable to that of Repeat Player lawyers, for only in that way is it likely that there will develop

*Leaving aside self-representation, which is not an effective solution in any but the simplest court cases

a body of lawyers specializing in defending consumers, tenants, and other unmoneyed people.

The universal availability of legal assistance is also the best (perhaps the only) way of assuring the proper operation of the adversary system, with both sides represented by counsel—the model on which the legal profession's ethic of duty-to-client-above-all-else is based.

Free legal help could be made available through a National Legal Service (NLS), comparable to the National Health Service in Great Britain. A person in need of NLS help could get it in either of two ways: through an NLS office, using the services of full-time, salaried NLS personnel (attorneys and paralegals); or by going to an independent attorney or paralegal whose services on behalf of the NLS would be compensated with government funds.

There could (and presumably would) be a third way of getting legal help. Those who could afford to do so could, as in England, purchase it privately, outside of the NLS scheme. Thus there would remain a private bar, alongside the government-supported NLS bar.*

The provision of government-paid legal services does not represent a totally new departure for America but rather a broadening of an already well-established principle, enunciated in the Sixth Amendment to the Constitution. That amendment guarantees to every criminal defendant "the assistance of counsel for his defense" and has now been extended, by court interpretation, to encompass misdemeanor charges. In 1977, more than 90 percent of

---

*Under such a dual system, privately paid lawyers would predictably receive higher pay than the NLS attorneys, and a large portion of the Best and the Brightest lawyers would gravitate to the private segment of the profession. To the extent that legal victories result sheerly from "better" lawyering, that discrepancy would dilute the ideal of equal justice. A NLS plan could, however, include measures to narrow the gap—such as, say, requiring all attorneys to take on a minimum amount of NLS work per year, as has recently been proposed by a committee of the New York City Bar Association.

all persons in New York City charged with state-law violations were defended either by Legal Aid or government-paid attorneys.

The NLS would, in essence, extend the principles of the Sixth Amendment from the criminal into the civil arena, a threshold this country has already crossed, with the active support of the Organized Bar, with the provision of government-funded civil legal help to the poor through the Legal Services Corporation. That extension recognizes that in today's society the consequences of a legal wrong in the civil area can be as serious as a criminal punishment (for example, illegal denial of public benefits to a disabled person can be a life-or-death matter).

There is also, now, a multi*billion*-dollar taxpayer subsidy of private legal expenses that dwarfs the $270 million budget of the Legal Services Corporation—but that is usually little talked about or noted. The fact is, however, that the tens of billions of dollars in legal fees paid by corporations and other businesses, being tax deductible, are in effect nearly half supported by taxpayer dollars. True, the dollars are not paid directly out of the U.S. Treasury, as with the Legal Services Corporation, but the revenue lost through the tax deductibility of business legal expenses produces precisely the same effect on all U.S. taxpayers as do direct outlays—as explained previously (pp. 133–34).

Would the NLS program proposed here be without problems and faults? Of course not; any system of law or government has its flaws, and so would the NLS. Whatever those might prove to be, though, they would be less, I am convinced, than those of the existing system of justice-for-sale.

Although providing government-supported legal help sets no fundamental new precedent in America, the notion of free legal help for all citizens will doubtless provoke deep fears and strong opposition. Here are some of the counterarguments that may safely be predicted:

ARGUMENT: *Free legal help for all comers will be colossally expensive and will cost far more than the country can "afford."*

A National Legal Service would unquestionably be costly. The precise price tag cannot be calculated until the final blueprints are drawn. But in the last analysis, what we can "afford" comes down to a matter of choices, of priorities, of what we are determined that we should have.

For example, the public has been persuaded that it is important to have a "strong national defense." Accordingly, the Pentagon routinely proposes, the President approves, and the Congress overwhelmingly ratifies Pentagon budgets well above $100 billion as well as new weapons costing $20 billion, $30 billion, sometimes more —with only the scantest questioning of whether or not we can "afford" those gargantuan sums. Quarter-billion-dollar "cost overruns" on multibillion-dollar projects (like the C-5A transport plane) are accepted with only the briefest of fuss.

If the public could be persuaded that "one nation . . . with . . . justice for all" is as important as a "strong national defense," does anyone doubt we would find ways of making a legal-aid program as "affordable" as C-5A transports and nuclear carriers and $30-billion mobile missile systems?

ARGUMENT: *The universal availability of free legal help will bring out the combative and the litigious, produce a torrent of ill-grounded lawsuits, and paralyze the court system, if not the entire economy.*

Before the British National Health System took effect, there was a comparable fear of overuse. But the reality proved less than the anticipation.* Since going to doctors' offices (like initiating and pursuing lawsuits) is time-consuming and often unpleasant, most of those who availed

*See note in the Notes and Sources section.

themselves of the new British health program proved to have good cause. Similarly, while there are doubtless some Americans who have nothing better to do than make mischief for their neighbors, it is not unreasonable to suppose that, over the long haul, the British medical experience would be repeated under a free legal-help scheme here.

Some aspects of a free legal-help program could *reduce* the amount of litigation. For example, with lawyers more widely accessible, advance planning and *preventive* legal advice aimed at forestalling disputes, now confined almost exclusively to business clients able to pay for it, might be more widely used. And with the knowledge that an adversary could get government-paid legal help, there would be less incentive for so-called "strike" or harassment suits, initiated in the hope of either wearing down an opponent or forcing an out-of-court settlement to avoid a protracted and costly trial.

The possibility of a litigation explosion cannot, of course, be ruled out. But it is, at best, a speculation. On the other hand, the present underrepresentation of tens of millions of Americans, which the NLS proposal is designed to correct, is a here-and-now certainty acknowledged by the Organized Bar. Moreover, if the NLS did result in a deluge of groundless lawsuits,* that would be the time to design curbs tailored to meet the then-known causes. Surely the mind of man can fashion penalties to discourage the mischief makers.

ARGUMENT: *It is unconscionable to allow General Motors and the Rockefellers to use taxpayers' money to pay their legal bills.*

First of all, we don't require the well-to-do to pay for other parts of the justice system (judges, courts, the police) even though they could well afford to do so. Hence, (it can

---

*An increase in *well-founded* actions should not be regarded as an evil, since that would, presumably, result in more justice.

be persuasively argued) lawyers' services—an equally essential part of that system—should likewise be available to all citizens without charge.

There is, too, the near certainty that GM and the Rockefellers and others who can afford to do so will, if permitted, hire their own lawyers and will use the NLS rarely if at all. On the other hand, it could be forcefully contended that the more the system is used by well-to-do and politically powerful citizens, who insist on high quality, the better the NLS will be. That argument finds graphic support in the experience of the public schools, which are demonstrably superior wherever they are attended by the children of the affluent.*

ARGUMENT: *If government dollars become the dominant source of legal fees, lawyering will fall prey to governmental control and political whim, and there will be less disposition and capacity to challenge the governmental hand that feeds.*

That argument does not apply to many, if not most, civil controversies (for example, contests over wills or contracts), which are between private parties. Nonetheless, that danger should not be brushed aside. The experience with government legal programs in the sixties and seventies leaves little doubt that when National Legal Service lawyers take aim at the White House, Congress, governors, and mayors, not to mention politically potent corporations and other Establishment institutions, there will be efforts at reprisals, fund cutbacks, and curbs on politically controversial lawsuits.†

---

*Even if there is no income ceiling for recipients of legal help, certain types of *cases* might be ruled out of bounds for NLS assistance. For example: (1) cases that result in large damage awards, and (2) cases where the legal fees are currently financed either by the losing party, as is often the case with private antitrust lawsuits, or through contingent-fee arrangements. I would hope, however, that the latter would be sharply reduced by the broadest possible adoption of the no-fault principle to personal injury cases. See Chapter 12.

†For example, as of 1979, Congress prohibited Legal Services attor-

Despite all the early sniping, the advent of government-paid poverty and Legal Services lawyers has given a legal voice to individuals and groups who never dreamed of having representation, and government programs have faced unprecedented legal challenges—a large portion of them brought by government-paid attorneys. To the extent that an expanded NLS program would make lawyers available to still more groups who are now unrepresented, and would give strong financial underpinning to the fragilely funded public-interest law movement (see pp. 15–24), we would have more diversity among lawyers and more challenges to official conduct, not less.

That proposition is the more convincing when one recalls the Organized Bar's behavior during the recent school desegregation battle and the assaults on Constitutional liberties during the so-called McCarthy era. While Senator McCarthy was a power in America, one searched the resolutions of the American Bar Association in vain for any protest against his trampling of Constitutional rights. And the ABA, far from upholding the Supreme Court on the school question, was mute while prominent attorneys in the South led the call for open defiance.*

Even acknowledging the danger of political control of a National Legal Service, is that sufficient reason to scuttle the entire NLS idea? If so, then it could be argued that we should forthwith terminate all publicly funded criminal-defense programs (which, as noted, would end most criminal-defense services in New York City). Under that reasoning, we should also lose no time in dismantling the Legal Services Corporation. Apparently, though, we regard the risks of political interference acceptable in pro-

---

neys from providing legal help in school desegregation and non-therapeutic-abortion cases.

*For examples, see p. 194. The defiance of certain Southern attorneys was, of course, counterbalanced by the often courageous support of the Supreme Court decision by many lawyers in all regions and by such groups as the Lawyers' Committee for Civil Rights Under Law.

viding legal help for the poor; if that's the case, why not for the rest of the population?

The answer lies not in discarding the NLS idea, but in devising the best possible buffers against the politicians. The courts could be one, and the NLS statute should be written in such a way as to insure court review of any charges of ·political interference. The preservation of a privately funded bar, alongside the NLS, would be a major insurer of diversity in the legal profession. And if the NLS program, with its availability to all comers, were to become popular with a large segment of the population, politicians would presumably be more reluctant to tamper with it than they are now, when the aid goes only to the politically feeble poor.

ARGUMENT: *(1) "Socialized law" will deny clients the right to an attorney of their own choice, and (2) publicly paid lawyers might not serve nonfee-paying clients with single-minded loyalty and zeal.*

Both are contentions traditionally advanced by the Organized Bar in opposing reforms aimed at lower-cost legal services, especially group and prepaid legal plans (pp. 105–11). But those arguments speak of disadvantages the bar elite seems to find quite acceptable when applied to the poor (via the Legal Services Corporation program, which the Bar supports), although a sensibly designed and operated NLS system would permit clients the maximum possible choice of attorneys. (Bear in mind, too, that the unprosperous, who currently can't find *any* affordable attorney, could hardly have less choice than they have now.)

Finally, does the Bar seriously suggest that loyalty to client is an attribute that has to be purchased with direct-from-the-client cash?

Skeptics will also doubtless argue that any proposal for universal free legal help is politically unrealistic, hopeless of enactment in the foreseeable future.

But the argument of political "impracticality," in addition to being speculative, hardly addresses the *merits* of the proposal.

Besides, who, not many years ago, would have predicted that government dollars would be paying for more than 90 percent of the criminal defense lawyering in New York City—and, even more striking, who would have envisaged the American Bar Association embracing "socialized" *civil* help (via the Legal Services Corporation)?

Whatever its validity, that argument does not provide a license to legal reformers to sit on their hands pending acceptance of a National Legal Service, for there is much that could be done *now* to alleviate many of the problems set forth in this book. Specifically, a variety of steps could be taken:

• To break up the Lawyers' Monopoly—that is, to end the Organized Bar's control of the conditions under which the public can obtain legal help.

• To introduce free-market competition into the legal services field and give people a choice as to how to go about resolving their legal problems.

• To make the legal profession accountable to the general public, and not just to itself.

• To lessen the imbalances now built into the American legal system against the unmoneyed and the unorganized.

Here, briefly, are some of the steps that could be taken to achieve those goals:

Breaking up the Lawyers' Monopoly and introducing competition into the legal services field: A crucial step here is to abolish the concept of "the *unauthorized* practice of law" (UPL) which, as we have seen, has been the Bar's principal weapon against would-be competitors. Wielding that weapon, the Bar has done its best to give people but a single choice when confronted with a legal problem: hire a full-fledged (and hence high-priced) lawyer, or do without legal help. The Bar should not have the power to deny people the option of solving their legal problems by less costly means. After all, the need is to protect consumers not from "unauthorized" help, but from *incompetent* legal help, whether provided by lawyers or lay people. And if those buying a home can effect that standard transaction with help from a broker or title company (as millions have done successfully) or can obtain an uncontested divorce or file for personal bankruptcy aided by a clinic manned by experienced nonlawyers or even by using a do-it-yourself kit, the Bar should not be able to impose a blanket ban on all such arrangements. If faulty legal advice results, the remedy should lie with the injured consumer (as it already does under malpractice law). It certainly should not depend exclusively, as it now does, on the self-interested Bar.

The Bar has traditionally disparaged such lawyer-avoiding arrangements with horror stories of cases involving some out-of-the-ordinary wrinkle unnoticed by a paraprofessional with unhappy consequences for the consumer. That can happen, of course; and there are cases requiring a full-fledged lawyer to hand-craft, say, a contract or a will. But that should not preclude the use of paraprofessionals by the millions of people whose problems are standard and can be well handled by a nonlawyer and who can't afford a full-blown expert anyway. After all, a custom-tailored suit admittedly fits better than a factory-made one; but for those who can't afford the custom suit, the off-the-rack model is satisfactory—*and surely far better than no suit at all.* The customer should have the same options in buying legal help as in buying clothes.

The same principle applies to courtroom representation. Does every consumer or landlord-tenant case require a full-blown law school graduate versed in Constitutional and criminal law and the rules of federal procedure? In fact, might a tenant be *better* represented in housing court by a trained paralegal specializing in landlord-tenant cases than by a full-fledged attorney handling his first such case? If so, why not grant limited licenses to paralegals intensively trained in, say, housing law and procedures to be advocates in housing court, with similar certificates granted to others to practice in family, bankruptcy, and other specialized courts?

Cutting costs by reducing people's dependence on legal experts: Legislative changes could, for example, extricate from court involvement as many undisputed matters as possible (for example, uncontested divorces and the probating of the overwhelming majority of wills that involve no disputes). America should also follow the example of other countries that made the transfer of land and homes —often a heavily-lawyered and expensive transaction in America (see pp. 42–50)—as simple as transferring title to an automobile.*

Even disputes customarily resolvable only in court can be de-lawyered. For example, companies dealing with consumers might be required, as a condition of their business licenses, to submit small consumer quarrels to unlawyered arbitration.

Long-recommended (and long-unadopted) steps could be taken to adapt small-claims courts to self-help use by the public,† and that current bane of small-claims court users—the often insurmountable task of *collecting* small-claims judgments even when they win—is solvable: borrow the technique applied to parking-tickets scofflaws and make the renewal of *any* state or local license (especially licenses to do business) contingent on satisfying all outstanding court judgments.

---

*There is a one-time cost involved in transferring any given home or property into a title-registration system, a cost that has stymied adoption of the title system in many localities. But the long-run benefits of such a system are so great that the one-time shift-over might appropriately be publicly subsidized.

†For example, those courts should sit in neighborhood locations at hours (nights and weekends) suitable for working people and should be amply manned with staff to guide citizens through deliberately-streamlined court procedures.

Making the legal profession accountable to the general public and not just to itself: That could best be accomplished, in my view, by subjecting the profession to control at all levels *by a majority of laymen.* Judging from the dramatic effect of introducing even a minority of nonlawyers to the regulatory process (for example, the quadrupling of lawyer disciplinary actions in Michigan noted earlier), this could mean significant changes in the profession's conduct.

Under lay-controlled aegis, the rules of conduct (the Code of Professional Responsibility) could be rewritten, (as has, at this writing, been proposed by an ABA committee) giving priority to the needs of the general public rather than those of the bar elite and their wealthy clients. For example, the rules regarding lawyer advertising should make it as easy for an aggrieved tenant or consumer to find a specialist in housing or consumer law as it now is, under specially written bar rules, for a bank or insurance company to identify experts in their fields.

With a majority of lay people on grievance and disciplinary panels (now typically made up entirely of lawyers), client complaints would get a less self-protective hearing and disciplinary actions would be less affected by fear of injuring professional brethren. And if the process by which lawyers are selected and trained for the bar were viewed afresh, through lay eyes, some basic questions might be asked, such as:

• Are college grades and performance on a single admission test really the best criteria for choosing humane and compassionate promoters of justice?

• Do lawyers emerge as proficient as law schools could make them in the skills the public most needs (skills of negotiation, document drafting, client counseling, and, most of all, courtroom advocacy)?

• Does the bar exam separate the fit from the incompetent by testing relevant lawyering skills; and does the character and fitness screening process really protect the public from morally deficient practitioners?

Lawyers would, no doubt, fear that their needs would be ill-considered, that lay people would not understand the subtleties of their professional needs *(what could laymen possibly know about designing a bar examination?)*. While there might be abuses and error, still, with up to half of any governing body consisting of attorneys, there would be ample opportunity for them to educate their lay colleagues; and where their arguments were reasonable, they would, I believe, be heeded.*

Lessening the imbalances against the have-nots that are built into the legal system: Most of the disadvantages suffered by have-not One-Shotters described in Chapter 13 are rooted in the superiority of the RPs in sheer dollar power. To that extent, any remedy short of universal free legal help will be, at best, partial. But pending enactment of such a program, two steps could be taken that would considerably diminish the imbalances between the One-Shotter and Repeat Players:

● *Legislation to facilitate class-action suits:* As recounted earlier, recent court decisions have hamstrung the capacity of similarly injured One-Shotters (for example, victims of an illegal price-fixing scheme) to band together in bringing a so-called class-action suit against the offending Repeat Player. The Congress could remove those obstacles by enacting laws overturning the offending court decisions.†

---

*Indeed, the history of regulatory bodies tells us the far greater danger is that the lay members will be unduly coopted by those they are supposed to regulate.

†Among the laws that could facilitate class-action suits are: (1) one that would permit courts to judge class actions on a basis of *aggregate* injury and damages to the class as a whole, using approved sampling techniques where necessary, thus lessening the burden of calculating and proving the injury to each individual member of the class on a person-by-person basis; (2) one that would reverse a 1977 Supreme Court ruling and enable retail consumers, and not merely wholesalers and other middlemen, to bring class-action antitrust suits where they feel they have been illegally overcharged; (3) one that would ease the financial burdens of notifying class-action members of the existence of

• *Facilitating the financing of public interest lawsuits:*
Many class-action and environmental lawsuits die a-born-
ing because the aggrieved One-Shotters, diffuse and unorganized, lack the means of raising the funds needed at the
outset of such lawsuits to collect evidence, question witnesses, and so forth. Enactment of a National Legal Service would remedy that, but in the meantime there are
other ways of closing the gap. For example, there could
be government-paid fees to lawyers bringing lawsuits that
seek to enforce an existing law or that benefit the public
at large (for example, an action to oblige a company pol-
luting a lake or strea m to abide by an environmental law).
Also, persons other than parties to a controversy could be
permitted to buy shares in class-action or other public-
interest lawsuits in return for a share of whatever money
damages might ultimately be won. That practice is currently prohibited by the rules of the Organized Bar out of
the concern that it would encourage frivolous or harassing
lawsuits.* But although that danger exists, it should be
possible to devise means of penalizing those who, upon
clear and convincing evidence, abuse the legal process.

While the interim reforms suggested in the preceding six
pages would be beneficial, they would not get at the root
cause of existing imbalances; nor would they answer basic
questions—such as *why* do law schools prepare most of
their students for the practice of corporate rather than,
say, consumer law, and, more importantly, *why do most
of the students want it that way?*
   The answer is: that's where the money is. As long as
legal help is strictly a for-sale commodity, the practice of
business and corporate law is likely to be the principal, if

---

the suit, so that they could "opt out" if they wished to preserve their
individual right to sue.
*The bar's concern about harassing legal tactics is not even-handed,
for, as described in Chapters 11 and 12, well-to-do litigants habitually
use legal as well as economic leverage against less prosperous litigants
without transgressing bar rules or triggering bar disciplinary action.

not the only, kind of practice in which lawyer prosperity will be found.*

Which brings us back, full circle, to the proposition put forward at the outset of this chapter: that the only way to make "justice for all" and "equal justice under law" more than empty rhetoric is to make legal help freely available to every citizen.

Yes, there are steps short of a universal legal-aid scheme that could moderate the existing imbalance of legal services—such as, say, a publicly run National Legal Insurance program, financed on as broad a scale as Social Security.

But even reforms of that magnitude would inevitably exclude some people—and would, therefore, skirt the fundamental question of whether access to the system of justice through the services of an attorney should not, like police protection and the courts themselves, be a basic governmental service accessible to everyone.

*The sole exception may be in the personal-injury field, where fees are based on a percentage of the damages awarded by the courts and where, for the most skillful attorneys, those awards (and the fees) are often very large.

Afterword

Through the centuries, lawyers have been looked upon with mistrust. The cry of Shakespeare's butcher, "The first thing we do, let's kill all the lawyers," is, unhappily, not an isolated example. Plato spoke of the "small and unrighteous souls" of lawyers; the Talmud refers to lawyers as "oppressors and robbers who did that which is not good among people"; Keats felt lawyers should be classed "in the natural history of monsters." Lawyers were entirely absent from Thomas More's Utopia; and a contemporary of Saint Ives, a thirteenth-century poverty lawyer and saint, made the remarkable observation, "He was a lawyer, yet not a rascal, and the people were astonished."

And a Harris poll has found lawyers, as a profession, ranking lower in public esteem than doctors, organized religion, the Congress, local government, the police—and garbage collectors.

One prominent member of the profession, former judge Marvin E. Frankel, believes that "the fundamental reason [lawyers] tend to be held in low esteem is the role so many play as hired guns . . . [there is] the vivid sense that we [lawyers] are not detached 'ministers of justice' . . . but self-seeking shopkeepers . . ."

Indeed, Judge Frankel says, "we staff a system in which justice is to a large degree for sale."

The best—perhaps the only—way to end, once and for all, the distrust of lawyers and of the legal system and to have the profession live up to its own ideals is: remove the 'for sale' sign.

That is also the way to make law the noble profession it aspires to be, has all too rarely been, but can—*always can*—be.

Acknowledgments

If I were properly to acknowledge the debts of appreciation incurred during the writing of this book a small sup-
plemental volume would be required. That being beyond
the bounds of practicality, I will do my best within reasonable space limits to convey my gratitude for the abundance of help and kindness extended to me.

A glance at the many pages of Notes and Sources will,
I trust, indicate the prodigious amount of research that
went into this book. That would have been impossible
without the able assistance of Joseph Ronan, Ira Wolf,
Matthew Valencic, Virginia Adams and, most especially,
Stephen Engel and Andrea Bolling, both of whom cheer-
fully tolerated the torrent of requests, were resourceful
sleuths, and provided the needed, and more.

The research would also have been impossible but for
the help of the New York Society Library, the library at
the law firm of Paul Weiss, Rifkind, Wharton & Garrison,
made available to me through the good offices of my respected friend Joseph Iseman, and, particularly, of Raymond Jassin and Anthony Burgalassi and the others in the
library of the Association of the Bar of the City of New
York. I am indebted to Adrian DeWind and to Paul De-
Witt of the Association for arranging for my use of its
excellent library facilities.

In writing this book, I have had to become versed in
several fields of considerable complexity, and it would be
difficult to convey my appreciation to the experts in those
fields who patiently sought to educate me, put up with an

endless stream of questions, often read and commented on manuscript drafts, and were, in every respect, splendid. These included Professor Richard Wellman in the field of probate; Professor Jeffrey O'Connell and Theodore Johnson on no-fault auto insurance; and David Hood, Michael Meltsner, and William Pincus in the arena of legal education. I owe special debts to Sandy DeMent in the field of group and prepaid legal services and to Beverly C. Moore, Jr. regarding class-action lawsuits. Each of them is an extraordinary "one-person-band" in his or her special field; both are endowed with special dedication and energy, and both extended patience and help far beyond any reasonable call.

So did Professor Stephen Gillers, a seemingly limitless source of ideas, insights, helpful criticisms, and challenges to muddy thinking, not to mention the most supportive personal friendship. It would be impossible to convey the extent of my appreciation for his help.

The same is true of my gratitude to others who patiently read and commented on draft manuscripts. These include my long-time friend, Arvin E. Upton; Robert C. Barnard; Charles Halpern; B. W. Nimkin; Jethro K. Lieberman, from whose marvelous book on lawyers' ethics, *Crisis at the Bar,* I have drawn heavily; and particularly, Gary Bellow, that inspirational bundle of brains and energy at the Harvard Law School; and Robert L. Gnaizda, one of the most effervescent and original men it has been my good fortune to know.

I hasten to absolve them, and all others listed in these acknowledgments, of all responsibility for errors that may have insinuated themselves into this book in spite of their (and my) most conscientious efforts.

For signal editorial improvement in the manuscript, I am indebted to Hugh Howard and, most particularly, to a special friend and wizard with an editorial pencil, Gilbert A. Harrison. I am indebted to him for instruction both in the use of language and in wise living.

Titling a book is a difficult and ordinarily thankless task. As a partial cure for the latter, I acknowledge and express appreciation for the helpful counsel of Victor Navasky and of Robert Stein.

I have drawn inspiration as well as helpful knowledge from two categories of attorneys: so-called public-interest lawyers and attorneys serving the poor as part of the Legal Services Corporation. Among the former are: Joseph L. Rauh, whose career would have been my model had I gone into the law; Philip Schrag; Mark Green; William A. Dobrovir and those associated with his remarkable good works, all of whom have been most kind and helpful; David L. Scull, an especially helpful source of information and advice; and, most particularly, Martin Lobel and his partners, Alan S. Novins and John Lamont —always welcoming and unfailingly helpful.

I consider my personal life enriched, as well as this book signally helped, by the Legal Services attorneys I have had the good fortune to meet in the past three years: Marjorie Fields, Douglas Ackerman, Pat Cooney, Philip Gassel, Andrew Zweben and, in particular, Jonathan Weiss, a man of exceptional acuity, dedication, and patience with pestering authors. In the Washington office of Legal Services, I received enormous assistance from Clinton Bamberger, Scott Price, and especially Harriet Wilson Ellis and her associates.

In the nongovernmental arena, I was fortunate to get to know some of the trail-breakers in two new areas of legal help: the so-called legal "clinics," and group and prepaid legal services, discussed in Chapters 10 and 11. Among the former, Stephen Z. Meyers and Leonard Jacoby in Los Angeles, together with their New York colleague, Gail Koff, were invariably hospitable and helpful; so were Floyd Kops in New York and Saul Sarney, Alan Waitkus, and Larry Trattler in Denver. In the field of group legal plans, in addition to the wondrous Sandy DeMent and her associates, Davida Maron and Charles Barron in Washington, I received the most generous assistance from many associated with that bellwether of group plans: the Municipal Employees' Legal Service plan in New York, led by the remarkable Julius Topol, as well as by Gerald Mann and John Renda, and several of their dedicated associates.

I was the beneficiary of the research and writing of three journalistic watchdogs of the legal profession: Tom Goldstein of *The New York Times,* Stuart Auerbach of *The Washington Post,* and Steven Brill, editor of *The American Lawyer.* I also derived great help from articles in the *New York Law Journal* and the *National Law Journal.*

The staffs of the American Bar Association and of the American Bar Foundation were uniformly cooperative and responsive to questions. I am especially indebted to Ross Hagen, Robert Glass, Fred Franklin, Donna Fossum, and Mary Redmond. And, while I ultimately concluded I could not fairly treat the massive subject of the American Bar Association within the compass of this book, I am indebted to those who endeavored to inform me about the ABA: Jonathan Adler, Roland Brandel and, in particular, Jerome Shestack and Bernard Segal, who gave most generously of their time and knowledge.

During the past three years, a great many people permitted me to tap their knowledge and information through personal interviews. Space does not permit listing each one, but I am grateful to all of them for their generosity with their time. I express particular appreciation to: Jeffrey Bauman, Jack Blum, Sam Buffone, Edgar Cahn, David Caplovitz, David Chambers, Abram Chayes, Ramsey Clark, Jerome Cohen, Martin Cole, Joe Covington, John Drinnan, Phyllis Eliasberg, Carl Felsenfeld, Jane Frank, William Fry, Leon Freedman, Monroe Freedman, Arthur Goldberg, Lewis Goldfarb, Eric Goldstein, John Heritage, Philip Hirschkop, Alger Hiss, Alan Houseman, Robert Joost, Harriet Katz, J. Anthony Kline, John Kramer, James Lorenz, David Lubell, Ted Mackey, Carey McWilliams, Duncan McDonald, Laura Nader, Carl Person, Jane Rosenberg, Douglas Rosenthal, Donald Ross, Donald Rothschild, Worth Rowley, Beardsley Ruml, Millard Ruud, Peter Schuck, Herman Schwartz, Richard Scupi, Doris Shaha, David Shapiro, Samuel Silverman, Joe Sims, Hugh Slate, John Slavicek, Morton Stavis, Harriet

Thayer, Michael Tigar, Jake Warner, Leon Wein, Michael Zander.

These have been three difficult years, made less so by the supportive kindness and friendship of countless people, to whom I extend heartfelt thanks. I would be remiss, however, not to convey my appreciation to David Ramage and Mel Cathcart of the New World Foundation and to Frank Dobyns and Linda Wilson of the Arca Foundation. They put up with a lot and helped in equal measure. I also gladly proclaim my debt to the Writers Room, that precious haven in midtown Manhattan for those seeking companionship in the miseries of writing. It was, for me, if not a life-saver, certainly a book-saver; and Abby Schaefer and my fellow sufferers in the corner room, Marjorie Iseman and Lucille Warner, were especially instrumental in helping make it so.

I owe special thanks to the staffs at 9 East 79th Street and 27 West 67th Street for unfailing patience and help; to Milton Horowitz for special wisdom; to Donald Brown for his unwavering friendship and supportiveness; to Ambrose Leo Craig for countless kindnesses; to my children, Henry, Michael, Holly, David, and Eve; to Mark L. and Jennifer M. Stewart; to Meta Markel; and, most specially, to a courageous, life-loving, and life-giving person, my mother, Edith R. Stern.

I have saved my greatest indebtednesses to last. First, there is Irene McCarrick, my evidently tireless, ever-patient, ever-resourceful secretary who has seen this labor through from beginning to end. Through its (and my) many ups and downs, through revisions and re-revisions, she has somehow remained steady, cheerful, perceptive, conscientious, and utterly unflappable, even when taxed with the umpteenth, "Mrs. McCarrick, where is that letter from? . . ." It is, of course, well known that there are certain utterly spoiled individuals in this world who would simply be unable to function without the help and support of someone like Irene McCarrick. I admit to being such an individual and happily acknowledge, to the extent words can do so, my debt to her.

And then there is my cherished wife, Helen, to whom this book is lovingly dedicated. No dedication of a book was ever more totally earned or more gratefully given. Beyond the qualities suggested in that dedication, there has been seemingly limitless patience, not merely in evaluating with a sure editorial eye and ear an interminable stream of experiments and missteps, of drafts and redrafts, and of redrafts of the redrafts, but also in tolerating the anxieties and the sometimes irksome (or even outrageous) behavior of a fellow writer. Blessed is the person who has such a loving and supportive partner. That I am thus blessed I am newly, acutely, and gratefully aware every single day.

—Philip M. Stern

Notes and Sources

Explanation of Major Abbreviations

ABA: American Bar Association

Balancing: Balancing the Scales of Justice: Financing Public Interest Law in America, a Report by the Council for Public Interest Law, Washington, 1976.

Bloom: Murray Teigh Bloom, *The Trouble with Lawyers* (New York: Simon and Schuster, 1968).

Citadel: Joel Seligman, *The High Citadel: The Influence of Harvard Law School* (Boston: Houghton Mifflin Company, 1978).

C.P.R.: The American Bar Association's *Code of Professional Responsibility,* embodying what were referred to, prior to 1969, as the Canons of Ethics. The Code is comprised of Ethical Considerations (ECs) and Disciplinary Rules (DRs). According to a "Preliminary Statement" to the Code, the Ethical Considerations are "aspirational in character and represent the objectives toward which every member of the profession should strive." There is, however, no reference to disciplinary action for failure to adhere to them. But "the Disciplinary Rules, unlike the Ethical Considerations, are mandatory in character," and "state the minimum level of conduct below which no lawyer can fall without being subject to disciplinary action."

Crisis: Jethro K. Lieberman, *Crisis at the Bar: Lawyers' Unethical Ethics and What to Do about It* (New York: W. W. Norton & Company, Inc., 1978).

Curran Report (Preliminary): Barbara A. Curran and Francis O. Spalding, *The Legal Needs of the Public: Preliminary Report of a National Survey* (by the Special Committee to Survey Legal Needs of the American Bar Foundation in Collabo-

221

ration with the American Bar Foundation), (Chicago: The American Bar Foundation, 1974).

Curran Report: Barbara A. Curran, *The Legal Needs of the Public: The Final Report of a National Survey* (Chicago: The American Bar Foundation, 1977).

DR: See C.P.R.

EC: See C.P.R.

F. Supp.; F.2d; U.S.: Denotes published opinions in decisions of federal courts: F. Supp. from District courts; F.2d from Courts of Appeal, U.S. from the U.S. Supreme Court. 433 U.S. 733, 739 indicates that the opinion appears in Volume 433 of the U.S. Reports, beginning at page 733, and that the passage or quote in question appears on page 739. P.2d denotes Pacific Reporter, 2nd Series, reporting on state-court cases in Western states.

L.J., L. Rev.: Law Journal or Law Review, one of the scholarly periodicals published by many leading law schools. 85 *Harvard L. Rev.* 426, 435 indicates that the article in question appears at Volume 85 of the *Harvard Law Review* at page 426, and that the quotation or passage in question appears at page 435.

New York Bar Report: "The Character and Fitness Committee," a report by the Special Committee on Professional Education and Admissions of the Association of the Bar of the City of New York and the Committee on Legal Education and Admissions to the Bar of the New York State Bar Association, 33 *Record of the Association of the City of New York,* (January/February 1978), pp. 20–90.

P.2d: See F. Supp., F.2d., U.S.

Steele and Nimmer: Eric Steele and Raymond T. Nimmer, "Lawyers, Clients, and Professional Regulation," *American Bar Foundation Research Journal,* 1976, no. 3 (Summer 1976).

U.S.: See F. Supp., etc.

Verdicts: Ralph Nader and Mark Green (eds.), *Verdicts on Lawyers* (New York: Thomas Y. Crowell Company, 1976).

Introduction

xv *New Yorker cartoon: The New Yorker,* December 24, 1973, p. 52, by Handelsman.

xvi *90 percent of lawyers serve 10 percent: ratio of law-*

yers in U.S., other countries: Carter speech to 100th Anniversary Lunch of the Los Angeles Bar Association, Los Angeles, May 4, 1978.

xvi *Two-thirds of earth's lawyers in U.S.:* See *Law and Judicial Systems of Nations,* Charles S. Rhyne, ed. (Washington: World Peace Through Law Center, 1978), which estimates world's lawyer population at about 750,000.

xvi *Right to criminal counsel:* See esp. *Gideon* v. *Wainwright,* 372 U.S. 335 (1963), and *Argesinger* v. *Hamlin,* 407 U.S. 25 (1972).

xvi *Nearly $1 billion in probate legal fees:* Internal Revenue Service Statistics of Income, Estate Tax Returns, 1969, Table 1, extrapolated for 1976.

xvi *Probate costs, England versus U.S.:* William B. Fratcher, *Probate Can Be Quick and Cheap: Trusts and Estates in England,* preface, p. i, cited in Scoles and Halbach, *Problems and Materials on Decedents Estates and Trusts* (Boston: Little Brown and Company, 1973), p. 442. The Fratcher study can also be found in Fratcher, *Fiduciary Administration in England,* 40 N.Y.U. L. REV. 12 (1965).

xviii *Hoyt Moore case:* See Lieberman, *Crisis,* pp. 197–199; also Joseph Borkin, *The Corrupt Judge* (New York: Clarkson Potter, 1962), pp. 167–186. *Lennox Hinds case:* See complaint of Middlesex County Ethics Committee, December 22, 1977, *In the Matter of the Alleged Unethical Misconduct of Lennox Hinds, Esq.*

xix *Bahamas bank "branch":* The Wall Street Journal, July 5, 1972, p. 26.

xix *Duty to represent clients "zealously":* C.P.R., Canon Seven.

xix *ABA on "not a money-getting trade":* ABA, Canons of Ethics, Canon XII.

xix *Burger quote:* Burger speech to American Law Institute, Washington, D.C., May 31, 1974.

xx *Statistics on lawyers' incomes:* Survey undertaken by the *Journal of the American Bar Association,* April 1978. *1974 Chicago lawyers' income:* ABA statistics appear in 1977 *New York Times Index,* p. 744. *Median income of doctors:* American Medical

Association, *Profile of Medical Practitioners,* Center for Health Services, Research and Development, American Medical Association, December 31, 1976, p. 285. The median income for doctors in nonmetropolitan areas was $54,000; for those in metropolitan areas with a population of under one million, $57,071; for those in areas with over one million people, $52,900.

2. Who Lawyers Do—and Don't—Serve
> 6 *Number of lawyers in Japan, D.C.: for Japan: Law and Judicial Systems of Nations,* Charles S. Rhyne, ed. (Washington: The World Peace Through Law Center, 1978); *for D.C.:* data by telephone from D.C. Bar Association.
>
> 6 *Statistics on poverty-law program:* Legal Services Corporation. "Background News Release," September 1979; "The Legal Services Corporation and The Activities of Its Grantees: A Fact Book," Spring 1979; "Selected Funding and Staffing Characteristics of Field Programs Supported by the L.S.C.—Start of 1979" (undated).
>
> 6–7 *Public interest versus Wall Street lawyers: Balancing* p. 5.
>
> 7 *Public Citizen Litigation Group budget:* Telephone interview with Litigation Group.
>
> 7 *Califano earnings:* White House press release on cabinet members' income, February 25, 1977, as reported in February 1977 *Facts on File.*
>
> 7 *Legal Service Corporation lawyer salaries:* Legal Services Corporation, "Funding and Staffing Characteristics," (see "statistics" note above) p. 7.
>
> 7 *Number of lawyers practicing before FCC:* Based on Federal Communications Bar Association *Directory,* January 1979, excluding attorneys listed as representing telephone companies and other non-broadcasters.
>
> 7 *Number of lawyers representing viewer and citizens groups:* telephone interviews, Media Access Group, Citizens Communication Center, Washington, D.C.

7–8 *$24 billion in corporate legal outlays:* Carter speech to Los Angeles Bar Associates, Los Angeles, May 4, 1978.

8 *Justice Department budget:* Budget of the U.S. Government, Fiscal Year 1980, pp. 445–88.

8 *New York Times on corporate crime:* July 15, 1979, pp. 1, 29.

8 *Number of attorneys, IBM versus antitrust division:* Letter from IBM General Counsel Katzenbach, September 12, 1979; telephone interview, U.S. Justice Department.

8 *Cravath's defense of IBM:* Arthur Lubow, "The Endless Trial of IBM," *New Times,* October 15, 1976, p. 60.

9 *New York Times report of IBM trial: The New York Times,* September 30, 1977, pp. D1, D10.

9 *Barr, Katzenbach salaries:* Letter from Thomas Barr, October 3, 1979; IBM 1979 Proxy Report, pp. 18–19.

9–10 *History of FTC oil antitrust case: The New York Times,* May 13, 1976, p. 47, and June 26, 1978, p. D1. *Fulbright and Jaworski lists oil and gas:* 1979 Martindale-Hubbell Law Directory, Vol. VI, p. 677B.

10 *Public's stake in antitrust enforcement: The New York Times,* July 15, 1979, pp. 1, 29.

10 *$1.3 billion legal battle:* See Consumers Union Petition for Special Redress, Case No. FSG–0037, decided February 18, 1977, 5 FEA ¶87,014.

11 *ABA survey of legal needs: Curran Report*

11 *Public's use of lawyers:* Curran Report (Preliminary) 1974, pp. 81, 83.

12 *Schell statement:* Orville Schell testimony before Subcommittee on Representation of Citizen Interests, Senate Committee on the Judiciary, Houston, Texas, February 3, 1974.

12 *ABA Statement:* American Bar Association; *Revised Handbook on Prepaid Legal Services: Papers and Documents Assembled by the Special Committee on Prepaid Legal Services,* p. 2 (1972).

12–13 *Grace Thompson case:* Based on Yaretsky v. Blum, 592 F.2d 65 (2nd Cir. 1979). The transfer trauma issue was dealt with specifically in a consent judgment entered in this case by Judge Constance Baker Motley (S.D. N.Y.) on October 17, 1979, in which the State of New York agreed that in the transfer of patients from one state institution to another, there was an obligation to perform a psychological appraisal of the patient and to make an express finding that the transfer would not result in psychological harm to the patient.

12–13 *Transfer trauma report:* Steven A. Hitov, *Transfer Trauma: Its Impact on the Elderly,"* 8 CLEARINGHOUSE REVIEW, (April 1975), p. 846.

13 *Charles Christian case:* Based on Rodriguez v. City of Philadelphia, 420 F. Supp. 893 (E.D. Pa. 1976), 529 F.2d 1231 (3rd Cir. 1977).

13–14 *Henry Swanson case:* Based on Montgomery County Office of Consumer Affairs v. Chrysler Credit Corporation, Montgomery County, Maryland, August 19, 1976. Settlement agreement reported at 10 CLEARINGHOUSE REVIEW 622 (November 1976).

14 *Frank Lacuzzi case:* Testimony of Mitchell Miller before American Bar Association Task Force on Advertising, New York City, August 3, 1978.

14–15 *Sarah Ellsworth case:* Based on Doe v. Kenny, 10 CLEARINGHOUSE REVIEW 626; Consent Decree issued October 12, 1976 in Federal District Court, Connecticut, Case No. 76–199.

15 *Black land-sale story:* "CBS Reports," July 5, 1978; 1978 Annual Report, The Emergency Land Fund, Atlanta, Georgia; letter to author from Emergency Land Fund, October 1, 1979.

16 *Gray Panthers suit:* Class Action Petition to Index Maximum Deposit Interest Rates to Inflation and/ or Provide Consumer Warnings to Depositors, before Board of Governors, Federal Reserve System, Federal Home Loan Bank Board, Federal Deposit Insurance Corporation and Federal Savings and Loan Insurance Corporation, October 19, 1978. *$42 billion loss to elderly:* Testimony of Treasury Secretary Blumenthal to Senate Banking Committee, June 21, 1979, p. 6; Also see testimony on behalf of

Gray Panthers before Senate Banking Subcommittee on Financial Institutions by Robert L. Gnaizda of Public Advocates, Inc., June 27, 1979. *Newsmen on Gray Panther suit's influence:* See Hobart Rowen, *The Washington Post,* September 13, 1979, p. A19.

16n *Pacific Legal Foundation: The New York Times,* February 12, 1978, p. 1.

17 *WLBT license challenge:* See Burger opinions in Office of Communication of the United Church of Christ v. FCC, 359 F.2d 994 (D.C. Cir. 1966) and 425 F.2d 543 (D.C. Cir. 1969); and Deirdre Carmody, "Challenging Media Monopolies," *The New York Times Magazine,* July 31, 1977, p. 21.

17–18 *Increase in TV minority employment:* Ralph M. Jennings, *Television Station Employment Practices, 1977: The Status of Minorities and Women* (New York: Office of Communication, United Church of Christ, April, 1978).

18 *Budgets of Media Access Project and Citizens Communication Center:* Telephone interview. *Fees by single Washington law firm:* According to the 1979 Martindale-Hubbell Law Directory, Vol. II, p. 141B, nineteen of the twenty-three lawyers in the firm of Cohn & Marks are members of the Federal Communications Bar Association, indicating significant revenues from FCC practice. Gross receipts calculated on assumption of $100,000 per lawyer.

18 *Coal-mine breathing apparatus case:* Council of the Southern Mountains, Inc. v. Mine Safety and Health Administration, Petition for Modification, Docket No. M–78–79–C.

18–19 *Northrop and Phillips cases:* Springer v. Jones (Northrop), Case No. 74–1455–F; Gilbar v. Keeler (Phillips), Case No. 75–611–EC.

19 *Public interest lawyers versus Wall Street firms: Balancing,* p. 5. *Proportion of lawyers in public interest work: Balancing,* p. 82.

19–20 *$1.3 billion oil price overcharge case:* See Consumers Union Petition for Redress, Case No. FSG–0037, Decided February 18, 1977, 5 FEA ¶ 87,014.

20–21 *Albert Kramer story:* See Deirdre Carmody, "Challenging the Media Monopolies," *The New York Times Magazine,* July 31, 1977, p. 21.

22 *Obstacles to public-interest support from foundations: Balancing,* pp. 226–245; *preference for "people they know":* p. 232; *discrimination suit:* p. 237; *foundations not principal source:* p. 240.

23 *Alaska pipeline case:* Alyeska Pipeline Service Co. v. The Wilderness Society, 421 U.S. 240 (1975).

23 *Cases failing for lack of funds:* See Vermont Yankee Nuclear Power Corporation v. Natural Resources Defense Council, et al., 435 U.S. 519 (1978) and, more particularly, Aeschliman v. Nuclear Regulatory Commission, 547 F.2d 622 (D.C. Cir. 1976), for role of the Saginaw Valley Nuclear Study Group in urging the Nuclear Regulatory Commission to adopt stricter safety standards for nuclear waste disposal and also in opposing construction of a nuclear plant at Midland, Michigan.

23 *ABA defeat of resolution:* 63 A.B.A. JOURNAL 174 (February 1977).

23–24 *Seattle lawyer reaction: Balancing,* p. 315

24 *New York Times editorial: The New York Times,* June 2, 1976, p. 36.

24 *Reginald Heber Smith proposal:* Smith, *Justice and the Poor* (New York: Charles Scribner's Sons, 1921), p. 237.

25 *Donations from private bar: Balancing,* p. 282.

25 *Nearly eight million poor lack minimum access:* Legal Services Corporation, "Background News Release," May 1978, p. 5.

25 *80% of legal needs of poor unattended:* Legal Services Corporation, "Background News Release," September 1979, p. 2. *Goal of two lawyers for every 10,000 poor:* Ibid.

25 *$11 million for New York's poor:* by telephone from Legal Services Corporation.

26 *AT&T Legal outlays:* AT&T Annual Report to the Federal Communications Commission for year ending December 31, 1977, pp. 60, 71. Report showed $19.4 million for company's own "law department" plus $6.9 million in outside legal fees.

26 *Legal Services turnover, "burn-out":* See, for example, Christina Maslach and Susan E. Jackson, "Lawyer Burn Out," *Barrister,* Spring 1978, p. 8.

27 *Number of lawyers in LSC specialized Centers:* by telephone from Legal Services Corporation.

27 *Per capita wealth, U.S. vs. other countries:* 1979 World Almanac, pp. 580, 588, 591. *Per capita expenditures for legal aid for poor:* Earl Johnson, Jr. et al., *Outside the Courts: A Survey of Diversion Alternatives in Civil Cases* (Denver: National Center for State Courts, 1977), p. 5.

3. Some Recent Changes—Apparent or Real?

29 *Statement by Cravath switchboard operator:* Telephone conversation with author, February 1979.

4. Where There's a Will, There's a Lawyer

33 *Burger statement:* Warren Burger, speech to American Law Institute, Washington, D.C., May 21, 1974.

33 *LaGuardia on high probate costs:* Quoted by Norman F. Dacey in *How to Avoid Probate!* (New York: Crown Publishers, 1965), p. 7.

33 *Legal fees versus funeral expenses:* Internal Revenue Service, Statistics of Income, Estate Tax Returns; *for 1962:* pp. 61, 79–80; *for 1969:* Table 5, p. 16; *for 1976:* Table 1. 1969 was the last year for which legal fees were separately published. The current legal figure is extrapolated from the 1962 and 1969 statistics.

33–34 *Probate costs, U.S. versus England:* Fratcher, *Fiduciary Administration in England,* 40 N.Y.U. L. REV. 12 (1965).

34 *Adele Conway example:* Murray Teigh Bloom, "Do It Yourself Probate—It's Here," *Readers Digest,* July 1975, p. 111. Author Bloom explains that Adele Conway is a composite of several actual cases he observed in Wisconsin.

34–35 *Probate fees of $481, $1,000 per hour:* "Where There's a Will", "60 Minutes," CBS Television,

6:00–7:00 P.M., EDT, June 3, 1973, transcript p. 4; *The New York Times,* March 30, 1979, p. D4.

35 *Estate Planning Guide:* Commerce Clearing House. 1977 Estate Planning Guide, ¶100, p. 4.

35–36 *Probate fee surveys, D.C. and Maryland:* See letter from David L. Scull to Fred Grabowsky; Bar Counsel, Disciplinary Board, District of Columbia Bar, October 7, 1977, p. 4, describing survey by a paralegal student of D.C. Register of Wills records and fees claimed in eighty consecutively filed 1975 estates and four hundred fifteen 1976 estates. Attorney Scull, a member of the Maryland House of Delegates, also caused his legislative aide to survey fees claimed in probating 74 estates in Montgomery and Anne Arundel Counties, Maryland, in 1977.

36 *Psychiatrist:* Personal conversation with author. *Attorney suspicion re probate fees:* Memorandum letter from William P. Cantwell, September 8, 1977, addressed to various persons concerned with probate reform.

36–37 *Austin Painter case:* In the Matter of the Estate of Austin M. Painter v. The First National Bank of Greeley Colorado and Its Counsel, William P. Southard, 567 P.2d 820 (July 21, 1977).

37 *Richard Bauer survey:* Bauer "Legal Fees in Probate: Survey Shows That Attorney Fees in Probate Proceedings Vary From State to State But Are Generally Reasonable," *Trusts and Estates,* September 1966, p. 850; quoted at *Bloom,* pp. 203 ff.

38 *Minnesota probate study:* Refers to the Minnesota Probate Administration Study, an analysis of the estates of all decedents in 1969 in four Minnesota counties, conducted under Professor Robert A. Stein, University of Minnesota Law School. It is described in, among other places, Robert A. Stein, *Probate Administration: Distinguishing Fact from Fiction,* 3 PROBATE & PROPERTY, No. 1 (Summer, 1974), p. 3.

39 *ABA and Uniform Probate Code:* R. V. Wellman, "Remarks re Uniform Probate Code" to Board of Governors, American Bar Association, January 24, 1969.

40 *Law forbidding probate staff aid:* "Certain Acts by Certain Officials Prohibited in Montgomery and Prince Georges Counties," Annotated Code of Maryland, Article Ten, §30.

40–41 *Helen Nelson story:* David L. Beal, "A Simple Will Still Elusive Despite Probate Reforms," *Milwaukee Journal,* February 13, 1977, p. 1.

41 *Walter Heiden quote:* Madison (Wisconsin) *Capital-Times,* August 11, 1972, pp. 1, 4.

5. Buying a Home? Legal Bills Ahead

43–46 *Berkely County (W. Va.) home-closing costs:* Public Hearing on West Virginia Administrative Regulations, Chapter 14–2, Series IV, Martinsburg, West Virginia, January 11, 1979 (typescript transcript).

46 *1972 government study:* "Mortgage Settlement Costs: Report of Department of Housing and Urban Development and Veterans' Administration," Committee Print of Senate Committee on Banking, Housing and Urban Affairs, March 1972 (hereafter HUD-VA Report). State variations in closing costs appear at pages 39–40.

46 *Title insurance losses less than 3 percent:* Burke, *Conveyancing in the National Capital Region: Local Reform With National Implications,* 22 AMERICAN U. L. REV. 527, 534–5 (1973); Whitman, *Home Transfer Costs: An Economic and Legal Analysis,* 62 GEORGETOWN L. J. 1311, 1323 (1974), cited by Martin Lobel, *A Proposal for a Title Registration System for Realty,* 11 U. RICHMOND L. REV. 501, 507 (1977). *1975 loss 9.7% and statement on "leaves us in the dark":* John C. Payne, *Some Thoughts About RESPA,* 29 ALABAMA L. REV. 339, 380 (1978).

46–47 *Annual home sales; legal fee estimates:* Payne, "Ancillary Costs in the Purchase of Homes," 35 *Missouri L. Rev.* 455, 491, (1970) cited by Bruce Owen, "Kickbacks, Specialization, Price Fixing and Efficiency in Residential Real Estate Markets," 29 STANFORD L. REV. 931, 932n (1977).

47 *Title registration commonplace in other countries:* HUD-VA Report, p. 22.

48 *Business Week on anticompetitive bar actions:* "Do Realty Closings Need a Lawyer?," *Business Week,* March 36, 1979, p. 98.

49 *Home purchase a "life stress event":* The Washington Post, June 4, 1977, p. E14.

49 *1972 behind-the-scenes picture:* Series by Ronald Kessler, *The Washington Post,* January 9–12, 1972.

49 *1972 report on "elaborate system of referral fees" etc.:* HUD-VA Report, p. 3.

49 *1974 antikickback law:* The Real Estate Settlement Procedures Act (RESPA).

49 *Washington Post re circumvention of law:* William Raspberry, "Insuring Titles: Less Risk Than Rip-off," *The Washington Post,* December 12, 1979, p. A19, citing *Post* series on title insurance by Michael Weisskopf.

50 *HUD official on kickbacks:* Telephone statement to author, April 1979.

6. The Lawyers' Monopoly

52 *Surety Title case:* Surety Title Insurance Agency v. Virginia State Bar, 431 F. Supp. 298 (E.D. Va. 1977).

52–53 *Joseph Sims:* Speech to Federation of Insurance Counsel, Scottsdale, Arizona, February 17, 1977.

54 *Lawyer in ABA Magazine:* Arnould and Courley, "Fee Schedules Should Be Abolished," 57 A.B.A. JOURNAL 655, 656 (1971). See also Roy S. Walzer, "Minimum Fee Schedules As Price Fixing: A Per Se Violation of the Sherman Act, 22 AMERICAN U. L. REV. 439, 454 (1973).

54 *Case and Comment:* Harold Brown, "Some Observations on Legal Fees," *Case and Comment,* May–June 1971, pp. 44, 45.

54 *Bar argues exemption from antitrust laws:* "The [Fairfax County, Va.)] Bar argues that Congress never intended to include the learned professions within the terms "trade or commerce' in §1 of the Sherman Act . . ." Goldfarb v. Virginia State Bar, 421 U.S. 773, 785–86 (1975).

54–55 *Idaho Bar President:* Blaine Anderson of Blackfoot, Idaho, addressing ABA annual meeting, Montreal, August, 1966. Quoted at *Bloom,* p. 201.

55 *New Jersey anticompetitive rule:* "Local Attorneys' Fees in Bond Issues," (The Center for Analysis of Public Issues, Princeton, 1971), p. 24.

55 *Monroe County Bar Association:* Monroe County (N. Y.) Bar Association, "Manual on Fees and Charges Including the Minimum Fee Schedule of the Monroe County Bar Association," April 1, 1970, from "Foreword—Factors Affecting Establishment of Legal Fees."

55 *ABA Lawyers' Practice Manual:* Mark Green, "The Gross Legal Product" in *Verdicts,* p. 68.

55 *Goldfarb case:* Goldfarb v. Virginia State Bar, 421 U.S. 773 (1975). *Number of lawyers approached:* 421 U.S. 776.

56 *Effect of advertising on eyeglass prices:* The New York Times, May 28, 1977, p. 1. See also Benham, *The Effect of Advertising on the Price of Eyeglasses,* 15 J. LAW & ECONOMICS 337 (1972).

56–57 *Bates case:* Bates v. State Bar of Arizona, 433 U.S. 350 (1977).

57 *Charges of "over-reaching":* New York Law Journal, January 31, 1979, p. 1.

57 *ABA survey on lawyer advertising:* 64 A.B.A. JOURNAL 673 (May 1978).

58 *Canons on unauthorized practice:* See C.P.R., Canon Three and Ethical Considerations and Disciplinary Rules thereunder. *Right of self-representation:* C.P.R., Ethical Consideration 3–7.

59 *UPL effort to close down lay-owned clinic: National Law Journal,* September 10, 1979, pp. 1, 12–13.

59–60 *Rosemary Furman case:* The Florida Bar v. Rosemary Furman, 1979 *Florida Law Weekly* 202 (May 10, 1979), Case No. 51,266 (Fla. S. Ct., filed March 19, 1977).

61 *Dacey:* Norman F. Dacey, *How to Avoid Probate!* (New York: Crown Publishers, 1965).

61 *Charles Sherman incident:* telephone interview with author.

62 *Footnote to ABA Code:* Cheatham, *The Lawyer's*

Role and Surroundings, 25 ROCKY MT. L. REV. 405 (1953), cited at Footnote 2, Canon Two, Code of Professional Responsibility.

62 *Illinois Bar advertisement:* published in the *Wood-lawn Booster,* July 31, 1963. Cited in Marc Galanter, "Why the 'Haves' Come Out Ahead: Speculations on the Limits of Legal Change," *Law and Society,* Fall 1974, p. 118.

62–63 *Marion Strong incident: The New York Times,* January 6, 1977, p. 22.

63 *Estimate of $4 billion in legal fees; comment by Robert Brown: The Washington Post,* June 11, 1967.

63 *British lawyers charging by the word:* see David Hapgood, *The Screwing of the Average Man* (New York: Doubleday, 1974) in Bantam edition, p. 82.

63 *Complaint against Blackstone:* quoted in Lieberman, *Crisis,* p. 45.

63 *Carl Felsenfeld, lack of litigation after Sullivan law: The New York Times,* April 1, 1979, Sec. 3, p. 1.

66 *Arkansas Supreme Court ruling:* Creekmore v. Izard, 367 S.W.2d 419 (1963), described at *Bloom,* pp. 121–22.

66 *Llewellyn quote:* Karl Llewellyn, *The Bar's Troubles and Poultices—and Cures?,* 5 LAW & CONTEMPORARY PROBLEMS 104, 107 (1938).

7. How Lawyers Are Accountable To No One

68 *Washington Post disclosures; Markow statement, McLaren statement: The Washington Post,* January 9, 1972, p. A12.

69 *Supreme Court justices are "attorneys all":* Bates v. State Bar of Arizona, 433 U.S. 350, 368 (1977).

69 *New York State judge: New York,* February 16, 1976, p. 85.

69 *Judge Joseph P. Willson:* Transcript of hearing on parties' motion for final settlement, William Shlensky, et al., v. Claude C. Wild, Jr., et al., Project on Corporate Responsibility, Inc., Case No. 77–1157 (3rd Cir.), November 18, 1976, p. 69.

69 *Mark Green on paucity of articles on ABA:* Green testimony at "The Organized Bar: Self-Serving or Serving the Public?" Hearing before Subcommittee on Representation of Citizen Interests of Senate Judiciary Committee, February 3, 1974, p. 105.

70 *New Jersey bond-lawyer study:* "Local Attorneys' Fees in Bond Issues: A Report by the Center for Analysis of Public Issues," Princeton, 1971.

70 *Nader-Green article: The New York Times Magazine,* November 20, 1977, p. 53; *Goldstein article on corporate law firms' response:* Ibid, p. 84.

71 *Proportion of lawyers in Congress: Congressional Quarterly,* January 30, 1979, p. 81.

71 *Karl Llewellyn:* Quoted by Ralph Nader in "An Overview," in *Verdicts,* p. ix.

8. Writing the Rules: By Lawyers, for Lawyers

72 *"Clearly excessive" fees:* C.P.R., DR 2–106 (A).

72–73 *Rule on kickbacks:* See ABA, Ethics Committee Opinion No. 320, December 1973, cited in Lieberman, *Crisis,* p. 119.

73 *Rule on solicitation:* C.P.R., DR 2–104 (A).

73 *Rule on naming dead partners:* C.P.R., DR 2–102 (B).

73–74 *Factors for determining "excessive" fees:* C.P.R., DR 2–106 (B).

74 *Rare instances of disciplining for overcharging:* Westchester County Bar Association v. St. John, 43 App. Div. 2d 218, 350 N.Y.S.2d 727 (2d Dept. 1974); Nebraska State Bar Association v. Richards, 164 Neb. 80, 90; 84 N.W.2d 136, 143 (1957).

74 *Kleindienst fee: The New York Times,* September 26, 1976, p. 61.

74 *$1,000-per-hour probate fee: The New York Times,* March 30, 1979, p. D4.

74 *Duty to make legal counsel available:* C.P.R., Canon Two.

74–75 *Special fee consideration for "brother-lawyer":* C.P.R., EC 2–18.

75 *"Adequate compensation necessary":* C.P.R., EC 2–17.

75 *Rule on "reputable" legal directory:* C.P.R., DR 2–
102 (A) (6).

76 *79% had "no way of knowing":* Curran Report
(Preliminary), p. 95.

76 *ABA insistence re "learned profession:"* Canon XII,
cited at 57 A.B.A. JOURNAL 655 (July 1971).

76 *The Attorneys' Register; Monroe Freedman comment:* Freedman, "Advertising and Soliciting: The
Case for Ambulance Chasing," in *Verdicts*, p. 98.

77 *Lieberman on cocktail party solicitation:* Lieberman, *Crisis*, p. 104.

77–78 *Primus-Williams case:* In re Primus, 436 U.S. 412
(1978).

78–79 *Auto fleet-discount case:* National Auto Brokers
Corp. et al. v. General Motors Corporation et al.,
1976–2 Trade Cas.(CCH) ¶61,211;

79 *Contingent-fee witness rule:* C.P.R., DR 7–109 (C);
also see Person v. Association of the Bar, 414 F.
Supp. 144 (E.D.N.Y. 1976); 554 F.2d 535 (2d Cir.
1977).

80 *White versus blue business cards:* Jethro K. Lieberman, "How to Avoid Lawyers," in *Verdicts*, p. 110.
Calendars on business cards: Opinion of Committee on Professional Ethics, New York County Lawyers' Association, *The New York Times*, October 24,
1976, p. 58.

80 *Partners versus associates on letterheads: New York
Law Journal*, April 18, 1977, p. 1.

80 *ABA actions regarding kickbacks; Lieberman
efforts to outlaw them:* Lieberman, *Crisis*, pp. 114–
19, esp. p. 118.

81 *Gillers on referral fees:* Stephen Gillers, "Lawyers
Paid for Doing Nothing?" *The New York Times*,
June 13, 1979, p. A25.

9. Lawyers as Their Own Policemen

83–84 *Clark report findings:* American Bar Association,
Special Committee on Evaluation of Disciplinary
Enforcement (Tom C. Clark, Chairman), *Problems
and Recommendations in Disciplinary Enforcement* Chicago: 1970, p. 1 (hereafter Clark Report).

84 *Manning comment:* Bayless Manning, *If Lawyers Were Angels: A Sermon on One Canon,* 60 A.B.A. JOURNAL 821 (1974); *Clark comment:* reported in Eric Steele and Raymond T. Nimmer, "Lawyers, Clients, and Professional Regulation," *American Bar Foundation Research Journal,* 1976, No. 3 (Summer 1976) (hereafter Steele and Nimmer), p. 942, note 38.

84 *New York Bar study: Ad Hoc* Committee on Grievance Procedures, The Association of the Bar of the City of New York (Leon Silverman, Chairman), *Report on the Grievance System* (1976) (hereafter Silverman Report), pp. 48–49.

84 *1976 American Bar Foundation Study:* Steele and Nimmer, p. 942.

84 *1977 disciplinary statistics:* American Bar Association press release, January 31, 1978.

85 *Four-state disciplinary statistics:* Steele and Nimmer, p. 982.

85–86 *Keiler incident: The Washington Post,* July 25, 1977, pp. C1, C5. *Thirty-day suspension of Keiler:* D.C. Court of Appeals Order, October 17, 1977, In the Matter of Joel I. Keiler, Case No. DP 17–75/S–52–77.

86 *Kleindienst suspension, censure:* National Organization of Bar Counsel, *Final Report of Special Committee on Coordination of Watergate Discipline,* August 1976, p. 5.

86n *Kleindienst testimony versus Nixon tapes:* J. Anthony Lukas, *Nightmare,* (New York: The Viking Press, 1976), p. 185 (Kleindienst), p. 132 (Nixon).

87 *Complaints dismissed as "fee disagreements":* Silverman Report, pp. 29, 30.

88–89 *Hoyt Moore case:* See Lieberman, *Crisis,* pp. 197–99; Joseph Borkin, *The Corrupt Judge,* (New York: Clarkson N. Potter, 1962), pp. 168–186; Hearing before House Judiciary Subcommittee, 79th Congress, 1st Session, pursuant to H.R. 406 and H.R. 138; House Report 1639, 79th Congress, 2nd Session, Feb. 25, 1946.

89 *Judge Johnson made Bar president:* Lieberman, *Crisis,* p. 199; Borkin, *The Corrupt Judge,* p. 186.

89 *Dallas Bar Association letter:* Letter of October 4, 1977 from Robert H. Mow, Jr., Chairman, Grievance Committee, Sixth Bar District, State Bar of Texas to Clinic of Lee, Sommers & Parks.

89 *Charges against Phyllis Eliasberg: The Wall Street Journal,* September 3, 1976, pp. 1, 19.

89–90 *Daniel Taylor, Philip Hirschkop cases:* Described by Martin Garbus and Joel Seligman in "Sanctions and Disbarment: They Sit in Judgment," in *Verdicts,* pp. 54, 55.

90 *Lennox Hinds case:* See Statement of Charges, In the Matter of the Alleged Unethical Misconduct of Lennox Hinds, Esq., filed in Middlesex County (N.J.) Ethics Committee, December 22, 1977.

90–91 *Bar discipline of George Spater: New York Law Journal,* April 25, 1974, p. 1; *of Orin Atkins and Harry Dent:* National Organization of Bar Counsel, *Final Report,* p. 1 (Atkins), p. 3 (Dent).

91 *Bar Foundation on disciplinary budgets:* Steele and Nimmer, p. 942.

91–92 *Field, Newman and Anonymous cases:* Matter of Field, 408 N.Y.S.2d 72 (1978); Matter of Newman, 409 N.Y.S.2d 158 (1978); In Re Anonymous, 32 A.D.2d 37 (1969).

92–93 *Nadjari, Epley, Perkins, Shea cases: The New York Times,* February 17, 1979, pp. 1, 26; *failure to disbar Perkins: New York Law Journal,* July 29, 1979, and *The New York Times,* July 23, 1979, p. B3. *Brill on Fortenberry: Esquire,* December 19, 1978, p. 23.

94 *New York Times on disciplinary backlogs: The New York Times,* February 17, 1979, p. 26.

95 *Quadrupling of discipline in Michigan; Garbus and Seligman comment:* Garbus and Seligman, "Sanctions and Disbarments," *Verdicts,* pp. 50, 58.

10. Legal Clinics: The Bar Fends Off the Future

97 *Leonard Schwartz: The New York Times,* November 26, 1976, p. 26.

97–100 *Jacoby & Meyers case:* See opinion of California Supreme Court in Jacoby & Meyers v. California State

Bar, 562 P.2d 1326 (1977). For an excellent account of this case, see Lieberman, *Crisis,* pp. 79–84.

100–101 *Bar charges leveled against legal clinics: National Law Journal,* February 12, 1979, p. 28.

101 *Cummins and Bader statements: The New York Times,* November 26, 1978, p. 26.

102 *Ronald Sharrow:* 2 *New Directions in Legal Services,* 115 (July–August, 1978).

102 *Timothy Muris:* Testimony before American Bar Association Task Force on Advertising, New York, August 3, 1978.

103 *National Law Journal survey; Huckaby view: National Law Journal,* February 12, 1979, p. 1, 27–28.

103–104 *Jacoby & Meyers expansion: The New York Times,* August 26, 1979, Sec. 3, pp. 1, 9.

104 *"We want to be like Sears": The New York Times,* November 26, 1978, p. 26.

104 *Sears advertising budget: Advertising Age,* September 6, 1979, p. 1.

11. The Bar's Battle Against Legal Insurance

105 *Case of Mrs. Katz:* Telephone interview with attorneys at Municipal Employees Legal Service, New York.

106 *ABA and auto clubs:* Lillian Deitch and David Weinstein, *Prepaid Legal Services,* (Lexington, Mass.: Lexington Books, 1976), p. 16.

106–107 *Supreme Court cases on group legal services: Virginia NAACP case:* NAACP v. Button, 371 U.S. 415 (1963); *Union workmen's compensation case:* Brotherhood of Railroad Trainmen v. Virginia, 377 U.S. 1 (1964); *Illinois mineworkers case:* United Mine Workers v. Illinois State Bar Association, 389 U.S. 217 (1967); *1971 case:* United Transportation Union v. State Bar of Michigan, 401 U.S. 576 (1971).

107 *Prebe Stolz:* Stolz, *Sesame Street for Lawyers: A Dramatic Rendition of United Transport Union v. State Bar of Michigan,* 36 UNAUTHORIZED PRACTICE NEWS 15 (November 1971).

107–108 *Stephen Gillers: The Civil Liberties Review,* Fall 1974, pp. 121–22.

108 *Open vs. closed medical plan costs:* Hetherington, et al., *Health Insurance Plans: Promise and Performance,* (New York: Wiley, 1975), cited in Frech and Ginsburg, *Public Insurance in Private Medical Markets: Some Problems of National Health Insurance,* (Washington: American Enterprise Institute, 1978), p. 50.

108–109 *William Pugh:* Letter to Frederick G. Fisher, Chairman-elect, American Bar Association Section on General Practice, July 3, 1974.

109 *"Chicago rule" on group practice:* C.P.R., DR 2–103 (D), esp. (D)(4).

109 *BankAmericard case:* See Cuyahoga County Bar Assn. v. Gold Shield, Inc., et al. In 40 UNAUTHORIZED PRACTICE NEWS 96ff (Spring–Summer 1976).

110 *Status of state bar rules on group practice:* National Resource Center for Consumers of Legal Services, *Papers for Regulatory Conference on Prepaid Legal Services,* January 19–20, 1978, pp. 16–17.

111 *Lieberman statement:* Lieberman, *Crisis,* pp. 75–76.

12. No on No-Fault: Adding Insult to Injury

112 *Statistics re Plan A versus Plan B:*
[1]"Motor Vehicle Crash Losses and Their Compensation in the U.S.," U.S. Department of Transportation, 1971, (hereafter "Crash Losses") p. 35.
[2]"Economic Consequences of Automobile Accident Injuries," U.S. Department of Transportation, 1971, (hereafter "Economic Consequences") pp. 90, 203.
[3]Assuming a pure no-fault system that fully compensates victims for their medical expenses and wage losses.
[4]"Crash Losses," p. 51.
[5]Assuming standards embodied in federal no-fault legislation introduced in 1978 and 1979, insurance company administration expenses plus costs of lawsuits and damages in cases of death or serious injury are generally considered to run around 30 percent. According to Congressman Bob Eckhardt (D-Tex.), data submitted to the House Subcommittee on

Consumer Protection and Finance by New York Insurance Commissioner Thomas A. Harnett revealed that "almost 75 percent of the no-fault premium dollar is being used to compensate accident victims." 123 *Congressional Record* No. #144, September 16, 1977.

[6]"Crash Losses," p. 52.

[7]Assuming pure no-fault system containing an absolute ban on private negligence lawsuits for pain and suffering.

[8]Assuming all drivers are required to—and *do*—purchase no-fault auto insurance, and that all comply with that law.

114 *44 cents of "fault" premium dollars returned to victims:* See Note 6 above.

115 *$1.8 billion paid to lawyers:* "No-Fault and Trial Lawyers' Lobby," *The Washington Post,* editorial, March 25, 1976, p. A18.

115 *Least injured got 4½ times losses:* "Crash Losses," p. 36.

115 *Most gravely injured recovered 5 percent:* "Economic Consequences," Table 31 FS, pp. 277–78.

115 *38% versus 61% recovery:* Sen. Philip A. Hart, *National No-Fault Auto Insurance: The People Need It Now* (hereafter "Hart article"), 21 CATHOLIC U. L. REV. 259, 265 (Table 2) (1972).

115 *John J. O'Brien:* Hearings on Automobile Insurance Reform before Senate Commerce Committee, Part 3, pp. 927–29, reported in Hart article, (see above note) pp. 289–90.

116 *Finneson testimony:* Hearings on H.R. 7514 and H.R. 241 before the Subcommittee on Commerce and Finance of the House Interstate and Foreign Commerce Committee, p. 158 (1971), cited in Hart article (see above note) at p. 295.

116 *Chief Justice Weintraub:* Unpublished remarks at a joint dinner of State Supreme Court Justices and members of the New Jersey Press Association, Newark, N.J., reported in O'Connell, *The Injury Industry,* (New York: Commerce Clearing House, 1971), p. 290, note 38.

117 *Decline in motor vehicle court cases in Massachusetts:* "Massachusetts No-Fault Hearing," Remarks of Rep. Bob Eckhardt (D-Tex.), 123 *Congressional Record* No. 109, June 23, 1977.

117 *Statements by Chief Justice Burger:* 1970 Message on the State of the Judiciary, 56 A.B.A. JOURNAL 929, 932–33; also see remarks at testimonial dinner honoring Chief Justice John C. Bell Jr., Philadelphia, November 4, 1970.

117 *Search of Chief Justice Burger speeches:* Letter to author from U.S. Supreme Court staff.

117 *Massachusetts Teamsters' advertisement, and political "tithing":* "Automobile Insurance Reform and Cost Savings," Hearing before Senate Interstate and Foreign Commerce Committee, May 6, 1971, testimony of Robert H. Joost, pp. 897 ff., esp. pp. 903, 913.

118 *Senator Moss: The New York Times,* April 18, 1976, p. 4.

118 *Miami doctor: Miami Daily News,* April 16, 1976, pp. A1, A4.

119 *State insurance cost comparisons:* Report by Conning & Co. prepared for American Insurance Association, November 1977, pp. 7, 26.

120 *No-fault bill passed by Senate:* S. 354, passed Senate May 1, 1974. *1974 Congressional Quarterly Almanac,* p. 315.

120 *ATLA amassed $400,000:* No Fault and the Trial Lawyers' Lobby," *The Washington Post,* editorial, March 25, 1976, p. A18.

120 *Political contributions by Attorneys Campaign Trust:* Senators receiving $5,000 contributions: Beall (R-Md.), Roth (R-Del.), Stafford (R-Vt.), Taft (R-Ohio). Senator Moss (D-Utah) received $2,500. From official reports filed with Federal Election Commission.

120–21 *ATLA contribution to Rep. Walgren:* Reports filed with Election Committee by Attorneys' Congressional Campaign Trust, July 10, 1978 and October 26, 1978, Schedule B, p. 3.

121 *Composition of ABA No-Fault Committee:* Mark

Green, "The ABA as Trade Association," in *Verdicts,* p. 8.

121 *ABA opposition to federal no-fault:* American Bar Association, "Policy and Procedures, 1978–79," p. 98.

121 *Trial lawyers foresee no-fault spread: New York Law Journal,* August 4, 1977, p. 1.

121 *New Zealand no-fault law:* See Geoffrey W. R. Palmer, *Accident Compensation in New Zealand: The First Two Years,* 25 AMERICAN JOURNAL OF COMPARATIVE LAW 1 (1977); also *The Wall Street Journal,* September 16, 1975, p. 1.

121–22 *Benjamin Marcus:* Letter to Senator Hart, June 28, 1971 in 117 *Congressional Record* S12,463 (Daily Ed.), July 29, 1971.

13. Stacking the Deck for the "Haves"

127n *Galanter article on One-Shotters vs. Repeat Players:* Marc Galanter, "Why the 'Haves' Come Out Ahead: Speculations on the Limits of Legal Change," *Law and Society,* Fall 1974, p. 95 ff.

128 *Default rates on tenants:* City of New York, Office of the Comptroller, "Performance Analysis of the New York City Housing Court," January 7, 1977, p. 9 (showing tenants unrepresented in 61 percent of cases.

128 *Default rates on debtors:* David Caplovitz, *Consumers in Trouble: A Study of Debtors in Default* (New York: Free Press, 1974), p. 221, Table 11.8 (showing default rates of 91 percent in Chicago and Detroit, and 92 percent in New York).

132 *Stewart Macaulay:* Macaulay, *Law and the Balance of Power: The Automobile Manufacturers and Their Dealers,* (New York: Russell Sage Foundation, 1966), pp. 99–101, cited in Galanter article (see note above) at p. 102, note 19.

132 *Swine Flu Litigation and Claim Reporter: New York Law Journal,* January 13, 1978, pp. 1, 2.

135 *Housing code violations:* City of New York, Office of the Comptroller, "Performance Analysis of New

York City Housing Court," January 7, 1977, Summary, p. v.

135 *Migratory Bird vs. Antitrust Law violators:* Remarks by Donald I. Baker, Assistant U.S. Attorney General, Antitrust Division, to Tenth New England Antitrust Conference, Boston, November 20, 1976, p. 10.

135 *Electric company fines:* Carl Stern, by-line report, "The Today Show" (NBC), November 23, 1976.

135 *Second conveyor belt accident: Seven Days,* February 28, 1977, p. 10.

136 *Insurance for Gulf executives: The New York Times,* November 12, 1976, p. D12.

136 *Small-claims court collection record: 50% collection record in two Manhattan courts:* Community Service Society, Special Committee on Consumer Protection, "Large Grievances About Small Causes," 1974, p. 16 (showing 50% collection record in two Manhattan small-claims courts); and Hollingsworth, Feldman and Clark, *The Ohio Small Claims Court: An Empirical Study,* 42 U. CINCINNATI L. REV. 469 (1974), Table 16 (showing 31% collection record in Hamilton County, Ohio); both cited in Galanter article, p. 109, note 33.

136 *C. Wright Mills:* Quoted by Beverly C. Moore Jr. and Fred R. Harris in "Class Actions: Let the People In," in *Verdicts,* pp. 171–84.

137 *Pfizer tetracycline drug cases:* See West Virginia v. Chas. Pfizer & Co., Inc. 440 F.2d 1079 (2d Cir. 1971) and 1973 Trade Cases ¶74.749, ¶74,827 (S.D.N.Y. 1972) (consumer and government entities); Alpine Pharmacy v. Chas. Pfizer & Co., Inc., 1973 Trade Cases ¶74,350 and 481 F.2d 1945 (2d Cir. 1973) (wholesalers and retailers); Hartford Hospital v. Chas. Pfizer & Co., Inc. 1972 Trade Cases ¶74,112 (S.D.N.Y.) (private hospitals and Blue Cross); and 410 F. Supp. 680, 704, 706 and 722 (D.Minn. 1975) (farmers, veterinarians and other wholesalers) all reported at 5 CLASS ACTION REPORTS 339, 340.

138n *Restrictive interpretations of Class-Action rule:* In the view of class-action proponents, the most im-

portant restrictions may be divided into the following categories:

(1) *Decisions barring broad scale class-action
suits on grounds of "unmanageability":* some
courts have declined to approve class-action suits
involving large numbers of aggrieved persons on
the ground (often unjustified, in the view of
Class-Action advocates) that the lawsuit would be
"unmanageable." See, e.g., Windham v. American Brands, Inc., 565 F.2d 59 (4th Cir. 1977) (suit
brought by tobacco farmers alleging tobacco
companies rigged auction markets so as to de-
press the price they paid for tobacco); Alabama v.
Bluebird Body Co., 573 F.2d 309 (5th Cir. 1978)
(suit alleging price-fixing of school buses).

(2) *Decisions limiting damages to be paid by defendants:* In many, if not most, successful consumer class-action suits, plaintiffs are able to
prove total damages by the defendants vastly
greater than the amount that will be actually
claimed by class members (owing to difficulties in
identifying and contacting them, and in getting
them, even where notified, to go through the
often burdensome and confusing steps of filing a
claim that may be only a few dollars). For example, in the Pfizer tetracycline price-fixing suit,
while the drug companies in effect acknowledged overcharges totaling at least $100 million,
only a small fraction of that amount was actually
claimed by overcharged purchasers of tetracycline. In that instance, the drug companies made
up a part of the difference in payments to various
states, which were devoted to improving public
health programs. In other class-action cases
where it was not possible to make refunds to
overcharged purchasers, defendants have been
ordered to make price reductions on future sales
of the same product. In short, in what is sometimes called a "fluid recovery" principle, the
amount to be paid by defeated defendants was
related to the total damages shown rather than to

the amount actually claimed by class members. But some recent court decisions have limited the payments to amounts claimed—thus, in the view of class action advocates, reducing the deterrent effect of such lawsuits. See, e.g., *In re Hotel Telephone Charges,* 500 F.2d 86 (9th Cir. 1974) (suit alleging hotel chains added arbitrary and hidden telephone charges to guests' bills); and Van Gemert v. Boeing Co., 553 F.2d 812 (2nd Cir. 1977) (securities fraud).

(3) *Decision limiting class-action antitrust lawsuits by overcharged consumers:* In 1977, a Supreme Court decision held that those guilty of illegal price-fixing could only be sued by their direct customers. Thus, manufacturers who fixed prices could only be sued by the wholesalers to whom they sold; wholesalers only by retailers; and consumers were precluded from suing either of them, their suits being limited to price-fixing by the retailer from whom they bought. See Illinois Brick Co. v. Illinois, 431 U.S. 720 (1977).

(4) *Decisions imposing burdensome or prohibitive "notice" costs on class-action plaintiffs:* In Eisen v. Carlisle & Jacquelin, 417 U.S. 156 (1974), the Supreme Court ruled that class-action plaintiffs must send individual notices of the lawsuit to each of the identifiable members of the aggrieved class (who, in the Eisen case, numbered in the millions). A lower court had held that the notice requirement could be satisfied by notifying a random sample of the class members. Class-action proponents argue that the notice costs required by the Eisen ruling preclude many otherwise valid class action suits by imposing prohibitive costs even before the matter is brought to trial on its merits.

(5) *Decisions limiting the ability to bring Class Action suits in Federal courts:* The Supreme Court, in Snyder v. Harris, 394 U.S. 332 (1969) and Zahn v. International Paper Co., 414 U.S. 291 (1973) interpreted federal rules in such a way

as to make it difficult for class-action plaintiffs to satisfy the requirement of $10,000 "in controversy" to sue in federal courts.

138–39 *Penfield housing case:* Warth v. Seldin, 422 U.S. 490 (1975).

139 *Experts on narrowing of court access by Burger Court:* See Carole E. Goldberg and Herman Schwartz, "Supreme Court Denial of Citizen Access to Federal Courts to Challenge Unconstitutional Or Other Unlawful Actions: The Record of the Burger Court," A Statement to the Board of Governors of the Society of American Law Teachers, 1976, reprinted in *Student Lawyer,* March 1977, p. 34; also Stephen Gillers, "Unequal Access to the Courts," *The Nation,* January 29, 1977, pp. 110–113.

14. How Lawyers Make Matters Worse

140–41 *Perot Amendment: The Wall Street Journal,* November 7, 1975, p. 1.

141 *Kleindienst fee: The New York Times,* September 26, 1976, p. 61.

142 *Ruckelshaus firm: The New York Times,* August 23, 1976, p. 40.

142–43 *Hutt, Coleman, Crowley "revolving door" incidents: The Washington Post,* October 10, 1978, p. A3.

145 *Fidelity Bank Bahamas "branch": The Wall Street Journal,* July 5, 1972, p. 26.

145 *Barracuda Tanker Corporation: Shipping, insurance companies: Fortune,* February 1969, pp. 96, 178. *"Captive" insurance companies: The Wall Street Journal,* May 26, 1971, p. 34.

146–48 *Chloromycetin hearing:* "Competitive Problems in the Drug Industry," hearing before Monopoly Subcommittee of Senate Small Business Committee (hereafter "Competitive Problems Hearings"), November 29, 1967, pp. 2139–2237.

146 *Estimates of chloromycetin deaths: The Washington Post,* November 7, 1967, p. A18.

147 *Soft-pedaling of ads, chloromycetin sales:* Richard

Harris, *The Real Voice* (New York: Macmillan, 1964), pp. 101–2.

147 *South American sales of chloromycetin:* "Rx for Tourists: Beware the Foreign Prescription Drug," by Dr. Milton Silverman, *The Washington Post,* March 13, 1977 (Travel section); also see testimony by Dr. Silverman in "Competitive Problems Hearings," p. 15444 ff., May 26, 1976.

147–48 *Parke-Davis brings practices into line: The Washington Post,* March 20, 1977, at "Competitive Problems Hearings," p. 15574.

148 *Cutler on "reasonable and responsible:" Juris Doctor,* October 1976, p. 40.

148 *Albe Watkins incident:* Dr. Watkins's testimony in "Competitive Problems Hearings," Part 6, pp. 2583–97. *Parke-Davis salesman's "perfectly safe" reassurance:* p. 2583. *"I might have done better [to shoot him]":* From Dr. Watkins's letter to Parke-Davis, May 5, 1952, at p. 2585.

150–51 *Panalba incident:* Mark Green, *The Other Government,* (New York: Grossman, 1975), pp. 125–30.

152 *Lawyers' oath not to delay:* American Bar Association, Oath of Admission to the Bar.

152 *Bromley speech on delays:* Bromley, *Judicial Control of Antitrust Cases,* 23 FEDERAL RULES DECISIONS 417–20 (1959).

152–53 *Court decisions in motion picture and gypsum cases:* U.S. v. Paramount Famous Lasky Corporation, et al., 34 F.2d 984 (S.D.N.Y. 1929) and 282 U.S. 30 (1930); *Footnote on ultimate Supreme Court ruling on illegality of block-booking:* 334 U.S. 131, 156–59; also U.S. v. Gypsum Co., 333 U.S. 364 (1948).

154 *Philip Schrag story:* Schrag, *Counsel for the Deceived: Case Studies in Consumer Fraud,* (New York: Pantheon Books, 1972), p. 10.

155 *Arthur H. Schwartz comment:* Schwartz, "What Is a Character and Fitness Committee?" *New York Law Journal,* November 1976, pp. 1, 24.

155 *ABA President on Bar's "desire to serve country":* cited by Leon Jaworski in *The American Bar Associ-*

ation: A Quasi-Public Institution, 58 A.B.A. JOUR-
NAL 917 (1972).

156 *"May" versus "must":* C.P.R., EC 7–9.

156–57 *Lawyer's unchanged duty in legislative and administrative settings:* C.P.R., EC 7–15.

159 *Lawyer's duty "to avoid needless harm":* C.P.R.,
EC 7–10.

159 *Ethical considerations "aspirational":* C.P.R., Preliminary Statement.

159 *John Dean observation:* Statement before Senate
Watergate Committee, quoted by Mark Green in
"The Organized Bar; Self-Serving or Serving the
Public?" Hearing before Senate Judiciary Subcom-
mittee on Representation of Citizen Interests, Feb-
ruary 3, 1974, p. 100.

159 *Weymouth Kirkland:* Speech by Donald Reuben,
partner in firm of Kirkland, Ellis, reported by Mark
Green in *The Other Government* (New York: Grossman Publishers, 1975), p. 289.

159 *Statement by hiring partner of Wall Street firm:*
Personal interview by author with lawyer to whom
statement was made.

15. Who Are Lawyers Trained to Serve?

161 *Robert Keeton story:* Keeton remarks to conference
of Society of American Law Teachers, New York
University Law School, December 4, 1976.

162 *Creditors' Rights; statistics on law teachers:* Association of American Law Schools, *Directory of Law
Teachers, 1977.* (St. Paul: West Publishing Co.), p.
943.

162 *Criticism by Carnegie Corporation:* Cited by Seligman in *Citadel,* p. 160; *by Jerome Frank:* see Frank,
A Plea for Lawyer-Schools, 56 YALE L. JOURNAL
1303–44 (1947); *by Arch Cantrall: Law Schools and
the Layman: Is Legal Education Doing Its Job?,* 38
A.B.A. JOURNAL 907, 908 (November 1952).

163–64 *Redlich on "law schools do not even pretend":* Norman Redlich, *Both People and Practice,* 53 N.Y.U. L.
REV. 2–3 (May–June, 1978), p. 592; *on three kinds of
jobs:* Remarks to Section on Legal Education and

Admissions to the Bar, American Bar Association Annual Meeting, Chicago, August 9, 1977.

164 *227 law schools in the U.S.:* American Association of Law Schools, *1978–79 Directory of Law Teachers.*

164 *All but five states require ABA accreditation:* American Bar Association, Section on Legal Education, *Law Schools & Bar Admission Requirements: A Review of Legal Education in the United States —Fall 1978,* pp. 6ff.

165 *Stevens on ABA admission requirements:* Robert Stevens, *Democracy and the Legal Profession: Cautionary Notes,* 3 LEARNING AND THE LAW, No. 3 (Fall 1976), pp. 12, 16.

165 *Statistics on minority students in law schools:* American Bar Association, *Review of Legal Education—Fall 1977,* pp. 49–50.

165 *Statistics on expectation of college, graduate degrees:* W. Vance Grant and C. George Lind, *Digest of Educational Statistics, 1975,* (Washington: U.S. Government Printing Office, 1976), cited in Seligman, *Citadel,* p. 101.

165 *ABA requirements for law school accreditation:* American Bar Association, *Approval of Law Schools: ABA Standards of and Rules of Procedure, As Amended, 1977.*

166–67n *ABA disaccreditation of law schools:* Stevens, *Democracy and the Legal Profession,* p. 68.

167 *Seligman on 2 of 162 schools "clinical":* Seligman, *Citadel,* p. 206.

167–68 *Proportion of students exposed to clinical instruction:* Speech by William Pincus, President of CLEPR, to the Conference of Chief Justices, Atlanta, Georgia February 12, 1979, reported in CLEPR *Fifth Biennial Report* (1977–78), p. 7. *Proportion of schools with ceilings on clinical courses:* See Council on Legal Education for Professional Responsibility (CLEPR), *CLEPR Annual Survey— 1977–78,* p. ix.

168 *One case in twelve appealed:* 1977: 130,567 civil cases filed in Federal court, 10,980 (8.4%) appealed; 1978: 138,770 cases filed, 11,162 (8%) appealed. Administrative Office of the U.S. Courts.

168 *Gary Bellow CRLA experience:* Interview with author, October 1976.

169 *Pincus on "capacity to respond":* William Pincus, *Clinical Training in the Law School: A Challenge and A Primer for the Bar and Bar Admission Authorities,* 50 ST. JOHN'S L. REV. 479, 483 (Spring 1976).

169 *Griswold speech:* Remarks, September 22, 1967, quoted in Seligman, *Citadel,* p. 6.

169 *Change in attitudes at Davis Law School:* Craig Kubey, "Three Years of Adjustment: Where Your Ideals Go," *Juris Doctor,* December 1976, p. 34.

169 *Langdell on law as a "science":* C. C. Langdell, *A Selection of Cases on the Law of Contracts,* 2d ed. (Boston: Little Brown & Co., 1879), vol. 1, "Preface to First Edition," p. viii, quoted in Seligman, *Citadel,* p. 36.

169 *Most law patterned after Langdell model:* See Seligman, *Citadel,* pp. 42–44; see also Justice Lewis F. Powell, *Clinical Education in Law School,* 26 SOUTH CAROLINA L. REV. 389, 390 (1974).

170 *Bernard Diamond on M'Naughten case:* Diamond, "Psychological Problems of Law Students," *Looking at Law School: A Student Guide from the Society of American Law Teachers,* ed. Stephen Gillers, (New York: Taplinger Publishing Co., Inc. 1977), p. 26.

171 Hatch v. Ford Motor Co. *(hood ornament case):* 329 P.2d 605 (1958).

171–72 *Scott Turow:* Scott Turow, *One-L,* (New York: G. P. Putnam's Sons, 1977), pp. 92, 102.

172 *Derek Bok and Law Review:* Bok quoted in *Harvard Law Record,* February 8, 1968, p. 5; reported in Seligman, *Citadel,* p. 179.

172–73 *Alan Stone:* Stone, *Legal Education on the Couch,* 85 HARVARD L. REV. 426 (1971), cited in Seligman, *Citadel,* p. 180.

174 *Langdell model of law teacher:* Quoted by Jerome Frank, *Courts on Trial: Myth and Reality in American Justice* (Princeton: Princeton University Press, 1949), p. 226.

174 *Andrew Watson on law teachers:* Watson, *The*

Quest for Professional Competence: Psychological Aspects of Legal Education, 27 CINCINNATI L. REV. 93 (1968).

174 *Bernard Diamond on role models:* Diamond, "Psychological Problems of Law Students," in Gillers, *Looking at Law School,* p. 21.

175 *Effect of LSAT scores on NYU admissions:* Association of American Law Schools and the Law School Admission Council, *78–79 Prelaw Handbook,* p. 235.

175–76 *Educational Testing Service on LSAT errors and variations: racial differences in results, Bowdoin versus Georgetown:* Steven Brill, "The Secrecy Behind the College Boards," *New York,* October 7, 1974, p. 67. For another critical view of the LSAT, see Peter James Liacouras, *Adding Up the LSATs: A Cheap Way of Avoiding Our Responsibilities,* 3 STUDENT LAWYER No. 7 (March 1975) p. 34ff.

176–77 *Seligman's "welcoming speech":* Seligman, *Citadel,* p. 181.

177n *Dean Griswold's welcoming remarks:* Griswold, "Hopes—Past and Future," Remarks to Visiting Committee of Harvard Law School, April 18, 1970; reported as customary welcoming remarks in Seligman, *Citadel,* p. 4.

177–78 *Six of 1,700 students at counseling competition:* Letter from Professor E. A. Sander, *Harvard Law Record,* April 14, 1978, p. 11.

178 *Turow on summer salary comparisons:* Turow, *One-L,* (see note pp. 171–72 above) p. 100.

16. The Bar Exam: Protector of the Public—or the Bar?

180 *Bar-waiver in five states:* ABA Section on Legal Education and Admission to the Bar: *Law School and Bar Admission Requirements: A Review of Legal Education in the U. S., Fall, 1978,* pp. 69–81.

181 *Variations in pass-fail rates:* "Admission to Bar by Examinations in 1977," *The Bar Examiner,* vol. 47, nos. 5–6, pp. 113–15.

181 *Bar Examiners confined to active practitioners:* Tele-

phone interview with Joe E. Covington, Director of Testing, National Conference of Bar Examiners.

181–82 *98 percent of applicants ultimately pass:* Edward F. Bell, *Do Bar Examinations Serve a Useful Purpose?* 57 A.B.A. JOURNAL 1215, 1217, citing findings regarding white bar applicants in Pennsylvania, 1955 to 1970. See also letter from Mario G. Obledo, Mexican-American Legal Defense and Education Fund, ABA JOURNAL, March 1972, p. 228.

182 *Oliver Morse: The Washington Post,* July 24, 1977, pp. C1, C4.

183 *Bar exam results, black versus white: Georgia:* Jerold Auerbach, response to letter, *Juris Doctor,* May 1976, p. 13, citing data gathered by the Southern Regional Office of the American Civil Liberties Union; see also Tyler v. Vickery, 517 F.2d 1089, 1092 (5th Cir. 1975); *Alabama:* See Parrish v. Board of Commissioners of the Alabama State Bar, 533 F.2d 942, 944 (5th Cir. 1976); *Pennsylvania:* Peter J. Liacouras, *Racial Discrimination in Administration of the Pennsylvania Bar Examination,* 44 TEMPLE LAW QUARTERLY 146 (1971). *Michigan:* Edward F. Bell, *Do Bar Examinations Serve a Useful Purpose?* 57 A.B.A. JOURNAL 1215, 1217 (December 1971). *South Carolina:* See Richardson v. McFadden, 540 F.2d 744 (4th Cir. 1976); 563 F.2d 1130 (4th Cir. 1977); *cert. den.,* 435 U.S. 968 (1978). Statistics reported in *Los Angeles Daily [Law] Journal,* April 18, 1978, p. 1. See also *Equal Protection Challenges to the Bar Examination,* 1975 ARIZONA STATE L. J. 531, esp. p. 563; and Symposium, *The Minority Candidate and the Bar Examination,* U.C.L.A. School of Law, May 1, 1976, reported in 5 THE BLACK LAW JOURNAL 120.

183 *Jane Kelso criticisms:* Kelso, "Solving Our Credentialing Problems by Drawing on the Medical Analogy," in CLEPR, *The Alternative Education and Licensing of Lawyers* (1976), p. 152, reported in Seligman, *Citadel,* p. 206.

183 *Less than one minute per Bar Exam question; testing on out-of-date divorce law: The Washington Post,* July 24, 1977, p. C4.

184 *Only four black Bar Examiners:* Edward F. Bell, *Do Bar Examinations Serve a Useful Purpose?* 57 A.B.A. JOURNAL 1215, 1218 (December 1971).

184–85 *Norman Redlich on "consumer fraud":* Redlich, "We Train Our Students to Work for Wall Street," LEARNING AND THE LAW, Winter 1977, p. 6.

17. Screening Out the Mavericks

186 *Character standards nowhere set forth: New York Bar Report,* p. 27.

187 *95 percent pass without doubts raised: New York Bar Report,* p. 29.

188 *Questions asked by Bar: New York Bar Report,* pp. 68–79.

188 *No effort to scrutinize information: New York Bar Report,* p. 26.

189 *Committee secrecy on screening results; factors that are "something to worry about": New York Bar Report,* p. 28.

190 *Questions asked in interviews: New York Bar Report,* pp. 35–36.

191 *Rudolph Schware:* Schware v. Board of Examiners, 353 U.S. 232 (1957).

192 *Terence Hallinan:* Hallinan v. Committee of Bar Examiners of State Bar, 421 P.2d 76, (1966).

192–93 *George Anastaplo:* In Re Anastaplo, 366 U.S. 82 (1960); see esp. Black, J. dissenting.

193–94 *Rosenberg review:* Telephone interview with author.

194 *Tom P. Brady:* John Bartlow Martin, *The Deep South Says "Never,"* (New York: Ballantine Books, 1957), pp. 17, 20.

194 *George Wallace: The New York Times,* May 22, 1963, p. 1.

194–95 *Topkis dissent: New York Bar Report,* p. 52.

18. What Should Be Done

196n *Supreme Court on lawyers as "essential":* Goldfarb v. Virginia State Bar, 421 U.S. 773, 792.

197 *Code's commandment regarding "ready access" to lawyers:* C.P.R., EC 1–1.

199n *Recent proposal for requiring "pro bono" work of all lawyers: The New York Times,* October 15, 1979, pp. B1, B7.

199–200 *90 percent of New York City criminal work by publicly-paid lawyers:* Marvin E. Frankel, "Justice: Commodity for Public Service?" published by the Poynter Center, Indiana University, 1978, p. 9. The figures were drawn from "available" but unpublished reports of the Office of Court Administration for New York State and official Reports to that Office by the Legal Aid Society and the Appellate Division of the State Supreme Court.

201 *Unrealized fear of overuse of British health system:* See Office of Health Economics, Department of Health & Social Security, "Scarce Resources in Health Care," 1979, pp. 5–8; also see Brian Abel-Smith, "The National Health Service, The First Thirty Years," Department of Health & Social Security, 1978, pp. 52–3. The comparison of the medical with the legal fields is clouded by the factor of new medical discoveries, not present in law, which can cause upsurges in the demand for treatment. *Restrictions on Legal Services Corporation:* Legal Services Corporation, Background News Release, September 1979 p. 8.

210n *Proposals to facilitate class-action suits:* See, e.g., H.R. 5103, 96th Congress, 1st Session, introduced by Representative Neal Smith (D., Iowa); *1977 Supreme Court decision:* Illinois Brick Co. v. Illinois, 431 U.S. 720 (1977). Case is decided in paragraph (3), p. 246, above. *Measure to overturn that decision:* See S. 300, 96th Congress, 1st Session.

Afterword

213 *Shakespeare's butcher:* Shakespeare, *Henry VI, Part II,* Act IV, Scene 2.

213 *Keats:* Letter to George Keats of March 13, 1819.

213 *Plato, Thomas More:* Cited in "Those # *X¶§!!! Lawyers," *Time,* April 10, 1978, p. 56.

213 *St. Ives:* Cited by Joseph A. Califano Jr., in "The Washington Lawyer: When to Say No," in *Verdicts,* p. 187.

213 *The Talmud:* Quoted in commencement address by Marvin E. Frankel, in *The New York Times,* June 11, 1979, p. B3.

213 *Harris Poll:* "Confidence and Concern: Citizens View American Government," Poll conducted for Subcommittee on Intergovernmental Relations of Senate Committee on Government Operations, December 3, 1973. Poll showed that 52 percent of respondents had a "great deal of confidence" in "people in charge of running" trash collection compared with 24 percent for people running law firms.

213 *Marvin E. Frankel:* "An Immodest Proposal," *The New York Times Magazine,* December 4, 1977, p. 92.

Index

259 *Index*

rule permitting special low rates for
fellow lawyers, 74–5
written entirely by lawyers, 52
Cantrall, Arch, 163
Capital Cities Broadcasting, 21
Carnegie Corporation, 163
Carter, Pres. Jimmy, xv
Center for Analysis of Public Issues,
70
Center for Law and Social Policy, 18
Center for Law and the Public Inter-
est, 19
Character and fitness
as bar admission requirement, 53,
186–95
personal interviews to determine,
189
questions asked as basis for apprais-
ing, 188
Chloromycetin, 146–48
Citizens Communication Center, 18,
21
Clark Report (on lawyer discipline),
83–4, 88, 91
Clark, Tom C., 83
Class action lawsuits, 136–37
proposals to facilitate, 210
Cleveland Bar Association, 109
Clinical legal education, 167–69
discouraged by nature of Bar Exam,
183
Clinics, legal. *See* Legal Clinics
Code of Professional Responsibility.
See Canons of Ethics
Cohen, Sheldon, 141
Coleman, Lynn R., 143
Columbia Law School, 183
Competition among lawyers
and Bar resistance to self-help kits
and books, 60–1
curbed by Bar rule against competitive bidding, 54
curbed by minimum fee schedules,
54
lack of in home-buying field, 29, 30
Connally, John B., 143
Consumers Union, 10, 20
Contingent fees
as equalizing factor in legal system,
78
prohibited for witnesses, 78–9

Corporations
lack of crackdown on corporate
crime, 8
legal fees for forming, 30
yearly expenditure for lawyers'
fees, 7
Council on Legal Education for Professional Responsibility (CLEPR),
167, 169
Council on Public Interest Law, 19,
22
Covington & Burling, 21, 142, 150,
151, 155
Cravath, Swaine & Moore, xviii, 8, 26,
29, 88, 152
Creditors' Rights textbook, 161–62
Crisis at the Bar (Lieberman), 77
Crowley, Frederick, 143
Cummins, Joseph H., 101
Cutler, Lloyd N., 146–48, 154, 157

Dacey, Norman F., 61
Dallas Bar Association, 89
Darrow, Clarence, 173
Dean, John, 159, 187
De-lawyering
and Bar resistance to self-help kits
and books, 60–61
Delaval Turbine Company, 135
Delaying tactics
by Bruce Bromley, 151–53
in Panalba case, 151
DeMent, Sandra, 59
Dent, Harry S., 91
Diamond, Dr. Bernard, 170, 174
DISC (Domestic International Sales
Corporation), 144, 155
Discipline. *See* Lawyers' Discipline
District of Columbia Bar Association,
86
District 37. *See* Municipal Employees
Union (District 37)
Donovan Leisure (firm of), 93
Douglas, Sen. Stephen A., 164

Educational Testing Service (ETS),
175–76
Ehrlichman, John, 187
Eliasberg, Phyllis, 89
Emergency Land Fund, 15
England, Chief Justice (Fla.) Arthur, 4
Epley, Marion J. III, 93

About the Author

Philip M. Stern is a Phi Beta graduate of Harvard with varied experience in government, politics, and journalism. He was, successively, reporter and editorial writer for the New Orleans *Item;* legislative assistant to Congressman (later Senator) Henry M. Jackson of Washington and to Senator Paul H. Douglas of Illinois; campaign aide to Adlai Stevenson during his 1952 presidential campaign; Director of Research for the Democratic National Committee; co-founder, editor and then publisher of *The Northern Virginia Sun* in Arlington, Virginia; and Deputy Assistant Secretary of State. Mr. Stern is the author of *The Great Treasury Raid,* a best-selling book about tax-loopholes; *The Shame of a Nation,* a photographic essay on American poverty, with pictures by George de Vincent; *The Oppenheimer Case: Security on Trial;* and *The Rape of the Taxpayer;* and co-author, with Helen B. Stern, of *O Say Can You See,* a book contrasting the tourist's view of Washington, D.C. with the neglected aspects of the capital. At the 1968 Democratic National Convention, he nominated Channing E. Phillips, the first black man in history to be placed in nomination for the Presidency at a major party convention.

In 1974, Mr. Stern became a special investigative reporter for *The Washington Post,* then enrolled, at the age of 49, as a freshman at Georgetown University Law School in Washington, which led to his writing of this book.

Mr. Stern is married to Helen Markel, an editor at *McCall's Magazine.* They make their home in New York City.